BEYOND THE CURSE

The Salvation Army
School For Officers' Training
Library
Chicago, Illinois

BEYOND THE CURSE

WOMEN CALLED TO MINISTRY

Aida Besançon Spencer

3606570024483

HENDRICKSON
PUBLISHERS
PEABODY, MASSACHUSETTS 01961-3473

To My Parents,
Aida Guzmán de Besançon
and
Frederick Heinrich Besançon
who always assumed the best for me,
an ambassador or a physician.
I did become an ambassador for God
and a physician of the spirit.

BEYOND THE CURSE
Women Called to Ministry

Copyright © 1985 by Aida Besançon Spencer

Hendrickson Publishers, Inc. edition

ISBN: 0-943575-29-X

reprinted from the 1985 edition originally published
by Thomas Nelson, Inc., Publishers

First printing, June 1989

All rights reserved.

Written permission must be secured from the publisher
to use or reproduce any part of this book, except for
brief quotations in critical reviews or articles.

All Scripture quotations are from the author's own translation or from
the Revised Standard Version of the Bible, copyrighted 1946, 1952, © 1971,
1973. Quotations from the Apocrypha are from *The New English Bible.* © The
Delegates of the Oxford University Press and the Syndics of the Cambridge University Press 1961, 1970. Reprinted by permission.

"A Gift of Sight: A Christmas Fable" by William David Spencer is reprinted
by permission from *Daughters of Sarah* (November, 1976), 8-9. "In Defense
of the First Church of Tootsie" is reprinted by permission from *The Wittenburg Door* 72 (April-May, 1983), 26-27.

Printed in the United States of America

Contents

26236

Preface

Women are cursed if they do and cursed if they do not. If we study women in our discipline, whether it be the Bible, history, psychology, or sociology, we are immediately classified as limited: "She only knows about women's studies!" However, if we do not study women in our discipline, then we are avoiding the issue and we are letting down our sisters. So, I published my first book on a supposed neutral topic, Paul's literary style. Of course, I will now fall into the everready trap. Nevertheless, I must share my findings on women and ministry. Like Jeremiah, I have a fire that burns within me which propels me to speak out. I am deeply saddened by the limitations placed on women. Why must women be misled to think that God (or at least the Scriptures) does not want them to be publicly acknowledged (and paid!) for the leadership they are giving in the church?

Sometimes people find it distasteful and uncomfortable and, thereby, unscholarly for other people to defend a thesis with zeal and personal interest. However, is the one who is personally affected by a study thereby necessarily unobjective and inaccurate? Or can that person have unusual insight? Both of course are possible. Yet justice and vindication are not alien to passion and study. I would want to be a careful and accurate scholar who adds to the ongoing discussion a new and helpful perspective. Sometimes matters are not seen because no one ever suggested they be looked for. For example, I am embarrassed to say that not until I was in my thirties did I notice that some "squirrels" lived in trees while others dug holes in the ground. When I reported this strange phenomena to my husband he kindly explained that I had been seeing chipmunks! (My own defense is that neither squirrels nor chipmunks live in the tropics where I spent my earliest years.) The next day as I walked I looked around to see if he was correct and, sure enough, I saw for the first time that these "squirrels" looked differently from one another. I never had noticed a chipmunk until I was told to look for it. Similarly, I, along with others, would like to invite my readers to look for these chipmunks who, incidentally, have been there digging all along.

If I could only do all my academic study like all "the boys" how easy life would be! However, you cannot have new people without new visions. I always insist on the use of primary sources. I have tried to study thoroughly the New Testament and the early Jewish sources so as to see anew what they have to say. I have quoted only secondary references which I have employed. What I have *not* done is amassed "documentation" from the guild of scholars, showing where earlier scholars have agreed and disagreed with my own views. I have tried to discuss ideas opposing my own, but I have not quoted other writers regularly and by name to reward or punish them publicly. People will speak about others in print in a manner they would never dare to do face to face. Genuine scholars do not need to parade their knowledge of names. Otherwise, we may become like the exorcists who tried to remove the evil spirits: "by the Jesus whom Paul preaches" (Acts 19:13). The wise reader will reply: "Jesus I know, and Paul I know; but who are you?" The real scholar is like a gourmet cook who sifts the flour. Authentic scholars are not like stock clerks, simply dumping a bag of flour on the kitchen floor. That is not to say I do not appreciate help in my kitchen. The best meal is like the best fought battle—a community effort. I have appreciated my coworkers.

Ever since we met hiking up a mountain by the Hudson River, I have appreciated the years of discussion with my husband, William David Spencer. He has taken to heart Paul's command to husbands to help their wives become mature ministering Christians. Only a man strong in himself could rejoice in his wife as he has done. His formal education, experience in ministry, and great integrative mind well equip him to write the afterword. Original drafts of parts of the book were published in *Free Indeed*, the *Journal of the Evangelical Theological Society, Daughters of Sarah*, and the *Evangelical Women's Caucus Update*. I began my study on women in 1970 when I entered Princeton Theological Seminary. If my otherwise excellent professors and peers had not kept talking about Man, man and men, I would never have begun to ask about my place in ministry. Pamela McDonald has been a thoroughly delightful person and skillful typist. I am thankful to Gordon-Conwell Theological Seminary for hiring her as a faculty secretary. Douglas Stuart, chair of our Biblical Division, has given me some good advice on publishing. Lori V. Johnson, who has served as my Byington scholar for two years, has spent much of her own time double-checking the bibliography. Julie Aldrich, my first Byington, organized the first draft of the bibliography. Rhonda Hoehn indexed the Scripture references. R. K. Harrison, consulting editor with Thomas Nelson, has gone out of his way to make a place for me in the scholarly guild. His greatness is shown not only by his scholarship but also by his humility. I am also grateful for the freedom and direction Thomas Nelson has given me. Most of the Bible translations are my own or they are from the Revised Standard Version of the Bible. The staff at Goddard Library has also been very helpful in obtaining references or books through inter-library loan. Nothing could be published without the help of our libraries. And, finally, I want to thank my parents. Who would ever think a dollar for every "A" would be so effective? Not that I learned for the dollar! Then, I would be like that unjust historian who as Lucian writes: "hopes to get a purple cufta, a gold necklet, and a Nisaean horse" (*How to Write History* [39]). No, I enjoy learning and I appreciated your appreciation of me. And I want to extend your appreciation of me on to other women and men.

And no one drinking old wine wishes new;
for he says, "The old is good."

—Jesus (Luke 5:39).

Introduction

One of the delights of living in the New York metropolitan area and in Louisville is to attend Shakespeare's plays at the park in the open air with our little friends, the mosquitos. In *The Winter's Tale* King Leontes asks his lords whether his wife the Queen Hermione is "honest" (Act II, Scene 1). What a strange question to ask in the midst of such turmoil! Has Hermione been siphoning off her husband's money? If the audience limits its understanding of the term "honest" to its contemporary use and ignores the context of the play, the scene and even the play will forever remain a mystery or be misunderstood. Of course, Hermione's *truthfulness* is not questioned, it is her *fidelity* which is unsure. Would it be inaccurate or even wrong to understand "honest" as used by Shakespeare as it is defined today rather than as it was defined in Elizabethan times? It certainly would be!

The Bible can be very easy or very hard to understand. The good news is, at its core, very simple and very profound: God became human so that humans can again approach God cleansed, perfect, and forgiven before the just Judge. Nevertheless, the very process which aids the contemplation of biblical truths—the division of books into verses and the memorization and recitation of those verses—can and does also aid the breakdown of truth. Some biblical passages have been so frequently quoted, the listener loses sight of the original context of that passage. A new concept has replaced the original reality. Then that new concept becomes understood as part of a new culture and the listener is now two further steps from reality.

Our goal as lovers of God and of God's revelation is to try to rediscover that original reality beyond our culture and our common understandings. The author who inspired the Bible is still available today through the Spirit. And truth is best approached in love.

However, when one begins to look at the Bible's teachings concerning the mutual roles of women and men, one is particularly in a dilemma. If we conclude that the Bible presents a "liberating" understanding of the roles of women and men, then those who challenge such a position charge that our view only follows from the impact of feminism in society. However, if we conclude that the Bible presents a "traditional/hierarchical" understanding of the roles of men and women, then feminists might charge that our view only follows from the basic conservative strain in our contemporary society; "the conservative reaction," which is so frequently mentioned. What is in truth at issue here is that the Bible's view of the relationships between men and women is at its core a very personal topic. All of us Christians are either women who must do what the Bible says or we are men who must have to relate to women in some capacity. This truth did not become evident to my husband until a number of years ago when I spoke on "Should women become pastors according to 1 Timothy 2:11-15?" at a seminary which does not allow women to pursue the pastor's degree. At the end of my presentation, as many people spoke to my husband as they did to me. The men asked him, "What is it like to be married to a minister?" and "How does such a marriage make you feel?"

God has made us with a will. The will is good. In the Bible, the heart symbolizes the will: "From among all things to be guarded especially watch your heart because from out of it is produced life" (Prov. 4:23). God wants us to have a will because with it we can will to do good or to do evil and will to love God or to hate God. So too when we come to the Scriptures we bring that will with us. Certainly no one can profess to be completely objective when studying the topic of male-female relationships which is so personal as well. The best one can do is analyze and become aware of one's feelings and try not to have one's feelings subconsciously decide conclusions. The writers' own assumptions when coming to the Bible are that God loves us and we, in turn, want to please God. God is loving and merciful and just. Whatever the Bible says must be good because the Bible comes from God. Moreover, God's truth will cut through all systems as a two-edged sword. The Bible is a revolutionary book because all are called to account.

My focus is the New Testament because we now live in the post-cross period of time. The law is our schoolteacher, our pedagogue, but now we are past justification by the law because Jesus has fulfilled that law. Moreover, the book has to be limited in scope in some way! What makes *Beyond the Curse* unique? In this book the authoritative and reliable Scriptures are exegetically studied in depth to ascertain exactly why women are and should be called to minister as leaders. Although the question of woman's ordination and church leadership has been discussed for years, only now is the conservative church beginning to take it seriously. The Bible offers a coherent system of principles to guide those individuals and churches who are willing to listen. To develop that coherent system of principles, the New Testament must be set in its context. Consequently, Chapter 1 discusses God's teachings before and after the fall, a foundation for ministry and marriage. Jesus' teachings and practices concerning women (Chapter 2) supply a context for the apostle Paul's teachings and practices concerning women (Chapter 3). Within the New Testament itself the teachings concerning women are proven by the many examples of authoritative women (Chapter 4). To test these conclusions we return to God's nature as we began. If humans were made in God's image, then God too will not hesitate to use feminine metaphors to help us understand God's nature (Chapter 5). All my findings are summarized in Chapter 6.

The early chapters of Genesis set a foundation for both ministry and marriage. However, I have not developed a biblical view of marriage in this book, although the questions of ministry and marriage are often intertwined in current discussions. The relationship between women and men in work and a man and a woman in marriage are two different questions. If the discussion of the relationship between men and women in the church is personal, the discussion of the relationship between a woman and a man is even more personal and subjective. I will show how the biblical use of the metaphor "head" does not limit women in ministry and, furthermore, how Jesus and Paul place ministry in higher priority over homemaking. Nevertheless, ministry should not destroy marriages. In the afterword my husband, the Reverend Doctor William David Spencer, will share how the New Testament encouragement of women in active Christian service can affect marriage, parenting, and church life. Moreover, since humans indeed are often led by their will rather than their reason, he explains experientially why people, but especially men, would be wise to encourage and affirm women as church leaders. Bill has requested that his experiential thoughts be separated from the biblical study because the Bible should be our authority for action, not our desires or experiences. Experience should confirm and add depth to biblical principles as those biblical principles are fleshed out in practice.

The book ends with a bibliography of works cited, an additional bibliography for further study, and suggestions for group study. I have tried to make the listing of historical and biblical studies on ministry as complete as possible. I have also included some theological and historical studies, some works on shared marriage, and other more popularly-written works.

What have I as a student of God's revelation discovered? The title and subtitle suggest the conclusions. I have discovered that we should and should not go beyond the curse. On the one hand, we should go beyond the punishments of Adam and Eve to begin to live lives affected by Christ's redemption. God is pleased with the shared or equal ministry of Christian men and women. Yet, on the other hand, at the very least we should never go beyond the implication of the curse by accepting more punishment than it metes out. However, as we travel on that road toward shared ministry, the means are as important as the end. Eve's problem was to desire foolishly to attain wisdom. Paul's answer was to focus on the wise way to attain wisdom.

1

Equal in Eden:
Foundation for Ministry
and Marriage

"How beautiful, then, the marriage of two Christians, two
who are one in hope, one in desire, one in the way of life they
follow, one in the religion they practice" Tertullian, *To His
Wife* (8).

Although this book focuses on the New Testament teachings on ministry, we are driven nevertheless back to the
early chapters in Genesis. Although Christ may have
changed our perspective toward the Old Testament's sacrifi-
cial laws he has by no means invalidated the authority and
pertinence of the Old Testament. Almost all foundational
questions find their answer in the early chapters of Genesis.
Male-female relations are no exception.

The Apostle Paul himself treats Genesis 1-3 authoritatively and as crucial for developing first-century principles
for women and men. His principles for women and men at
Ephesus and at Corinth conclude with the following ration-
ales:

"For Adam was formed first, then Eve; and Adam was not
deceived, but the woman was deceived and became a transgressor" (1 Tim. 2:13-14 RSV), "For man was not made from
woman, but woman from man" (1 Cor. 11:8), "The two shall
become one flesh" (1 Cor. 6:16), and "The first human Adam

became a living being" (1 Cor. 15:45). Paul also refers to the early chapters of Genesis when he writes the Ephesians and the Romans: "For this reason a man shall leave his father and mother and be joined to his wife, and the two shall become one flesh" (Eph. 5:30 RSV) and "Therefore as sin came into the world through one human and death through sin, and so death spread to all humans because all sinned" (Rom. 5:12). Since Paul refers to Genesis in his arguments, contemporary students of the New Testament must as well refer to them.

Outside of imitating Paul's own example, another reason we study the early chapters of Genesis is because many contemporary writers on women and men refer back to these chapters, and for good reasons. In a speech at Wheaton College, reprinted in *The Christian Reader*, Elisabeth Elliott challenged the audience:

The Nicene Creed begins, "I believe in one God, the Father Almighty, maker of all things visible and invisible." That's where we start. There is an intelligent Creator, a created order, a design. This design includes a hierarchy of beings such as cherubim, seraphim, archangels, angels, men ("a little lower than the angels"), animals, insects, things like paramecia and microbes. Every creature is assigned its proper position in this scale and glorifies God by being what it is. There is no reason to believe that a fox glorifies God less by being a fox than Michael does by being an archangel. I understand that women, by creation, have been given a place within the human level which is ancillary to that of men, and I am glad of this. The Genesis account calls woman a "help, meet"–that is, fit, suitable, for man. I do not hold all men to be so strong, so intelligent, so competent, and so virtuous or holy that they deserve a superior position. I simply see that the place is theirs not by merit but by appointment.[1]

Elisabeth Elliot has highlighted a crucial thought. God's intention at creation is neither affected by culture nor by the fall. No amount of study of the influence of the temporal ef-

[1] Elisabeth Elliot Leitch, "Called to be Liberated Women," *The Christian Reader*, November/December, 1975, 44.

fects of culture or of the influence of the fall versus the re-
deeming grace of God upon the roles of women can alter the
will of God before humans fell in Eden, a supracultural situation. She concludes that women should be submissive to
men because that was God's intention at creation. Acting on
similar principles, in June 1984 the Southern Baptist Convention resolved to exclude all women from pastoral func-
tions and leadership entailing ordination: "to preserve a
submission God requires because man was first in creation
and woman was first in the Edenic fall."[2] Women should be
homemakers and men should be breadwinners. Elliott and
others have voiced a common sentiment. God has planned
for men and women to have distinct and hierarchical roles.
These conclusions are exemplary, not unique, nor are they
merely contemporary. Augustine teaches as well in *The
Good of Marriage* that the union of male and female is: "a
kind of friendly and genuine union of the one ruling and the
other obeying" (ch. 1).

Such an apparent consensus of understanding of Genesis
2 has even influenced many Christian feminists. For instance, Evelyn and Frank Stagg conclude: "There are at
least two creation narratives in Genesis, woman having
equality with man in one (1:24-30) but subordinated to man
in the other (2:7-25)."[3] They have agreed with persons such
as Elliott that Genesis 2 teaches the submission of women
to men. However, in contrast to chapter 2, Genesis 1 teaches
the equality of female and male. Consequently, depending on
what conclusions they wish to foster, exemplary and devout
Christian scholars like these have tended to focus either on
chapter 1 of Genesis or on chapter 2. If they favor the equality of women and men they prefer chapter 1. If they favor the
submission of women to men they prefer chapter 2.

---

[2]See Richard Groves, "Conservatives Dominate Southern Baptist Meeting," *The Christian Century,* July 18-25, 1984, 701-03 and the Southern
Baptist Convention Annual (104th).

[3]Evelyn and Frank Stagg, *Woman in the World of Jesus* (Philadelphia:
Westminster Press, 1978), p. 16.

Must the Bible become a see-saw in which the heaviest person maintains control? Must we choose Genesis 1 over Genesis 2 to support the equality of male and female? In a letter to the editor of *Christianity Today*, Richard Laribee has voiced a frequent point of view:

> Regardless on which side of the issue one stands, one should be able to recognize by now that the real issue is no longer the rights and responsibilities of men and women within their respective roles. Rather, the issue on which we must each decide is the issue of ultimate authority in our lives and in our theology: are we going to be subject to the Scriptures or are we going to subject the Scriptures to our current cultural whims? [4]

It is evident that understanding Genesis 1-3 is foundational for understanding the New Testament and for developing principles for marriage and ministry. What indeed does Genesis teach about the relation between Adam and Eve at creation? Was there any power or authority distribution? Was there a hierarchy or lack of hierarchy? What kind of accountability was there? What did it mean for Eve to be Adam's "helpmate"?

What I have discovered is that the first two chapters of Genesis do not have conflicting messages. Genesis 1 does not have a contradictory view of women to Genesis 2. Before the fall God created man and woman to share in ministry and marriage. God intended Eve and Adam to have equal participation.

Before the Curse: The Blessings

God's Image and Command (Genesis 1)

Genesis 1:26-27 reads:

And God said, "Let us make Adam in our image, according to our resemblance, and they will rule over the fish of the sea and over

---

[4]Richard Laribee, "Letter to the Editor," *Christianity Today,* June 4, 1976, 24.

the birds of the sky and over the animals and over all the earth and over all the moving things which move upon the earth." And God created the Adam in his image in the image of God he created him, a male and a female he created them.

These verses teach the reader certain basic facts. "Adam" is made in the image of God. Who is "the Adam"? "The Adam" is a "they." The clause "he created him" is parallel to the following clause "he created them" indicating that the "him" is synonymous with the "them." "The Adam" is a "male and female." Thus "the Adam" could be translated "Human" or "humanity"; however, the effect of the synecdoche would be lost. The synecdoche "Adam" is a singular which represents the plural "male and female." By having the one "Adam" represent the two "male and female," the writer has emphasized the essential unity and diversity of Adam and Eve. Their relationship is foundational. Synecdoches emphasize relational values. Thus, if "Adam" is made in the image of God then "male and female" have been made in the image of God. Conversely, in order to understand God's nature, males and females together are needed to reflect God's image. The image of God is a double image.[5]

Moreover, the contextual significance for the image of God is displayed in relationships. Thus even as the Adam is singular but yet plural, so too God is singular but yet plural. God who is One says "let *us* make Adam in *our* image, according to *our* resemblance." Male and female reflect the plurality of God as Trinity. The interrelationship between male and female symbolizes the interrelationship within God. There is no possibility, according to these verses, that Adam, the male, could by himself reflect the nature of God. Neither is it possible for Adam, the female, by herself to reflect God's nature. Male and female are needed to reflect God's nature. In a broader sense, relationship in itself between different people reflects God's nature.

---

[5]See also Rolf E. Aaseng, "Male and Female Created He Them," *Christianity Today*, Nov. 20, 1970, 5-6.

Did the fall modify the double image of God at creation? After the Fall, the truths elaborated in verses 1:26-27 are repeated in 5:1-2:

> This document is the family register of Adam in the day God was creating Adam; in the resemblance of God he made him, a male and a female he created them. And he praised them and he named their name Adam in the day of their being created.

Again we have the parallel clauses, "he made him" and "he created them." As well, the writer adds that God "named *their* name *Adam.*" The male and female have one name, "Adam." The fall has not changed the woman's ability to reflect God's image.

Sometimes people think that in some way males more fully reflect God's image than females. Even C. S. Lewis, at the conclusion of his magnificent novel *Perelandra*, has the King reflect the deity Maledil more fully than the Queen. However, in Genesis 1:26-27 male and female are too interrelated to become separated in this manner. Even the New Testament writers are always careful to describe Jesus with the generic Greek term "human" or *anthropos* rather than the term "male" or *aner*. Although God became a male, God primarily became a human; otherwise, in some way males would be more saved than females. At creation, conversely, male and female form a unity. It is that unity which mirrors God's likeness.

In Genesis 1:28 the reader learns even more about Adam and male and female. The text reads:

> And God blessed them and God said to them, "Bear fruit and become many and fill the earth and subdue it and rule over the fish of the sea and over the birds of the sky and over all the moving animals upon the earth."

In verse 26 God describes "Adam" as a "they" who will rule. In verse 28 God commands them, not merely the male, to subdue the earth and to rule over the fish, the birds, and all moving animals. "Subdue" is almost a synopsis of the second longer clause "rule over." The verb "rule" (*radah*) takes the preposition "over" (*b*) to emphasize the aspect of ruling. Consequently, according to Genesis 1, not only are male and female needed to reflect God's image, but also rulership (and with it authority) and work are not merely designated but commanded for man and woman. Not jointly to rule would be to disobey God's command. The nature of male and female is consistent with the practice of male and female. Male and female share in power and authority, even as they share in dignity.

"Help meet" (Genesis 2)

Genesis 1 provides an overview of all creation. Genesis 2 now focuses back on one period, the end of day six. Can we draw the same conclusions about chapter 2 as we did about chapter 1? Or, does the description of the female as "an help meet" for the male prove that the female was to be submissive to and to obey the male and never was the male to be submissive to and to obey the female? Not until one day when I was studying the Hebrew text did the full impact of Genesis 2:18 strike me. The verse literally reads:

And the Lord God thought it was not good for the Adam to be by himself; "I will make for him a helper as if in front of him."

In this verse "the Adam" is used to describe the male. What the King James Version translates "meet for him" and the Revised Standard Version translates "fit for him" in Hebrew, is one word, *knegdwo*. This one word occurs in this form only in verse 18 and is repeated in verse 20. The word is made up of three thought units: the prefix *k* the preposition *neged*, and the suffix *wo*. The prefix *k* signifies comparison, similarity, or proportion. The suffix *wo* is a pronoun signifying "him." The prefix asks the question, what is the comparison between the helper and "him"? How may the helper be described in comparison to Adam? The preposition *neged* which lies between the prefix and the suffix answers the question. The helper is *neged* to him. What does *neged* mean? The basic root literally describes physical relationships. It refers to "the front" or "the visible." The preposition *neged* means "in front of," "in sight of," and "opposite to." Thus, God has made for Adam a helper "as if in front of him." Does the phrase appear to suggest a submissive relationship or a lower hierarchy? In Hebrew, prepositions, verbs, and nouns tend to be concentrically related to their root meaning. The meaning of a verb or a noun or a preposition can enlighten the meaning of any other word in the group. "Front" or "visible" seems to suggest superiority or equality. Is this possible? The same preposition when converted into a noun (*nagid*) signifies "a leader, ruler, prince, or king," an "overseer." Literally it signifies the "one in front."[6] *Nagid* is the term used to describe David's and Solomon's role as ruler over Israel.[7]

Neged is not the only possible word to signify "front" which could have been used in verse 18. In 2:8 *qedem* is used. It too means "what is in front," "to go before, anticipate, meet, encounter." When the preposition is converted to an adverb or noun it means "in the east." In Hebrew the direction indicated by "the front" is to us "the east." The garden was in Eden "in the east." The writer of Genesis was aware of at least two words for "front." *Qedem* certainly would have had less authoritative connotations than *neged.* However, the writer chose the unusual combination *knegdwo* instead. Moreover, the text claims this word is the word God chose to describe the female.

If Eve had been created in an inferior position, the writer should have used a term to mean "after" or "behind"; such as the preposition *'ahar,* or even a more neutral term such as "for" (1): "a helper *for* him." The Hebrew language is not limited in possibilities. It is a metaphorical language. The Hebrews were a figurative people, as many older cultures today are quite dramatically symbolic. One set of our grandparents, one of whom was a contemporary Greek, recalled the traditional Greek practice which required a man's wife to

---

[6]Francis Brown, S.R. Driver, and Charles A. Briggs, *A Hebrew and English Lexicon of the Old Testament* (Oxford: Clarendon, 1907), pp. 617-18.

[7]1 Sam. 9:16; 13:14; 1 Kings 1:35.

walk down the street behind him and the children after her to symbolize their respective subordination.

The Bible, however, even Genesis 2, which some suppose to teach the hierarchy of male and female, grammatically reveals that there is no subordination of the helper to the Adam. Rather, God created woman to be "in front of" or "visible" to Adam, which would symbolize equality (if not superiority!) in all respects. Even more, one can argue that the female is the helper who rules over the one she helps! In effect, God has inaugurated a mutual submission, even at creation.

I have not, as an isolated exegete, read too much into the Hebrew grammar. The definitive *A Hebrew and English Lexicon of the Old Testament* by Francis Brown, S. R. Driver, and Charles Briggs has the same understanding of the verse: "A help *corresponding to* him" is, in other words, "equal and adequate to himself."[8] The early church father Irenaeus (second century) also says that God made "a helper equal and the peer and the like of Adam" *(Proof of the Apostolic Preaching,* ch. 13). Moreover, when the Hebrew text was translated into Greek around 250 BC, the Septuagint translators also made sure to express this idea of equality. They translated *knegdwo* (KJV "meet for him") in verse 18 with the Greek word *kata* followed by the direct object, which signifies horizontal rather than perpendicular direction.[9] The phrase is used to express equality and similarity. The Septuagint translated verse 20 with a different but parallel word, *homoios,* which means "of the same nature, like, similar." Within the general fabric of likeness, *homoios* also signifies equality in force and equality of rank.[10] Walter

---

[8]Brown, Driver, Briggs, p. 617.

[9]A.T. Robertson, *A Grammar of the Greek New Testament in the Light of Historical Research* (Nashville: Broadman, 1934), p. 608.

[10]Henry G. Liddell and Robert Scott, *A Greek-English Lexicon,* eds. Henry S. Jones and Roderick McKenzie (9th ed.; Oxford: Clarendon, 1968), p. 1224.

Bauer cites Genesis 2:20 as an example of the latter meaning. In Genesis 2:20 *homoios* signifies: *"equally great or important, as powerful as, equal (to)"*.[11]

Genesis 2 never calls woman inferior or subordinate to man. Rather, both the Hebrew and Greek texts accentuate the equality and similarity of the woman to the man. The Hebrew text even literally signifies that the woman is "in front of" the man or "over" him! Much contemporary confusion over the understanding of male and female at creation arises from the term "helpmate." If the woman is the "helpmate" to the man, is she not like the "handmaid" or "servant" to a mistress/master? Of course, the term "helpmate" arises from the absurd combination of "a help" and "meet." Eve is a "helpmeet" or "helpmate" to Adam. (The term "helpmate" in English is also sometimes applied to a husband.) "Helpmate" is a satisfactory word to employ if we understand "meet" to signify "equal and similar."

However, does the fact that the woman is called "a helper" or "a help" to the man change or alter the apparent lack of subordination in the "meetness?" Currently, there is a movement to propose that women are indeed equal to men, but are appointed to a subordinate position in the home and in the church. Perhaps in many cultures being a "helper" inherently signifies subordination. However, in the Bible the term *'ezer* ("one who helps") does not at all imply inherent subordination. The term "helper" most frequently refers to God (thirteen times) and sometimes refers to military protectors and allies (four times). As the Psalmist sings:

> I will lift up my eyes to the hills
> From whence does my help come?
> My *help* comes from the Lord,
> who made heaven and earth (121:1-2 RSV).

---

[11]Walter Bauer, *A Greek-English Lexicon of the New Testament and Other Early Christian Literature,* trans. and eds. William F. Arndt and F. Wilbur Gingrich (Chicago: University of Chicago, 1957), p. 569.

Moses' father-in-law, Jethro, names his second son Elie*zer* for "The God of my father was my *help*, and delivered me from the sword of Pharaoh" (Exod. 18-4 RSV). If being "one who helps" inherently implies subordination, then, in that case, God would be subordinate to humans! In contrast, God rebukes the Israelites for seeking the protection of the Egyptians rather than that of the Lord. The Egyptians are a people who bring "neither *help* nor assistance" (Isa. 30:5). At no times does *'ezer* indicate a subordinate helper unless the two references to "helper" in Genesis 2:18, 20 are considered exceptions.[12]

To denigrate the term "helper" is to ignore the total context of chapter 2. Woman was created not to serve Adam, but to serve *with* Adam. Apparently, God did not want Adam to handle his assignments by himself. In Genesis 2:15 God leaves Adam in the garden of Eden to till it and to guard it. Three verses later God is recorded as thinking that it was not good for the man to be by himself. Consequently, God says: "I will make for him a helper equal to him." To be "by himself" is not necessarily to be lonely. Adam had not expressed loneliness. It was God who thought it was not good for Adam to be alone. Not all aloneness is lonliness! God decides Adam should not be by himself. Then God proceeds inductively to educate Adam so that he might appreciate the newest creation.

One clear contextual reason for God not wanting Adam to be "by himself" is that Adam needs a helper. The suspense in Genesis 2 increases to a climax. Eden is first described as having no one to till the ground (v. 5). Then the Lord takes Adam and places him in Eden to till and guard it (v. 15). God then presents the animals to Adam to name them. At the

---

[12]R. David Freedman suggests that the term "helper" etymologically signifies "a power (or strength)" who can save. The word comes from the two roots: "one ʿ-z-r meaning 'to rescue,' 'to save,' and the other g-z-r meaning 'to be strong.' Therefore Eve is 'a power (or strength) equal to Adam.' "Woman, A Power Equal to Man: Translation of Woman as a 'Fit Helpmate' for Man is Questioned," *Biblical Archaeology Review* 9 (January/February, 1983): 56-58.

same time God allows Adam to discover whether any of the animals can serve as Adam's helper. None, of course, are appropriate (vv. 19-20). God wanted help for Adam, because God perceived Adam as needing help to till and guard the garden. Moreover, not just any help would suffice for the man. He needed another human, equal and corresponding to him, a friend. Adam and Eve together were to serve God. Consequently, the suspense mounts until the climax of chapter 2. Only someone formed from Adam's very side could cause him to exclaim: "This, this time is bone from my bone and flesh from my flesh!" The writer draws out the significance of the creation of a "helper equal to him" in verse 24. Because Adam's helper came from his own side or flesh, the helper becomes a person to whom Adam sticks. He abandons even his own parents, the two becoming one flesh. The unity between husband and wife is greater than between a son and his father and mother.[13]

Thus, Genesis 2 does call woman a "help meet" for the man. But, the "help" highlights Adam's insufficiency. By himself he is not able to fulfill God's command to till and guard the garden. Moreover, in no way does the context imply that Eve's duties as "one who helps" are different from the one she helps. Rather, the context strongly develops the need to till and guard and the fulfillment of that need by the creation of Adam and then Eve. To "help" here means "to share the same tasks" and "meet" means to do so as "equal and similar."

In a more concrete manner, Genesis 2 reiterates the mes-

---

[13]John Skinner, in *A Critical and Exegetical Commentary on Genesis*, comments that the verse would presuppose "the primitive custom called *beena* marriage" in which "the husband parts from his own kindred for good, and goes to live with his wife's kin,...But this would imply an almost incredible antiquity for the present form of the narrative; and, moreover, the dominion of the man over the wife assumed in 3:16b is inconsistent with the conditions of *beena* marriage." However, if Genesis is not a composite of later writings and the dominion of the husband over his wife is an unnatural result of the fall, then the verse may indicate a primitive *beena* marriage where the husband lives with the wife, rather than vice versa. *The International Critical Commentary* (2d ed.; Edinburgh: T. & T. Clark, 1930), p. 70.

sage of chapter 1. "To till and to guard" the garden is one way in which humans "rule over all the earth." Their similar tasks necessitate the work of equals. Eve and Adam are equal in rank, equal in image. Genesis 2, like Genesis 1, declares and explains male and female equality, joint rulership, and interrelationship.

God's original intention for women and men is that in work and in marriage they share tasks and share authority. Females as well as males are needed in positions of authority in the church to help people better to comprehend God's nature. God's image needs male and female to reflect God more fully. The biblical text also guards against excluding either females OR males from the task of ministry. In addition God may be described as neither male nor female (in other words, Spirit) or both female and male. If God's "maleness" is accentuated to the extent of eliminating God's "femaleness," then we have now created a male god from whom women may feel aloof. This male god is not the God who created and who sustains all heaven and earth! However, to seek a female goddess is to eliminate the truth that men too reflect God's image. Moreover, when God assigns to females and males tasks without differentiated roles, then that assignment implies that essential maleness and femaleness are not derived from roles or tasks. When a woman rules and works she has not lost her femininity. She has regained it. When a man cooperates as a joint worker he too has not lost his masculinity. God originally intended for Adam, male and female, as one to rule and to work in ministry and in marriage.

After the Curse

God may have intended Adam and Eve to rule and work jointly. Some may say, however, Eve did not show herself capable of fulfilling God's intentions. Did the fall irreparably eradicate the dignity and rulership of the man and woman in creation? Did the fall change their original equality? In order to ascertain the situation after the curse, the fall and the curses themselves must first be studied. What were Eve's and Adam's respective parts in the fall? What is the curse as it relates to men and women?

The Fall: The False Way to Wisdom

Eve and Adam may have both received negative repercussions for having disobeyed God's command to eat from the tree of the knowledge of good and evil, however, many people feel that it was Eve who was primarily responsible for the disobedience. In some rabbinical literature, commentaries on Genesis for instance, Eve was not created simultaneously with Adam because God foreknew that later she would be a source of complaint. Therefore, the Lord delayed forming her until Adam should express a desire for her (*Genesis Rabbah* XVII). In the Apocalypse of Moses Eve confesses to having brought pain to Adam:

> My lord Adam, rise up and give me half of thy trouble and I will endure it; for it is on my account that this hath happened to thee, on my account thou art beset with toils and troubles (IX. 2).

One to two centuries before our Lord's birth, Jesus ben Eleazar ben Sirach wrote: "From a woman did sin originate, and because of her we all must die" (Wisd. of Sol. 25:24). Eve and consequently all women now become responsible for the presence of evil in the world. Eve has become a totally ignoble character.

However, Eve may not have been so totally evil nor so totally culpable as many conceive her to be. First, who is present in that historic dialogue between the serpent and Eve (Genesis 3)? Of course, only the serpent and Eve speak. However, when the serpent speaks to the woman it uses the plural "you," not the feminine singular "you." Contemporary English employs only the one word "you" to signify one or more than one person. The King James Version, though, retains the now archaic plural "ye": "*Ye* may not eat," "*Ye* will surely not die," and "*ye* will be like God." As well, the text reads: "*your* (pl) eyes will be opened." God had used the singular "you" ("thou") in Genesis 2:16 when speaking only to Adam. Thus, the serpent is not merely repeating God's command. Probably the serpent employs the plural "you" because it wants to ensure Adam falls along with Eve. It may also be possible that the serpent employs the plural "you" because it addresses Adam as well as Eve. Adam may have been present although not speaking.

The possibility that Adam is present during the dialogue is confirmed in verse 6. After Eve eats the fruit, she gives it to her husband "with her," as in the King James Version. Many English translations tend to omit the words "with her" (*'mmah*) because they are difficult to translate. In English they appear unnecessary. But, in Hebrew they are also unnecessary, unless the writer wants to specify that Adam was present with Eve. Consequently, although the dialogue of chapter 3 is between the serpent and Eve, Adam may very possibly have been present. His lack of action signified his consent to the train of thought. That consent is overt in Adam's act of disobedience: "and he ate." Thus, Eve apparently was not totally at fault. Both Eve *and* Adam appear to have been present during the dialogue.

Second, what is Eve's sin exactly? Was everything she did totally wrong? Eve is often considered either to have been totally wrong *or* totally right in her actions. A contemporary well-known undergraduate institution of learning attempted to raise money by suggesting "Eve had the right idea. Surrounded in Eden by an infinitely varied, deliciously fascinating environment, she rejected the haven of blissful ignorance and reached for knowledge—of herself and the world around her." The concept of a happy fall is well expressed, albeit Christianized, in the sixth or seventh century song: "O fortunate crime which merited to have such and so great a redeemer." The sin of Adam, in the Roman Missal, is presented as "fortunate" so that the Redeemer might come. Of course, this conclusion that Eve and Adam did well to have eaten from the tree of the knowledge of good and evil arises completely external to the biblical data.

Eve, together with Adam, had been created in God's image. Therefore, she had known good. However, after her decision to eat the fruit, together with Adam, ironically, she takes on the *serpent's* likeness, not God's, and instead of knowing good and evil learns only evil.

Eve and Adam learn the knowledge of shame, independence, and irresponsibility. Not until *after* Adam covers himself does he explain to God: "I was afraid, because I was naked, so I hid myself." Adam literally no longer was naked. Adam was ashamed before the righteous eyes of God before whom no amount of clothes would suffice. Also, Adam and Eve lose that fundamental sense of interrelationship which they had before the fall. Before the fall Eve talks about their mutual actions in the first person plural: *"we* may eat." After the fall Adam and Eve employ only the singular: "I heard," "I feared," "I was naked," "I hid." Their unity has disappeared. And finally Eve and Adam no longer take responsibility for their actions. When God asks Adam: "Have you eaten of the tree which I commanded you not to eat?" Adam, in those memorable words, blames Eve: "The woman whom you gave me—it is her fault." (For us to continue to blame Eve for all culpability is simply to imitate Adam in his own sin.) Eve, however, in turn blames the serpent: "the serpent beguiled me—it is his fault." Adam and Eve became like the serpent, knowing and doing *evil.* In Hebrew the serpent is called *'arum* (v. 1): "cunning, sly, crafty." Adam and Eve become *'erom* (v. 7): "naked" or "half-dressed." The word play on the basic root (*'rm*) indicates to the reader that the serpent's slyness is really akin to shame. Consequently, despite the assertion of the Roman Missal, in no way is the fall desired by God. It is not a "happy fall." God may have wrought a victory through the incarnation. However, to bring about a victory despite an unhappy situation is in no way to intend and desire that unhappy situation.

Nevertheless, there is a certain way in which Eve did have "the right idea." Before she eats the fruit the reader is told in verse six: "And the woman saw that the tree was good for food and that it was a delight to the eyes and the tree was desirable to be wise." Eve perceives in the fruit certain commendable assets. The tree provides good food to eat. It is nutritious. It is not unhealthy nor cancer producing. It is not "junk food."

As well, the tree is beautiful. Eve was not only a primeval nutritionist, she also was aesthetically inclined. She appreciates beauty. Finally the tree helps her education. She is concerned to become a wiser and more educated person. What could be better than taking care of her body, choosing something pleasurable and beautiful, becoming wiser and more educated, and moreover, at the same time? Is God against food, beauty and education?

According to Genesis 2:9 all of Eden is full of trees which are pleasant to the sight and good for food which God had said could be freely eaten. Thus, God certainly values and wants Eve and Adam to enjoy nutritional and aesthetic delights. In addition, throughout the Bible, God's desire for humans to appropriate wisdom is central to the Lord's character. For instance, Proverbs 3:19-20 reads:

> The Lord by wisdom founded the earth;
> by understanding he established the heavens;
> by his knowledge the deeps broke forth,
> and the clouds drop down the dew (RSV).

And Proverbs 3:13-14 says:

> Pronounce happy a person who finds wisdom,
> and a person who obtains understanding,
> for its gain is better than gain from silver
> and than gold its profit.

Therefore, God would confirm Eve's desire for wisdom, aesthetic, and nutrition.

However, the nutritional, aesthetic, and educational values of the fruit are used by Eve as excuses or rationalizations to disguise or to augment her real desire. Her real desire is to be as God, knowing good and evil. Only *after* the serpent suggests that "You both will be as God knowing good and evil" (3:5) does Eve think of other benefits of the tree: it is "good for eating, pleasant to the eyes, and desirable for wisdom." In addition, Eve does not have to eat from the tree of the knowledge of good and evil in order to eat and in order to eat something attractive. The one distinctive characteristic of the fruit perceived by Eve is its desirability for intelligence, wisdom, and success. Eve desires wisdom. She thinks that by becoming like God, having the knowledge of good and evil, she would reach her goal. Her goal is not as wrong as her means. For Eve to desire wisdom is not as wrong as for her to pursue it by disobeying God and desiring to replace God. God had planned and encouraged the humans to eat good food and enjoy beauty. Would the Lord have kept them from wisdom? But, rather than receive her wisdom from God, Eve seized it in order to become God.

Wisdom is good, but there is a foolish and a wise way to wisdom . Unfortunately, Eve (and Adam) takes the foolish way. She was wrong to want to try to become the Creator. When the created tries to replace the Creator, what is newly created is not beautiful. God asks Eve: "What is this you created! " Eve, together with Adam, creates shame, independence, and irresponsibility. They become like the serpent. However, Eve was not totally evil. She valued nutrition, aesthetics, and wisdom, goals which many could learn to appreciate. Yet, the means toward those goals are as significant, or even more so, than the goals themselves. When Paul writes the Ephesians (1 Tim.2:11-15) many years later, he wants them, too, to take the wise way to wisdom.

The Curses

In several Bible passages God is described as intending to alter previously established plans. Human wickedness is so great during Noah's time God regrets having made humans (Gen. 6:6). And, God decides not to destroy Nineveh because of the national repentance of the Ninevites (Jonah 3:10). After the fall, did God change the commands made before the fall? God does not alter the commands initially made. "The Adam" is still commanded to till the ground after leaving Eden (Gen. 3:22-24). However, the fall has serious repercussions.[14] Every curse is a recasting of a pre-fall condition. The punishment is comparable to the sin. Moreover, every participant in the fall receives a separate punishment, following the order of their wrongdoing.[15] Each is responsible directly to God.

The serpent had been "more" sly than all the animals of the field which God had created (3:1). After the fall, the serpent is "more" cursed than all the animals (3:14). The serpent had encouraged Eve and Adam "to eat" from the fruit of the tree of the knowledge of good and evil. Now the serpent will himself "eat," but it is *dust* he will eat all the days of his life. Although in a normal Hebrew sentence the verb precedes the noun, for emphasis in verse 14 the noun "dust" precedes the verb "you will eat." In addition, the pre-fall understanding between the serpent and Eve is reversed by enmity. Instead of a loving dominion over animals as in 1:28, Eve now has to fight the serpent and its progeny.

God may allow this very fight to become the means for redemption. "Her [seed] will bruise your head and you will bruise its heel" (v. 15), God tells the serpent. Possibly here is the *Protevangelium*, "the first glimmer of the gospel." The "seed" of the woman may allude to the messianic line, which begins with Adam and Eve and continues through the line of Seth, but not in the line of Cain. The woman in the very process of living out the curse becomes an instrument for redemption rather than damnation. The subtle reference to the messianic line in Genesis may also be imitated by Paul's subtle reference to "the child-bearing" in 1 Timothy 2:15. The

---

[14]The word "curse" is used only for the serpent and the ground. However, *'arar* can be used of humans (e.g. Gen. 9:25; 27:29; Deut. 27:15 ff.). In Genesis 3 all the results for disobeying God's commands are "curses" in the sense that future generations cannot eradicate them by their good deeds. A mere punishment, in contrast, is often a temporary and an educational measure. Children, for example, are punished so that they may become good and mature adults (e.g., Prov. 22:15; 23:14).

[15]Philo explains: "The serpent was the first to deceive. Second, the woman sinned through him, yielding to deceit. Third the man (sinned), yielding to the woman's desire rather than to the divine commands" (*Questions and Answers on Genesis*, 1.47).

very seed which bruises the serpent becomes the seed which saves Eve.

The curses that the woman has to endure, like the serpent's curses, may each be compared to her pre-fall condition, and her punishments are comparable to her sins. Adam and Eve were to be fruitful; however, now Eve would bear children in "toil" (*'eseb*).[16] The basic command to be fruitful has not changed. Now the fulfillment of that command is hard work. Eve had been created to be a ruling helper to Adam. Her sin had been to want to take God's own commanding role. To that wrong end she took a commanding role in the fall. Her curse was now to be ruled, perversely to long for her husband and he to rule over her. She would want to be dominated by her husband and he would submit to this desire. God does not command Adam to rule or govern his wife. Rather, the curse is Eve's. The ruling is a consequence of Eve's longing and her fall.

Susan T. Foh has the interesting idea that "longing" (*tshuqah*) in Genesis 3:16 means that Eve desires to possess or control Adam in the same way that in Genesis 4:7 sin desires to enslave Cain.[17] Cain is commanded to rule over sin. Therefore, the woman's curse is *not* to be the willing slave of man nor to desire only what her husband desires. Rather, "These words mark the beginning of the battle of the sexes." Men and women now fight for control. Her thesis is possible. Although Foh employs her findings to support "the headship of the husband over his wife," her interpretation of the text does not necessarily suggest those conclusions. Adam's "governing" is not necessarily good in contrast to Eve's "devouring." Rather, both Eve's longing and the husband's rul-

---

[16]Ironically, "the curse" is sometimes employed colloquially to refer to menstruation. The pain ("premenstrual syndrome") associated with menstruation might be more appropriately called "the curse" as it represents the pain associated with childbirth. All such pain in the world is a result of the fallen nature of this planet. For example, see the satire by Karen Osman, "PMS Versus the Curse," *Daughters of Sarah*, May/June, 1985, 16-17.

[17]"What is the Woman's Desire?" *Westminster Theological Journal* 37 (Spring, 1975): 376-83.

ing are part of the fallen world. Foh presupposes that the leadership of the husband over the wife is part of the creation order. Therefore, her understanding follows from that presupposition. Furthermore, the redemptive answer to Eve's desire to possess Adam and "the battle of the sexes" would be for the wife and the husband to be mutually submitted to one another. Mutual submission would end the conflict of one to control, the other to be controlled, the direct results of the curse of God from which Christ has now freed us.

Eve's curse, then, is to desire to be ruled or to desire to rule. Both tendencies certainly are operant today. Women want to dominate men and they want to be subservient to men. Women even want to dominate men by insisting that men take on an apparent commanding role which the women then secretly manipulate. Either type of behavior by women and men's resultant rule over women are clearly part of Eve's and her descendants' curse.

Although today Eve's curse summons up the most interest, Adam's curse is the longest. So, God certainly sees Adam as responsible for his actions in the fall. Is Adam punished because he obeyed his wife? God tells Adam, "because you listened to the voice of your wife and you ate from the tree which I commanded you saying "do not eat from it' cursed is… " (3:17). Adam's obedience cannot be separated from his eating the tree God commanded him not to eat. The "and" (*waw*) connects the two clauses "Adam obeyed his wife" and "he ate" from the wrong tree. Consequently, God contrasts Adam's obeying his wife rather than his obeying God. Adam's wife had commanded him to disobey God. It was the nature of Eve's command which was wrong, not the command in itself.

Adam is cursed in three ways. First, the relationship between Adam's source ("ground of being") and himself is broken. Adam was formed from the ground (*'adamah*). Now the ground is cursed. In the same way, Adam had been the source for Eve. The woman (*'ishah*) was formed from the man (*'ish*). The word-plays of *'Adam* and *'adamah* and *'ish* and *'ishah* highlight the interrelationship between a creation and its source. We have seen as well how the woman's relationship with her source, the man, is now broken.

Second, it is the ground which helps sprout up the trees, the trees which Adam must tend and guard. Adam has misused those trees, eating from forbidden ones. Since Adam now lives in enmity with the ground (his source and potential for happiness), the ground now will fight his work:

> In toil you will eat from it all the days of your life and a thorn and a prickly plant it will cause to sprout to you and you will eat vegetables of the field in the sweat of your nose, you will eat from it till you return to the ground because from it you were taken because you are dust and to dust you will return (3:17-19).

The same word for "toil" (*'eseb*) is used for Adam as was used for Eve (3:16). Work, and child bearing, were not intended to be laborious. The ground had produced trees bearing fruits; now it produces thorns and prickly plants. Adam had eaten the fruit. Now he will eat vegetables, no longer in pleasure but in sweat or literally in "heavy breathing." Adam receives his desire to eat, but now it is with difficulty. Adam, who probably had a laissez-faire attitude (did not he allow Eve to talk with the serpent while he listened?), now is chained to the responsibilities of slaving for his food and of ruling over his wife. In this new world Adam can not subsist by merely plucking off his meals from a tree.

Third, Adam returns to dust. On the one hand, the dust is the very thing the snake will eat (3:14). So the snake's consumption of Adam, his life and his happiness, will always be symbolized. On the other hand, the dust is Adam's source. The ground over which Adam was to rule becomes his ruler. He becomes dust again and loses his independence. Adam's curse to be from the ground yet subserviently to return to it parallels Eve's curse to be from her husband yet subserviently to return to him.

The ground and the man were the source for both Adam and Eve. Because of the fall, the sources rule their successors rather than serve them. Eve symbolically returns to

Adam. He becomes her "longing" and her ruler. Adam is driven to try to master the ground, but he is mastered by it in the end. All relationships, like the image of God, have been ruptured, although not extinguished.

Does God command Adam to work and Eve to bear children? No, rather, Adam's work and Eve's childbearing are assumed. In no way is God's pre-fall joint command to bear fruit and subdue the earth changed. However, now the progeny that Eve and Adam each develop (children and vegetables) become difficult to produce. If anything, bearing children and planting have become cursed occupations.

Beyond the Curse

God created man and woman to share in ministry and marriage. They were commanded to share tasks and to share authority. Male and female are together needed to reflect God's image. Eve was created to share Adam's task as equal and similar to Adam (or as the helper who rules over the one she helps). Both Eve and Adam are fully responsible for the fall. Eve's particular sin was not so much what she valued (nutrition, aesthetics, and education) but her manner of seizing wisdom and trying to become God. The curses result in a new antagonism between each human and the material from which each was created. From rulers they became servants. Harmonious relationships become embattled ones. However, can people go beyond the curses in any way? Or, should the curses be lovingly welcomed?

First, Eve's curse was to long for *her* husband (*"your man"*). Her curse did not give sanction for any man to rule a woman or for all men to rule women. Women who want all men to rule over them amplify the curse even beyond its own boundaries. Men who choose to rule all women cannot employ the woman's curse in Genesis 3:16 as a rationale. Even as the serpent extended and misrepresented God's command to the overwhelmingly impossible command, "You may not eat from any of the trees in the garden," which Eve corrected to the still untrue "you may not eat and touch the tree in the midst of the garden," so similarly people extend and misrepresent the curse to the ruling by all men of all women.

Second, Christ's redemption has lifted many of the effects of the fall. After the fall, people are still characterized by shame, independence, and lack of responsibility. Death is still required of every human. However, Jesus' death and resurrection can save from the "sting" or "victory" of death any who choose to participate. As the Apostle Paul so eloquently tells the Corinthians:

> When the perishable puts on the imperishable, and the mortal puts on immortality, then shall come to pass the saying that is written: "Death is swallowed up in victory. O death, where is thy victory? O death, where is thy sting?" (1 Cor. 15:54-5 RSV).

"The sting of death is sin," Paul adds. Jesus has cleansed everyone of the eternal repercussions of Adam and Eve having disobeyed God. Jesus' redemption has also reintroduced the potentiality of mutual concern, interdependence, and responsibility. Humans who regret their inability to love others and who both privately and publicly acknowledge that the resurrected Jesus is God can be given the power to become loving toward others (Rom. 10:9-10; John 1:12). A continual New Testament theme is that the church should be united even as God is one (e.g. John 17:11-23). Paul commands the Corinthian church: "If one member suffers, all suffer together; if one member is honored, all rejoice together" (1 Cor. 12:26). God grants gifts to individual Christians so that other Christians can be assisted (1 Cor. 12:7). Jesus' redemption has certainly eliminated the need to appear in shame before God. As John writes:

> For everyone who does evil hates the light, and does not come to the light, lest his deeds should be exposed. But he who does what is true comes to the light, that it may be clearly seen that his deeds have been wrought in God (John 3:20-21 RSV).[18]

---

[18]Bill J. Leonard speaks eloquently against applying curses to groups today in "Forgiving Eve," *The Christian Century,* Nov. 7, 1984, 1038-40.

The world has not returned and cannot return to an Edenic, pre-fall state of natural "attire"; however, the essential sense of shame before God can be eliminated.

Jesus redeems not just humanity's curse but nature's curse as well. In Eden, a tree gives death. Jesus hangs on a tree, bearing human sin on his body (1 Pet. 2:24). Christ redeems all humans from the curse of the law, being made a curse because cursed is everyone that hangs on a tree (Gal. 3:13; Deut. 21:23). That very tree can now receive new life. Symbolically Jesus has redeemed the very tree and ground upon which he died. Thus, all creation as well as all humanity groans in childbirth waiting for its new life (Rom. 8:22).

God's redemption effected through the incarnation is presaged in God's immediate response in Eden. God treats each participant in the fall responsibly. God is the first to clothe the humans (Gen. 3:21). God still calls the two humans by one name, "the Adam" (Gen. 3:22). Furthermore, God acts on the essential equality and importance of the female to the male established before creation throughout the book of Genesis. Genesis shows God's concern to establish the covenant. In the majority of instances the choice of the woman is as important as the choice of the man in determining the covenant line.[19] Genesis 1-5 recount Adam and Eve as the proper patriarch and matriarch. Genesis 12-25 present Abram and Sarai, rather than Hagar, as the necessary succession. Chapter 25-35 include Isaac and Rebekah; chapters 37-50, Jacob, Rachel, and Leah. At every major link in the line the wife is as important as the husband. For instance, God promises Abram that he will make of him a great nation. Such a promise seems to become unlikely when Sarai is taken to Pharaoh. But she is delivered (ch. 12). Abram then complains to God that he is childless and the heir of his house is Eliezer of Damascus, his slave (ch. 15). Would

---

[19]In the case of intermarriage, interestingly, only those children are Jewish whose mothers are Jewish (*m. Kid.* 3:12). Even as of this century, a Jewish father alone is insufficient for inclusion in Judaism, while a Gentile father does not negate the claim.

Eliezer become the patriarch of the messianic line? No, the heir has to be Abraham's. Sarai then becomes concerned since she appears not to be able to have children. She has Hagar, her maid, and Abraham conceive a child, Ishmael. However, the heir has to be not just Abraham's but also Sarai's. God promises that Sarai (now "Sarah") will bear a son (17:15). Abraham's heavenly visitors also repeat that Sarah will bear a child in the spring (18:9-10). Abraham again takes Sarah to Abimelech, but she is delivered. Finally, in their old age Sarah and Abraham are given their own child, Isaac (ch. 21). The heir could be neither Eliezer nor Ishmael. It had to be the child of Sarah and Abraham. (See also Isa. 41:2.) To perpetuate God's blessings not just the male but also the female is important.

If God's acts of redemption lift the effects of death, shame, independence, and irresponsibility, is it not also possible that Adam (and all men) can try to make work more pleasurable and that Eve (and all women) can try to make labor more pleasurable? The central message of Ecclesiastes is centered in the recurring sentence: "It is God's gift to humanity that everyone should eat and drink and take pleasure in all their toil" (3:13) The work that a person performs and the food one eats should be *pleasurable*. If then it is possible for men to try to enjoy their work and to develop technology to make it more pleasurable, in the same way, Eve and all women are justified in trying to regain their relationships of equality with their husbands, and in the cooperation of childbirth techniques and through new technology ease the pain of their labor to make child bearing more pleasurable. She too is entitled to go beyond the curse. The cross shines in two directions: after Jesus' death and before Jesus' death. We should not go beyond the curse by affirming more than it does. Yet we should go beyond the curse to live lives affected by Christ's redemption.

2

The Torn Curtain: Jesus' Teachings and Practices Concerning Women

"Woman, sister, there are some things which you do not execute as well as your brother, man; no, nor ever will. Pardon me if I doubt whether you will ever produce a great poet from your chairs, or a Mozart, or a Phidias, or a Michael Angelo, or a great philosopher, or a great scholar" Thomas Dequincy, 1847, on "Joan of Arc," *Tait's Magazine,* author of *Confessions of an English Opium-Eater.*

On a hill, overlooking the city of Jerusalem, stood the beautiful white temple built by Herod and his sons between 19 BC–AD 64. The temple was a central concern for Jesus during his life on earth. The Messiah's triumphal entry into Jerusalem is first followed by the cleansing of the temple. The first recorded act of ministry of the youth Jesus occurs while teaching at his Parent's House (Luke 2:42-49). The symbols to which God's temples have hearkened were fulfilled in the Messiah. The sanctuary was not primarily a place of worship, rather it was primarily a place where God dwelled. God told the Israelites: "Let them make for me a sanctuary and I will dwell in their midst" (Exod. 25:8). Paul, too, told the Corinthians: "Do you not know that you (pl) are a sanctuary of God and the Spirit of God dwells among you?" (1 Cor. 3:16). John tells us that Jesus was conscious of how his very body represented God's sanctuary, God dwelling among humans: "Destroy this sanctuary and in three days I will raise it up" (John 2:19).

The very structure of Herod's temple can help crystallize the priorities of Jesus' ministry on earth. Several courts connected by steps and gates preceded entrance into the innermost sanctuary. Gentiles were welcomed for worship at the temple in Jerusalem,[1] however they could not pass beyond their court. The "pure" Jewish men and women could step up through a gate into the Court of Women. The women could not pass that court.[2] The men could continue up to the Court of the Israelites, but only the priests could step up to the Court of the Priests. Only those priests who were chosen by lot could step up to the porch and enter the Holy Place.[3] Beyond a curtain stood the Holy of Holies, which was entered only once a year by the High Priest after an elaborate service on the Day of Atonement (Yom Kippur). The Holy of Holies was the sanctuary wherein humans could meet their Creator.

When Jesus died the curtain barring entrance into the Holy of Holies was torn in two, from top to bottom (Matt. 27:51). That torn curtain signifies that now God's Spirit no longer dwells in a place but in a people. The people of God have become a movable tent, the sanctuary of God.

And as the Spirit of God moves out from the Holy of Holies, the barrier between the Holy of Holies and the Holy Place is swung back. Then God moves out from the Holy Place to the Court of the Priests, eliminating the specially chosen priest. Then the barrier between priest and layperson is eradicated as God moves to the Court of the Israelites.

---

[1] Philo, for example, says: "And those of other races who pay homage to them [the Jews] welcome no less than their own countrymen, while those who either break them down or mock at them they hate as their bitterest foes" *The Embassy to Gaius* XXXI (211).

[2] Josephus, *Antiquities* XV. 11.5

[3] The temple is described in *m. Mid.*

44

The barrier between man and woman is removed as God moves to the Court of Women. At last, the final gate collapses when the Court of the Gentiles is reached. The movement outward that the Spirit made from the innermost sanctuary to the peripheral courts in the temple signifies the priority Jesus had on earth in dealing with different groups of people.

The torn curtain signifies that humanity's sins need no longer keep it from approaching a holy God. Jesus' first priority was to enable humans again to approach their Creator directly but without harm to themselves. For God's holiness is like a fire which destroys all impurities. When, in the Exodus, the Spirit moved from the tent to the periphery of the camp, people were destroyed.[4] Jesus' redemption of humanity, however, extends further than the porch. Now as well the next barrier between priest and layperson has been destroyed. All people can now fulfill that holiness demanded previously of only an officiating priest (1 Pet. 2:5-10). Jesus became an example to all when he spent his days with the religious priest and scribe as well as with the common people of the land who failed to observe all the Jewish laws of ritual purity and tithe. Jesus touched the sinner and the ritually unclean (e.g., Luke 7:36-50, Mark 5:25-34). Finally, in his earthly lifetime Jesus broke the barrier between male and female.

Before his death, Jesus did not break the ultimate barrier between Jew and Gentile, although he presaged that future action. Jesus chose twelve among all his disciples to represent the original twelve tribes of Israel.[5] Although Jesus healed Gentiles and praised their faith, during his life on

---

[4]Num. 11:1-3; John 1:14; Heb. 7:20-8:14.

[5]Luke 22:28-30; Matt. 19:28. See also a similar symbolism among the Essenes, *The Scroll of the Rule* VIII (1). If Jesus' choice of twelve male disciples signifies that females should not be leaders in the church, then, consistently his choice also signifies that Gentiles should not be leaders in the church.

earth he did not stress their entrance into God's presence. As he told the Gentile women from Syrophoenicia: "I was sent only to the lost sheep of the house of Israel" (Matt. 15:21-28; Mark 7:25-30). Paul highlights this fact in his letter to the Romans describing Jesus as "a minister to the circumcised for the sake of God's truthfulness, in order to confirm the promises given to the ancestors, and in order that the Gentiles might glorify God for the sake of his mercy" (Rom. 15:8-9). Even the seventy-two/seventy disciples recorded by Luke may refer to the seventy/seventy-two elders chosen by Moses (Num. 11:16) or to the seventy/seventy-two members of the Sanhedrin, the ruling council of Jewish religious life.[6] Jesus' ministry to the Jews was not intended to exclude Gentiles forever, but simply to prepare the way for their entrance. The close of Jesus' ministry leaves him commanding his disciples to make more disciples but now of *all* the nations (Matt. 28:19).

While on earth, Jesus did challenge the practices built on religious dogma which restricted Jewish women from full participation in the public domain. The extent to which Jesus broke the traditional Jewish barriers between men and women cannot be appreciated except by looking in depth at how the Jewish laws worked in first century society.

First-Century Jewish Thought and Practice

The Mishnah, a collection of authoritative early traditions of rabbis, indicates some of the beliefs in the Jewish religious mainstream thought during the first and second centuries AD. *Aboth* 5:21, possibly by Samuel the Younger who was active in the later half of the first century AD, says:

---

[6]E.g., see *m. Sanh.* 1:5; Luke 10:1.

At five years old [one is fit] for the Scripture, at ten years for the Mishnah, at thirteen for [the fulfilling of] the commandments, at fifteen for the Talmud, at eighteen for the bride chamber, at twenty for pursuing [a calling], at thirty for authority.

Although men were exhorted to pursue actively their religious training, women were not similarly required. The formal study of the Torah was not normally officially forbidden to women. Rabbi Gamaliel taught the Torah to his daughter, Imma Shalom, wife of Rabbi Eliezer ben Hyrcanus (e.g., *b. Sanh.* 39a). In the second century AD, Beruria, the wife of Rabbi Meir, even took the three-year rabbinical training. However, women learned in Jewish teachings were unusual, since women were not obligated to study the law, nor did they receive any merit in studying the law, nor was anyone obligated to teach them![7] They were exempt from the necessity to learn Torah. *The Mishnah* explains:

The observance of all the positive ordinances that depend on the time of year is incumbent on men but not on women, and the observance of all the positive ordinances that do not depend on the time of the year is incumbent both on men and women (*Kidd.* 1:7. See too *m. Hag.* 1:1; *m. Sukk.* 2:8).

In other words, women were exempt from any requirement which necessitated their leaving the home for any period of time. Consequently they were exempt from attending school, as well as traveling to Jerusalem at the feasts of

---

[7]Roslyn Lacks adds: "The very structure of the academy tended to exclude [women]. Scholars would often travel long distances to spend months and years of study with their mentors and colleagues, while wives (of necessity?) remained at home....The semimonastic *ambiance* of the academy together with that climate of camaraderie in intellectual discourse essential for a real grasp of Talmud precluded the participation of women—except in rare instances—in Talmudic debates and decisions" *Women and Judaism: Myth, History, & Struggle* (Garden City: Doubleday Co., 1980) p. 123.

Passover, Pentecost, and Tabernacles.[8]

The Babylonian Talmud records a teaching by Rabbi Aha ben Jacob which comments on Exodus 13:9. Rabbi ben Jacob says:

> Scripture saith, "And it shall be for a sign unto thee upon thine hand, and for a memorial between thine eyes, that the Torah of the Lord may be in thy mouth," hence the whole Torah is compared to phylacteries. (Also R. Meir, *b. Kidd.* 34a-35a; cf. *m. Sanh.* 11:3.)

Phylacteries are small leather boxes with scripture verses worn on the head and the left arm during prayer. A woman had as a counterpart a *mezuzah* on her doorpost at home. Women, slaves and minors were exempt from wearing phylacteries (*m. Ber.* 3:3). The Torah was comparable to phylacteries. Consequently the Torah and phylacteries were applicable only to people who traveled about in their daily life.

According to much Jewish thought, the performance of a good act which is not obligatory has *less* merit than if it is obligatory. For example, Rabbi Hanina said: "He who is commanded and does, stands higher than he who is not commanded and does" (*b. 'Abod. Zar.* 3a). How then could women earn merit before God? *The Babylonian Talmud* records that Rab said to Rabbi Hiyya:

---

[8]Note however how Mary went anyway [Luke 2:41]. Nathan Drazin says that "girls were not admitted as pupils in any of the schools, and women were not allowed as teachers" (p. 128). Since females were not required to study the Torah, therefore compulsory education was not necessary. Parents *might* teach a daughter elementary skills at home: reading (of Scripture), writing, prayers, and some grammar, arithmetic, geography and history. *History of Jewish Education From 515 B.C.E. to 220 C.E. (During the Periods of the Second Commonwealth and the Tannaim).* (Baltimore: Johns Hopkins, 1940). See also *m. Ned.* 4:3. Philo speaks metaphorically of, "mother, the instruction in the elementary learning of the sophist" in contrast to wisdom which entails, "long meditation on the truth by the knowledge of right reason" (*On the Cherubim* III [10]). Although the wisdom he describes are the words spoken by Sarah and Abraham, he alludes to the literal practice of girls receiving elementary training (from their mothers?) as opposed to the lengthier and more advanced formal education received by the boys. In *The Embassy to Gaius* XVI (115) Philo explains that children are trained by parents, tutors, and instructors.

Whereby do women earn merit? By making their children go to the synagogue to learn Scripture and their husbands to the Beth Hamidrash (Talmud stage of advanced learning after fourteen years of age) to learn Mishnah, and waiting for their husbands till they return from the Beth Hamidrash (*b. Ber.* 17a).

Women did attend synagogue services. They participated in worship and were present in the prayer hall, "House of the Book," or *sabbateion.* Technically women could even read the Scripture aloud before the congregation. However *The Talmud* records:

Our Rabbis taught: All are qualified to be among the seven [who read], even a minor and a woman, only the Sages said that a woman should not read in the Torah out of respect for the congregation (*b. Meg.* 23a).

However, they did not participate in the "House of Study" which was called *andron* or "of males." In the House of Study scribes and disciples discussed the Jewish law. Even in the prayer hall women may have been separated from the men by some sort of barrier or grillwork. At least by the second century AD, if not before, women may have sat in a gallery above the sides and rear of the prayer hall. *The Palestinian Talmud* describes a scene in AD 116 when Trajan destroyed a famous synagogue in Alexandria. After he killed the men, Trajan offered mercy to the women at the price of their honor. They replied: "Do to those above as you have done to those below" (*t. Sukk.* V.1). Even the Court of Women in the temple at Jerusalem came to have a gallery: "so that the women should behold from above and the men from below and that they should not mingle together" (*m. Mid.* 2:5). One rationale for women being separated from the men during worship in the synagogue was to make it a little more difficult for the women to benefit from the homily in the service. According to Deuteronomy 31:12 and Joshua 8:35 all people were exhorted to attend regularly the reading of the Law:

Assemble the people, men, women, and little ones, and the so-journer within your towns, that they may hear and learn to fear the Lord your God, and be careful to do all the words of this law (RSV).

However, *The Talmud* explains that while men came to learn the Torah, women came to hear, but not to study it fully (R. Eleazar b. Azariah, active at the end of the first century AD (*b. Hag.* 3a).

Why, despite the clear scriptural injunction, were women to be exempt from formal training in the law? The rabbinic law on "positive ordinances that depend on the time of year" and the stationary nature of a *mezuzah* highlight the principle that these rabbinic laws were constructed to ensure that women were not encouraged to leave their homes. The location of women (and slaves) seems to be the underlying concern. Rabbi Jeremiah explained that "a woman generally stays at home, whereas a man goes out into the streets and learns understanding from people (men)" (*Midrash Rabbah*, Genesis 1, ch. XVIII.1).

Philo, who especially had in mind daughters of wealthy families in Alexandria, said:

Market-places and council-halls and law-courts and gatherings and meetings where a large number of people are assembled, and open-air life with full scope for discussion and action—all these are suitable to men in both war and peace. The women are best suited to the indoor life which never strays from the house, within which the middle door is taken by the maidens as their boundary, and the outer door by those who have reached full womanhood. Organized communities are of two sorts, the greater which we call cities and the smaller which we call households. Both of these have their governors; the government of the greater is assigned to men under the name of statesmanship, that of the lesser, known as household management, to women (*On the Special Laws,* III, ch. 31 [169-170]. See also *Flaccus* XI [89]).

Women were exempt from learning the Torah first because their role as homemakers was seen as primary and second because the culture feared the possibility of unchastity. The Rabbis differed on whether women were capable of learning the Torah. Rabbi Eliezer declared: "There is no wisdom in woman except with the distaff" (*b. Yoma* 66b). Rabbi Jose thought, "women are of unstable temperament" and therefore easily succumbed to torture (*b. Sabb.* 33b). And Josephus thought women could not be witnesses because of "the levity and temerity of their sex" (*Antiquities* IV. Ch. 8:15 [219]). The more enlightened Rabbi Hisda thought that God "endowed the woman with more understanding (or intelligence) than the man."[9]

First century Jews, like twentieth century Americans, also differed on whether women were more easily deceived than men. Philo explains in *The Embassy of Gaius* that: "the judgments of women as a rule are weaker and do not apprehend any mental conception apart from what their senses perceive" (XL [319]). Philo based his perceptions on women on the principle he outlines in *On the Account of the Creation of the World Given by Moses*: "For in human beings the mind occupies the rank of the man, and the sensations that of the woman" (LIX). However, Philo's contemporary Ben Azzai wanted women to learn the law so that they could avoid deception:

A man ought to give his daughter a knowledge of the Law so that if she must drink [the bitter water] she may know that the merit [that she had acquired] will hold her punishment in suspense (*m. Sot.* 3:4).

Although not presenting any consistent analysis of woman's essential character, early Jewish law did present a consistent belief in the necessity for women to be centered around their household. If women spent their time in the

---

[9] *b. Nid.* 45b. So too R. Eleazar in the name of R. Jose b. Zimra, *Midrash Rabbah*, Genesis I, ch. XVIII.1. R. Ishmael b. Kimhith said: "All women are valiant but the valor of my mother exceeded them all" b. Yoma 47a.

study of the law, it was feared, their care of the household would suffer. [10]

Wives were required themselves to sustain a household's economy, unless they had servants to direct. For instance in *The Mishnah* a wife is required to grind flour, bake bread, wash clothes, cook food, nurse her child, make ready her husband's bed, oversee the Sabbath celebrations, and spin wool (*m. Ketub.* 5:5,9). Women were trained in domestic arts, especially needlework and weaving. Even young girls looked after their younger brothers and sisters.

Women were so intimately associated with the house and homemaking that Rabbi Judah said that "his house" is a synonym for "his wife" in Leviticus 16:6 (*m. Yoma* 1:1). Rabbi Jose, commenting on *Yoma* 1:1, proudly adds that: "Never have I called my wife by that word [i.e. 'my wife'], but always "my home.' " Even a woman's body came to be perceived as constructed for homemaking. Rabbi Hisda interprets Genesis 2:22 wherein God takes Adam's rib and "builds (it) into a woman":

"This teaches that the Holy One, blessed be He, built Eve in the shape of a storehouse.
As a storehouse is [made] wide below and narrow above so that it may contain the produce, so was [the womb of] a woman [made] wide below and narrow above so that it may contain the embryo" (*b. 'Erub.* 18a-b).

Second to the importance attached to the woman's role in the home was the fear of immorality. First century Judaism was part of an Eastern culture where women participated little in public life. The woman who did take an active part in

---

[10]See also a Cohen, *Everyman's Talmud* (New York: E.P. Dutton & Co., 1949), p. 159. The character Rabbi Small, created by Harry Kemelman, suggests that even today Jewish women are exempt from commandments at a particular time because these commandments would interfere with their work of managing the home and the family. He adds that the center of the Jewish religion is the home. It is there that the Sabbath, Feast of Passover, and Succah are celebrated. *Thursday The Rabbi Walked Out* (New York: Fawcett Crest, 1978), Ch. 7, pp. 58-59.

public life was in danger of a charge of promiscuity. Rabbi Eliezer, who was active during the end of the first century AD, declared: "If any man gives his daughter a knowledge of the law it is as though he taught her lechery" (*m. Sota.* 3:4). Why "lechery"? A woman who knew the law would become active in public thereby indirectly inviting sexual advances. Even women and unmarried men were not desirable as teachers of children because then the rabbis feared that the teacher and the parent of the child might resort to promiscuous behavior! Any man whose business was with women was told that he should not remain alone with women (*m. Kidd.* 4:12-14).

Two centuries earlier Jesus ben Sirach (ca. 180 BC), in Ecclesiasticus, summarized well this oriental fear of immorality:

A daughter is a secret anxiety to her father,
and the worry of her keeps him awake at night;
when she is young, for fear she may grow too old to marry,
and when she is married, for fear she may lose her husband's love;
when she is a virgin, for fear she may be seduced
and become pregnant in her father's house,
when she has a husband, for fear she may misbehave,
and after marriage, for fear she may be barren.
Keep close watch over a headstrong daughter,
or she may give your enemies cause to gloat,
making you the talk of the town and a byword among the people,
and shaming you in the eyes of the world.
Do not let her display her beauty to any man,
or gossip in the women's quarters.
For out of clothes comes the moth,
and out of woman comes women's wickedness.
Better a man's wickedness than a woman's goodness;
it is woman who brings shame and disgrace (42:9-14 NEB).[11]

Not every Jewish father was like Jesus, son of Sirach. However, his attitude was not that different from his later

---

[11]See also Testaments of the Twelve Patriarchs T. Reuben 3:10, 6:2; T. Judah 17:1, T. Issachar 4:4.

Egyptian compatriot Philo. Certainly Jews in Macedonia and Italy might have a more gracious attitude toward women. However, the fear of immorality to varying degrees was a constant element of ancient Jewish culture.

A woman could be divorced without any financial settlement (*Ketubah*): "If she goes out with her hair unbound, or spins (wool) in the street, or speaks with any man" (*m. Ketub.* 7:6). If a woman spoke with a man on the street she was presumed to have had intercourse, unless proven otherwise (*m. Ketub.* 1:8). Rabbi Meir who lived in the middle of the second century AD, said, however, that "most men do not mind their wives talking with their brothers and relatives" (*b. Gitt.* 90a).

Women normally did not eat with men whenever there was a guest present nor did the women normally serve the men if a boy or a slave were available.[12] Leonard Swidler comments:

The same custom persists in the villages of Palestine today. While in Israel in 1972 I was in a number of houses of Arabs, Christian, Druze and Muslim, for meals, and never met the wives, or any other women; my friends had many similar experiences.[13]

However, customs would vary depending on the wealth of the family and the locality. Simon's mother-in-law personally served Jesus and his disciples after her recovery to health. Was such a practice possible in the countryside? Women did travel more freely in the countryside than in the cities. A respectable woman would try to avoid stepping outside during busy times of day such as noon. They had to draw water from the wells; they might help their husbands work in the fields, sell olives at their doors, sometimes keep shop, and of course, they could attend worship services (e.g., *m. Ketub.* 5:9, 9:4).

---

[12]E.g., *b. Kidd.* 70A, The Essenes described by Philo did have women eat with men but at different sides of the room, *On the Contemplative Life* VIII-IX [68-9].

[13]*Women in Judaism: The Status of Women in Formative Judaism* (Metuchen, N.J.: Scarecrow, 1976), p. 125.

The Jews certainly had female rulers. Queen Alexandra Salome was so renowned and loved by the Pharisees that her reign in 76-67 BC is called the "Pharisaic Golden Age." When Jesus was a child, he would have known that Salome, Herod the Great's sister, ruled over several cities by the coast of Jamnia, Phasaelis, and Azotus.

Probably, the women disciples who followed Jesus traveled in a group, thereby making it possible for them to appear respectable (e.g. Mark 15:41; Luke 8:1-3). Nevertheless, the norm for women was to be localized around the household or courtyard. Activity in public was to be done only when necessary and then to be done very carefully. In other words, respectable women did not travel alone nor with their hair unbound or unveiled.[14]

Since women were usually encouraged to remain at home limiting the possibility of promiscuity and maintaining the home instead of getting formal religious training, their participation in the public domain was then affected. Jose ben Johanan of Jerusalem, who lived around 160 BC, declared, "talk not much with womankind. They said this of a man's own wife: how much more of his fellow's wife! Hence the Sages have said: He that talks much with womankind brings evil upon himself and neglects the study of the Law and at the last will inherit Gehenna."[15] Men were encouraged not to converse too much with women because women were not

---

[14]E.g. *m. Ketub.* 1:10, 7:6, Num. 5:18. In *m. B. Qam.* 8:6 a man who unloosed a woman's hair in the street is fined 400 zuz (or 250 denars). R. Ishmael b. Kimhith's mother was rewarded with seeing two high priests in one day because she covered her hair even in her own house. She said: "Throughout the days of my life the beams of my house have not seen the plaits of my hair," *b. Yoma* 47a.

[15]*m. 'Abot.* 1:5. The learned Beruria in the second century A.D. in humor refers to the sayings of the Sages. *The Babylonian Talmud* records: "Rabbi Jose the Galilian was once on a journey when he met Beruriah, 'By what road,' he asked her, 'do we go to Lydda?'—'Foolish Galilean,' she replied, 'did not the Sages say this: Engage not in much talk with women? You should have asked: By which to Lydda?'" (*b. 'Erub.* 53b). See also *b. Ber.* 43b, *b. Hag.* 5b. R. Eliezer even declared that women cannot be possessed of good manners because they are "not familiar with the Torah" Kallah 50b, *The Minor Tractates of the Talmud.*

trained in the Torah. There was no more edifying topic than
the law. For instance, Rabbi Hananiah ben Teradion, who
died in AD 135 in the Bar Cocheba Revolt, said:

> If two sit together and no words of the Law [are spoken] between
> them, there is the seat of the scornful, as it is written, "Nor sitteth
> in the seat of the scornful." But if two sit together and words of the
> Law [are spoken] between them, the Divine Presence rests between
> them, as it is written, "Then they that feared the Lord spake one
> with another: and the Lord hearkened, and heard, and a book of re-
> membrance was written before him, for them that feared the Lord,
> and that thought upon his name." Scripture speaks here of "two";
> whence [do we learn] that if even one sits and occupies himself in
> the Law, the Holy One, blessed is he, appoints him a reward? Be-
> cause it is written, "Let him sit alone and keep silence, because he
> hath laid it upon him."[16]

Many persons have referred to the Jewish daily prayer as
proof of the low view of women in all Jewish eyes:

> "Blessed be He who did not make me a Gentile;
> Blessed be He who did not make me a woman;
> Blessed be He who did not make me an uneducated man (or a
> slave)"
> (Tosephta 7:16-18 on *t. Ber.* 13b or *b. Menah.* 43b).

However, the prayer of thanksgiving is given not so much
because Gentiles, women and slaves are inherently inferior
but because they are not obliged to fulfill the commands to
study the law. Rabbi Judah explains that a woman is "under
no obligation to keep the commandments" (*t. Ber.* 13b). Consequently, an "uneducated man" would be similar to a Gentile, woman, or slave.

In summary, Jewish women were discouraged from having
formal higher education in the law. They were not required to
pursue religious training nor did they receive any merit in

---

[16]*m. 'Abot* 3:2. *m. Kidd.* 1:10 similarly reads: "He that has a knowledge of
Scripture and Mishnah and right conduct will not soon fall into sin, for it is
written, 'And a threefold cord is not quickly broken.' But he that has no
knowledge of Scripture and Mishnah and right conduct has no part in the
habitable world." See also *m. Pe'a* 1:1.

study. Furthermore, no one was required or encouraged to teach them. They were not admitted into Jewish schools. Even in the synagogue service they were not to "study fully." These exemptions were made for woman because she was to be primarily a homemaker and to be protected against unchasity. Consequently, women were often treated as persons who had little edification to share in conversation and who had little preparation to withstand the temptations of public life.

Jesus' Thought and Practice in Light of First-Century Jewish Culture

How did Jesus' teaching and practice compare with those of the people to and from whom he was called to serve? Although Jesus supported the Jewish concern for God's intention in the Old Testament laws by fulfilling them in his own life, he highly criticized the misuse of God's laws and the addition of many encumbering oral laws. And when Jesus' teachings came to affect women, they were such as to cut away totally the thorn vines which were choking the ancient tree. God's intentions could flourish again. What women could do, and the priorities in their lives, Jesus completely restored!

Jesus' dinnertime conversation with Mary and Martha has become such a common aspect of popular culture that Luke 10:38-42 has lost much of its original power. Upon hearing of Mary and Martha we may either agree that, yes, Mary did well to learn about spiritual truths rather than to do housework or we may, probably in boredom, react that Martha has been misunderstood. Martha worked very hard to serve Jesus and the disciples and has been overlooked and underestimated by the church. Jesus was not speaking derogatorily about housework. He was simply comparing metaphorically a life of works and a life of contemplation.

Luke sets an interesting scene before the reader:

And while they were traveling [Jesus] entered into a certain village; and a certain woman by the name of Martha welcomed him as a guest. And she had a sister called Mary, who having been seated at the Lord's feet she heard his word.

"To sit at someone's feet" in the United States conjures up memories of childhood, such as sitting around an adult or sitting at a campfire hearing stories. However, to sit at someone's feet for a first-century Jew (or other ancient person) would be an act to symbolize higher level formal education. Sitting at a rabbi's feet was a position typical of rabbinic students expressing respect to their rabbi. As Jose ben Joezer of Zeredah, who lived *ca.* 160 BC, said: "Let thy house be a meeting-house for the Sages and sit amid the dust of their feet and drink in their words with thirst" (*m. 'Abot* 1:4). Since teachers sat on a raised place in order to teach (as Jesus did in Luke 4:20-21), students had to sit on mats on the floor to be in a lower position than their teacher. The Apostle Paul describes his own rabbinic learning in similar language. He told a crowd of his fellow Jews that he was reared in Jerusalem "having been instructed at the feet of Gamaliel according to [the] strictness of the law of the ancestors" (Acts 22:3).[17] Consequently, Luke is indirectly telling his readers that Mary was taking a position typical of a rabbinic pupil, a position unusual for a woman and moreover usually disapproved.

Luke goes on to describe Martha:

[She] became overburdened (or distracted) concerning much service; and having approached, she said, "Lord, is it not of concern to you that my sister has left me to serve *alone*? Therefore tell her that she might help me."

---

[17]S. Safrai adds: "Sitting on the floor was very uncommon, being reserved for mourners and those under a ban. Only at public assemblies or large gatherings of students around their rabbis would people sit on mats spread on the ground because of lack of other seats or out of respect for the speaker." S. Safrai and M. Stern, eds, *The Jewish People in the First Century: Historical Geography, Political History, Social, Cultural and Religious Life and Institutions,* Compendia Rerum Iudaicarum ad Novum Testamentum, Section One (Philadelphia: Fortress, 1976), p. 737. See also *b. Mo'ed Katan* 16b.

While Mary sits in rabbinic fashion at the Lord's feet hearing his words, Martha not only is working around the house but she also becomes overburdened and mentally distracted by the many things she has to do. Luke chooses a colorful word to describe Martha. *Perispao* literally means "I draw around" and metaphorically means in the passive tense "I am driven about." Martha stresses in her question that she is all alone. Naturally, she becomes angry at the Lord ("is it not of concern to you"!) because he appears as if he does not care that she alone has such a great burden. She then commands Jesus to tell Mary to help her. Apparently, Martha had had no success in commanding Mary herself! Martha does not plan to relegate all the work to Mary. She employs *sunantilambanomai*, which signifies "I help *with* another." Martha wanted Mary to help along with herself.

How can the Rabbi Jesus respond to such a situation? The use of the word *perispao* does indicate that Martha had become mentally distracted and thereby had allowed her work to overcome her. However, Luke did tell the reader that she had *much* service and she was by herself. Also, Martha allowed her frustration to turn into anger against the Lord and she inappropriately came to command him to do her bidding. Nevertheless, Martha's indignation was perfectly understandable in the light of her culture. A Jewish woman's primary role was that of homemaker. She was exempt from rabbinic training and received no merit from learning the law. Should not Martha's request that Mary help her in service *supersede* Mary's desire to learn?

How does Jesus respond in light of the educational assumptions of his time? Jesus could have reprimanded Martha for being distracted and angry and yet asked Mary to help her: "I do not mind your wanting to learn, Mary, but your first obligation is the home!" What did Jesus say?:

Martha, Martha, you are anxious and troubled concerning many things, but one is needed: for Mary the good share has chosen which will not be removed from her!

Jesus uses two additional descriptive words to describe

Martha. *Merimnao* literally means "I am drawn in different directions," and metaphorically it signifies "I am anxious or unduly concerned." Such an anxiety is not necessarily wrong. Paul recommends Timothy to the Philippians as a person who is "anxious" about them and he encourages the Corinthians to become "anxious" about one another (Phil. 2:20; 1 Cor. 12:25). Apparently such excessive concern is a desirable trait if the object is people, but it is not desirable otherwise. Martha was not concerned about Mary's spiritual growth nor about the one concern Martha should have had. The second word Jesus uses to describe Martha is *thorubazo*, which comes from "confusion" and means "I make a noise, uproar, or distrubance as a crowd would make." Jesus perceives Martha as troubled with cares, drawn in different directions, making an uproar in her troubledness. But his love for her is shown by the tender way in which he repeats her name and shows her what she is feeling.

Although Jesus does show a concern for Martha's feelings (he does not want her to be anxious and troubled), he declares it is Mary who has selected the good share and, moreover, that share will not be taken from her! Mary, not Martha, has made the right choice. And Jesus would not allow Martha, or anyone else, to stop Mary from learning as his male students would learn. Jesus has completely reversed the priorities and the consequences of those priorities in Jewish ancient life. Not only does Jesus *not* think women are exempt from learning the Torah, but also they do *best* to learn God's law. Moreover, this new rabbi will not allow anyone to take this learning process away from those who sit under his feet!

Moreover, in choosing between a woman's role in homemaking and a woman's role in education, which Martha and Mary represent, in contrast to contemporary Jewish practice, Jesus has concluded that a woman's role as homemaker is *not* primary. Jesus has returned to that original injunction in Deuteronomy 31:12: "Men, women, children and strangers are to learn to fear the Lord and do all the Lord commands." The same point is made in Luke 11:27-28. More blessed are those women who hear and do God's word than those who nurse the wisest of all teachers. Apparently, Jesus thought women received more merit from attending the School of the Rabbis than sending men to the School of the Rabbis. Moreover, in his whole ministry he constantly stressed the importance of allegiance to his name over allegiance to one's family, if such a choice needed to be made (e.g., Luke 12:51-53; 14:26). As well, Jesus did not allow the fear of immorality to prohibit women from learning. Consequently, he demanded the highest chastity from the men: "Everyone that looks on a woman in lust already has committed adultery in his heart" (Matt. 5:28). Jesus was assuming that women indeed were intellectually capable of learning. (As their Creator, Jesus should know!) Since Martha had "much service," Martha and Mary must have had quite a crowd of disciples at their house. Yet even so, Mary was face to face (*pros* is the preposition used in v. 39) with Jesus. She apparently was not at the back of the crowd.

If the Jewish system of discouraging women to participate in formal higher education affected the way women were publicly treated, so too Jesus' new principle of encouraging women to seek religious training affected the way he publicly treated them. Jesus spoke to women directly and in public in defiance of Jewish custom. Consequently John tells us that Jesus' desciples "marveled" when they found him speaking with a woman, the Samaritan woman at the well (John 4:27). Jesus spoke often to women in public. Before a large crowd he told the widow at Nain: "Do not weep" (Luke 7:12-13). He demanded to know and to speak to the woman who touched him in the crowd, the woman who had bled for twelve years (Luke 8:45). As he was teaching in a synagogue during the sabbath service, he addressed, touched, and healed a bent woman, a "daughter of Abraham" (Luke 13:10-16). Even as he was on his way to death he did not hesitate to speak to the many women in the crowd who lamented his death (Luke 23:27-31).

Moreover, Jesus had a female group of disciples who, along with the men, followed him wherever he went to learn from him. The angels reminded Mary Magdalene, Joanna, Mary the mother of James, and Salome, mother of the sons of Zebedee, James and John, that they were part of the disciples whom Jesus had taught in Galilee telling them that he would "be delivered into the hands of sinful humans and be crucified and by the third day arise."[18] Mary showed her awareness of Jesus' teachings on suffering when she anointed the Messiah "for the day of [his] burial" (John 12:3-7). And these very women were chosen by Jesus to be the first witnesses to his resurrection. They were the first to see the empty tomb. Mary Magdalene is the first person to see the resurrected Jesus (John 20:11-18), then the other women meet him (Matt. 28:8-10). After these encounters, Jesus meets Simon Peter (Luke 24:34). When Paul repeats the list of official witnesses to the resurrection in 1 Corinthians 15:5-8 he mentions specifically only the men because according to Jewish law, only certain men could testify officially about a person.[19] The tension between the ramifications of Jesus' good news and the temporary accomodations necessary to communicate that good news were already being felt. Jesus though has shown the consistency between his teaching and his practice. His male disciples were confounded by his consistency and even questioned the reliability of the witnesses he chose (Luke 24:10-11, 22-24). Jesus in contrast wanted women to learn and to testify before others about God's actions on earth. He wanted these women whom he had taught to go on to take authoritative leadership positions themselves. That is why they were chosen to be the first witnesses to the resurrection.

The very barriers Jesus had dismantled were later to be rebuilt: barriers between priest and layperson, man and woman, Jew and Gentile. The dead animal skin that was the tent has become living human flesh. The moveable tent has

---

[18]Luke 24:6-7; 9:22; Matt. 17:22-3; Mark 9:30-1. Lori V. Johnson, "Galilean Women Disciples of Jesus: And They Remembered His Words," (Unpublished paper, Gordon-Conwell Theological Seminary, 1983).

[19]*m. Sheb.* 4:1-6. See also *m. Ros. Has.* 1:8 and *m. Sanh.* 3:3-5.

become alive. The body of Christ, God's sanctuary, is God's people. However, after the third century AD, Christians began constructing buildings in imitation of that old marble temple. The sanctuary or "holy of holies" became the pulpit set on a porch above the people. No longer were women or lay people allowed to enter that "holy of holies" and there hear and speak God's message. The raised place became reserved again for certain purified males. The priesthood of all believers became the priesthood of males again.[20] The good news for all became the good news for the powerful and the rich. The good news for the women became the good news for the men. Today some seminaries maintain the old style of encouraging men first, women second, or women not at all to learn and teach. The antipathy between Jew and Gentile is often still with us. However, no matter how extensively people try to pour cement into that former foundation, the living temple will grow up and crack the imitation!

---

[20]Apparently, Western Christendom tended to restrict women before the East did. By the second century some Christians were being taught that it was the prophets not the people who were "your high priests" (*The Didache* XIII.3). By the fourth century Chrysostom, although he assumed women could carry "on the race Apostles and Evangelists ran" and teach, even a wife could teach her husband when she became wiser than him, yet he thought women should not publically speak from the "bema" (a raised platform) (*The Epistle to the Romans* XXXI). Toward the end of the fourth century sentiments such as Chrysostom's were beginning to appear as decisions in synods. The Synod of Laodicea in Phrygia (AD 343-81) concluded, "Women may not approach near the altar" (Canon 44). The supposed fourth Synod of Carthage (398) concluded: "A layman may not teach in the presence of the clergy, except at their command. A woman, however learned and holy, may not take upon herself to teach in an assembly of men. A woman may not baptize" (Canons 98-100). Margaret Howe, Elizabeth Tetlow, and Mary McKenna trace some of the changes in Christianity which tended to return its organization from the priesthood of all believers to the church leader as priest. E. Margaret Howe, *Women and Church Leadership* (Grand Rapids: Zondervan, 1982), chs. 5-6; Elizabeth M. Tetlow, *Women and Ministry in the New Testament: Called to Serve* (Lanham: University Press of America, 1980); Mary L. McKenna, *Women of the Church: Role and Renewal* (New York: Kenedy, 1967).

3

The Altered Prayer: Paul's Teachings and Practices Concerning Women in Ministry

> Blessed art thou who hast not made me a Gentile,
> Blessed art thou who hast not made me an uneducated man,
> Blessed art thou who hast not made me a woman
> (*Palestinian Talmud Ber.* 136b).

The Jewish three-fold daily prayer is often a Gentile's first introduction to the status of women in Judaism. Such a prayer shows, however, as we have shown, more a love for the opportunity to study the law than a depreciation of Gentiles, slaves, and women. Many persons[1] have suggested that it is this very prayer which Paul paraphrases and negates in Galatians 3:27-28:

---

[1] E.g. Leonard Swidler, *Women in Judaism: The Status of Women in Formative Judaism* (Metuchen: Scarecrow, 1976), p. 81. Wayne A. Meeks also mentions that the Greeks (originally Thales or Plato) would be thankful they were "born a human being and not a beast, next, a man and not a woman, thirdly, a Greek and not a barbarian." "The Image of the Androgyne: Some Uses of a Symbol in Earliest Christianity," *History of Religions* 13 (February, 1974): 167. If the Jews derived their prayer in response to such a Gentile gratitude, then they changed the three groups (beast, woman, barbarian) into three groups of humans who were exempt from study of the law (Gentile, slave or uneducated man, woman). Ironically, the Jews were thankful they were not *Greeks*. Women made both lists!

For whomever into Christ is baptized, wears *Christ;* there is neither Jew nor Greek, there is neither slave nor free, there is neither male and female; for all of you are one in Christ Jesus.

However, we do not have a clear example of this Jewish prayer in the early first century. It occurs in the later Palestinian and Babylonian Talmuds. The prayer is not found in the authoritative Mishnah but in the Tosephta, the competitive Mishnah which did not gain authority. Rabbis Judah and Meir are associated with the benediction. They lived during the second century AD. Possibly, though, the prayer was an informal or not fully accepted benediction which later was accepted into the Jewish mainstream. Or possibly the prayer was a Jewish response to Paul's proclamation, which became well known through Christian evangelism. Whatever the case, the sequence of Gentile, ignoramus or slave, and woman is a similar sequence in Galatians and in the Palestinian Talmud.

One Because We Wear Christ: The Theory (Galatians 3:27-28)

The sequence Paul follows in Galatians reflects Paul's own priorities in ministry, even as the temple layout reflected Jesus' priorities in ministry. Paul's first priority was to help Jew and Gentile to see each other as "Christ," and therefore "one." If a person wears "Christ," then it is "Christ" who is seen, not one's Jewishness nor Gentileness. Interestingly, Paul's priorities begin where Jesus' priorities left off. At the end of his life on earth, Jesus challenged his disciples to go to all the Gentiles. The foundational God-human, priest-lay, male-female barriers had been overturned. All the gates were opened, even the gate excluding the Gentile. Paul's call was to extend the ministry of the living Christ past, while not excluding, the "lost sheep of Israel" to the lost wild "dogs" of the world. His second and third priorities were to help slave and free and then male and female be one as well.

Paul explains that he was entrusted with the gospel to the

"uncircumcised," or the Gentiles.[2] Such a conviction was not an immediate one for Paul. Devout Jews distinguished themselves from their Gentile neighbors by observing the Sabbath and other festivals such as Passover, Tabernacles, Purim, and Hanukkah, by dietary restrictions, and by circumcision. Pharisees, such as Paul, distinguished themselves from other Jews by diligently observing the rules of cleanness and uncleanness and the rules of tithes. Now Paul was commissioned with good news for the Gentiles that Jew and Gentile were one. No doubt Paul thought deeply about his new calling during his years in Arabia, his self-imposed theological training (Gal. 1:17). Moreover, even when he did begin his preaching tours, he followed in Jesus' steps by preaching first to the Jews. When the Jews rejected his message, then he and his associates turned to the Gentiles.[3]

Is it possible that, although Paul may have seen Jew and Gentile as "one" and both wearing the same "Christ," the privileges of the Jew in the religious area did not have any social implications at all? In other words, could Paul simply have been declaring that neither being Jew nor being Gentile gave a person an advantage when approaching God, yet in social life a Jew could and should have advantages over Gentiles? Does Jesus' good news to the oppressed pertain only to the spiritual realm but not to the earthly realm?

In Galatians 2:11-14 Paul reprimands Peter and Barnabas because they refused to eat with the Gentiles when the circumcision party of the Jews appeared. Paul specifically opposed Peter for his inconsistency. Peter was not a model of his own teachings (v. 14). The Jews who were compelling the Gentiles to fulfill the laws of ritual cleanliness were also wrong. Are not these *social* as well as religious practices? And, what is the reason Paul cites for the rebuke? Jews *and* Gentiles are both justified by faith in Christ Jesus (2:15-16). The oneness of Jew and Gentile affected their social prac-

---

[2]Acts 9:15; Rom. 15:16; 11:13; Gal. 2:2-9; Eph. 3:7-9; 1 Tim. 2:7.

[3]E.g. Acts 13:44-7; 17:1-2; 18:6-9, 19; 28:17-23.

tices and requirements toward one another.

Indeed, Paul's call itself to preach to the Gentiles had social and political implications for Paul's own life. Paul
preached to Gentiles and taught them the good news (Acts
16:14; 17:16f.). Titus, a Gentile, became an equal and authoritative minister with Paul. Paul was continually harassed
both by some Jews and Jewish Christians, those of the circumcision party. The Jews from Antioch and Iconium
stoned Paul (Acts 14:19). Even though Peter had already explained why Gentiles had become followers, the circumcision
party again raised similar concerns later in Jerusalem before
Paul and Barnabas (Acts 11:1-3; 15; 21). Finally, Paul's Jewish opposition had him arrested in Jerusalem.

Gentiles were not only perceived as equal to Jews before
God, they were also treated as equal to Jews by the early
Christians. Always, theory precedes practice. Or, practice
assumes an already held theory. The theory that justification by faith creates an equality between Jew and Gentile,
slave and free, male and female precedes the practice. Trans-
ferring the theory into practice takes time. To be "one" in
Christ Jesus is never simply a spiritual instead of a social
statement. Oneness is always spiritual and social. Because
God is one God, the church is to be "one" in unity, its members living in harmony, economically and spiritually interdependent, serving the interests of others in humility, even as
Jesus Christ, to the extent of death.[4] James reinforces the
necessity for mental assent of oneness to be an experiential
assent as well: "You believe that God is one; you do well.
Even the demons believe and tremble with fear. And, do you
wish to know, O foolish person, that faith apart from works
is useless?" (James 2:19-20).

Paul placed less priority on eradicating the social inequali-
ties between slave and free and male and female than he did
between Jew and Gentile. However, he made sizeable contri-

---

[4] E.g., John 17:11, 22-3; Acts 4:32; Rom. 12:4-5; 15:5-6; 1 Cor. 3:8; Eph. 2-4;
Phil. 1:27, 2:2-8.

butions to these groups, too. Slaves, like women, were exempt from learning the Torah and from wearing phylacteries (*m. Ber.* 3:3;7:2). They also were exempt from celebrating the Feast of Tabernacles and were ineligible as witnesses (*m. Sukk.* 2:8; *m. Ros. Has.* 1:8). The early Roman Empire specialist and numismatist Harold Mattingly says:

"Christianity made no attempt to abolish slavery at one blow, but it undermined its basis by admitting slaves into the same religious fellowship as their masters."[5]

In the immediate context of Galatians 3:28, Paul explains one basic theory of education: "the law became our instructor until Christ, in order that out of faith we may be justified" (3:24). Paul employs the word *paidagogos* for "instructor." *Paideia* originally signified an art that pertains to children. A *paidagogos* was a slave hired by wealthy parents to escort their child to school, conversing with him in Greek while supervising his conduct until he became an adult. The law is analogous to such a tutor, supervisor, or governess. Being sinful, ready to do evil, humans need to be educated and restrained. If we desert our governess too soon, we sin because we are not ready yet to handle freedom. However, faith having come, Paul says, we are no longer under a pedagogue (3:25). Why not? "For all of us are sons (or descendants) of God through faith in Christ Jesus" (3:26). Adults no longer need pedagogues. Moreover, a "son" or "descendant" is an automatic heir. Few were the slaves like the wise slave of Proverbs 17:2 who "share the inheritance as one of the brothers." Paul now directly defines the image of sons (*huios*) in verse 26 with the category of "the heir" (*kleronomos*), the descendant of Abraham (v. 29). An heir is not like a slave, nor like a child under guardians and tutors. The heir Paul has in mind refers to the heir in possession of the inheritance. With such an heir a father could not even

---

[5]Harold Mattingly, *The Man in the Roman Street* (New York: W. W. Norton, 1966), p. 131.

sell his possessions because, proleptically, the son was the owner (*m. B. Bat.* 8:7). Paul was declaring that Gentiles, slaves, and females now, too, were heirs along with Jews, free citizens, and males.

Could women become heirs in first-century Jewish society? When Mahlah, Noah, Hoglah, Milcah, and Tirzah, the daughters of Zelophehad, lost their father they asked Moses if they could inherit his land and possessions. And Moses asked the Lord. The Lord said the women were right: "If a man dies, and has no son, then you shall cause his inheritance to pass to his daughter. And if he has no daughter, then you shall give his inheritance to his brothers" (Num. 27:8-9 RSV). The Mishnah records an almost identical statute. This is the order of inheritance:

> the son precedes the daughter, and all the son's offspring precede the daughter; the daughter precedes the brothers (of the deceased) and the daughter's offspring precede the brothers (*m. B. Bat.* 8:2).

Even if a father wanted, he could not have his daughter inherit when he had a son, according to *The Mishnah:* "for he has laid down a condition contrary to what is written in the law" (*m. B. Bat.* 8:5). But the Bible has no such statute. Job in his enlightened state gave an inheritance to his three daughters, Jemimah, Keziah, and Kerenhappuch, along with his seven sons (42:13-14). Rabbi Eleazar ben Azariah, who taught toward the end of the first century, expounded the law before the Sages in the vineyard at Jabneh: "The sons inherit and the daughters receive maintenance" (*m. Ketub.* 4:6). But no, Paul declares, now the daughters inherit too!

What did it mean to be an heir during Paul's life? What were the rights of an heir? As now, an heir, of course, would receive the inheritance. The daughters of Zelophehad received their father's land. Christ's heirs receive his inheritance which is described in Galatians as the Spirit, freedom from the law, justification, and the right and privilege to rule over Christ's estate. An heir not only receives an inheritance but also reigns over an inheritance. The world is the Lord's and again humans have been given the world to oversee as was done once before in Genesis 1-2.

Paul repeats his metaphor in Galatians 4:5. The time has come wherein female, slave, and Gentile along with male, free, and Jew have been "adopted as sons or descendants" (*huiothesis*). To receive adoption in ancient cultures was not only to gain parents but also to gain and to reign over an inheritance. The Roman Gaius Caligula and his cousin Tiberius Gemellus both had the right to inherit Tiberius' rulership as Emperor. Gaius had been legally adopted as a grandson of Tiberius while his cousin was a blood-relative of Tiberius. However, since Gaius was older and more aggressive, he grasped sovereignty earlier, saying, "you see yourselves that he is still a mere child and needs guardians and teachers and tutors (*paidagogos*)." Nevertheless Gaius promised (deceitfully), "I will be more than a guardian, a tutor and a teacher, I will appoint myself to be his father and him to be my son" (Philo, *The Embassy to Gaius,* IV [26-27]). Gaius here alludes to the same practices and images to which Paul alludes. A child, not an adult, needs a pedagogue. Moreover, to be appointed or adopted as son or descendant signifies that one is to reign upon reaching maturity. Gaius never meant to fulfill his clear promise. Philo explains Gaius' deceit: "The adoption was a snare to assure not the sovereignty which he expected, but the loss of that which he held already. And Gaius proceeded to plot against his fellow-heir and true partner" (*Embassy,* V [28]).

God employs similar imagery. In Psalm 2:7 the Lord says, "You are my son, today I have begotten you." These words have been fulfilled at least twice. At the time they were spoken they were fulfilled in David. The same words are repeated in 2 Samuel 7:14. In that context the sentence clearly refers to God's appointment of David as king. A similar imagery is employed in Psalm 89:26-27. When God declares God is someone's "Father" then that person is made "the first-born, the highest of the sovereigns of the earth." To be someone's "son" is to become that person's heir.

In Psalm 2:7 the Lord's decree also predicts a future fulfillment in the perfect Ruler and Messiah, Jesus. The author of Hebrews in 1:5 and 5:5 explains that these words were fulfilled when Jesus ascended to the right hand of majesty and was appointed as high priest forever. Paul points out as well in Acts 13:33 that Psalm 2:7 was fulfilled when Jesus resurrected from the dead.

Consistently the clause "you are my son" means "you are my descendant and rightful ruler over all I own." To be "adopted" was to become part of a new family, to receive the inheritance of that family, and finally to have sovereignty over that family. Paul did not say that men were to become the heirs, the inheritors, the rulers alone. Rather, women too have the full rights of descendants. They are reigning heirs. They too have full sovereignty over God's creation and they too fully receive God's blessings.

One Because We Obey Christ: The Practice (1 Timothy 2)

Paul saw the practical ramifications of the oneness of Jew and Gentile. Did he as well see any practical ramifications for the oneness of male and female? Often Bible students have posited a disparity between the attitudes of Jesus and Paul toward women—Jesus the feminist, Paul the chauvinist. 1 Timothy 2:11 is probably the primary pericope employed as proof for Paul's regression: "Let a woman in silence learn in all submission."[6] Has Paul ignored Jesus' adamant support of Mary learning in a rabbinic fashion recorded in Luke 10:38-42? No, Paul in 1 Timothy 2:11 is obeying the example and commands Jesus has already set forth. Considered in his time, and considering as well that he

---

[6]The author is aware of the debate over the authorship of the Pastoral Epistles, but concurs with the traditional argument that the Apostle Paul wrote 1 Timothy after being released from prison in Rome *ca.* AD 61-62. 2 Timothy was written during his second Roman imprisonment before his death *ca.* 67-68. See Aida Dina Besançon Spencer, "Eve at Ephesus: Should women be ordained as pastors according to the First Letter to Timothy 2:11-15?" *Journal of the Evangelical Theological Society* 17 (Fall, 1974), 221 n. 2.

was a zealous Pharisee, Paul like his master was quite radical.

Verses 11-15 are part of the larger chapter 2. What are Paul's goals? He tells his readers in verse 4 that God our savior "desires all people to be saved and to come to the knowledge of truth." Such a desire is not easily met. By the time 2 Timothy was written Paul employs the same phrase (*eis epignosin aletheias elthein* 3:7) to refer to "weak women" who may not obtain that knowledge of the truth. They learn from anyone and are burdened by sins.

How then does Paul prescribe that all people come to a knowledge of the truth? First of all, Paul urges the Ephesians to pray for all people (2:1-7). Paul employs four different synonyms for prayer: prayer for needs (*deesis*), prayer of a sacred nature (*proseuche*), prayer as intercession (*enteuxis*), and prayer as thanksgiving (*eucharistia*). All such multiple prayer is focused on one object: "that we may lead a quiet and silent life in all ways godly and respectable" (2:2). "Quiet and silent" is a pleonasm. Paul doubles two synonyms for the same concept for emphasis. Leading a "quiet and silent life in all ways godly and respectable" helps all people to come to a knowledge of the truth. Prayer is the first way to reach these multiple goals.

Before Paul proceeds to the second and third ways to help people come to a knowledge of the truth, he repeats and thereby emphasizes his own status as an apostle, and thereby a person worthy to be obeyed: "I myself was appointed a preacher and an apostle—I say the truth, I do not lie—a teacher of Gentiles in faith and truth" (2:7; cf. 1:1). Paul probably emphasized his own appointment because what he was about to command might easily have been disobeyed. If Paul's first command had to do with the need for prayer, his second command has to do with the practice or lifestyle while praying. What types of behavior are *not* examples of a "quiet and silent life in all ways godly and respectable"? When men pray while angry and quarreling they are not leading a "silent" life. The Jewish synagogue worship service had one section called "the prayers" or "the lifting up of hands." In the synagogue service, anyone could pray, men, women, children, and slaves (*m. Ber.* 3:3). Paul was not commanding the men only to pray. Such a command would contradict his assumptions in 1 Corinthians 11:5 and his own customs. In fact, verse nine of 1 Timothy 2 may have an ellipsis or omission of "I wish to pray the..." thereby connecting the exhortations to the men and to the women. Paul wants the men to pray without arguing and, "likewise," the women to pray in befitting deportment. Paul assumes that both men and women are praying but each of them has a different improper practice to remedy.[7] Paul writes a similar parallel construction in chapter 3. The main verb and article, "it is necessary the" [bishop] from verse 2, is indispensable to begin the exhortation to ministers (or deacons) in verse 8. "Likewise" (*hosautos*) is employed as a connective between both parallel introductions in 3:8 and 2:9. Paul was commanding the men to pray in a certain manner, without anger or quarreling. Josephus records one example in his own life when the men began to quarrel during the prayer section of the synagogue service:

> We were proceeding with the ordinary service and engaged in prayer, when Jesus rose and began to question me about the furniture and uncoined silver which had been confiscated after the conflagration of the royal palace, asking who had the keeping of them (*The Life* 57 [295]).

The quarrel between Josephus and Jesus (not Jesus of Nazareth) became quite extensive. Josephus and Jesus had numerous rejoinders with the rest of the worshippers participating as they could get in a word. The Christian men would certainly have had examples of quarreling during prayer.

---

[7]Although Paul differently exhorts the men and women at Ephesus, the qualities they are to develop are not unique to either sex. Bishops are all to be respectable (*kosmios* 3:2) as are the women in deportment or dress (2:9). Euodia and Syntyche at Philippi need to agree as do the men in prayer at Ephesus (Phil. 4:2; 1 Tim. 2:8).

When women adorn themselves immodestly and in inappropriate and expensive apparel, they too are not leading "silent" lives. Good deeds and modest attire are the best apparel for god-fearing women.[8] Paul's overriding concern, like God's concern, was for all people to come to learn the truth. The ways that Christians were behaving would directly affect whether or not outsiders obtained a proper understanding of Christianity. Anger, quarreling, and costly and immodest attire did not achieve that "silent" life which would appeal to outsiders.

Paul now proceeds with the third way to help people reach a knowledge of the truth. The practice of "silence" has two aspects. Lifestyle is important. In addition, women, rather that focusing too much on their external adornment, should rather participate fully in education. *The Living Bible* paraphrases verse 11: "women should listen and learn quietly and humbly." In this rendering Paul's focus seems to be on the *manner* in which women, as opposed to men, should learn. However, Bible students often ignore the import of the Greek verb. Paul does not simply say that women "*may* learn" or "*should* learn" or that woman should be "*allowed* to learn." Woman *must* learn. By implication, women must be instructed. The word *manthano* signifies "to learn," but especially by study in a rabbinic school, as in John 7:15. Paul is commanding that the women, as the men, must not merely *hear* the truth but also *study* the truth. Women were not exempt from learning the Christian truth; rather, they were required to learn that truth. The division between the Jewish male and female was no longer to be a division in Paul's eyes.

But Paul does not only command women to learn. He also commands them "in silence" to learn. The sentence which includes verses 11 and 12 begins and ends with the same phrase, rendered literally: "a woman *in silence* let learn...but

---

[8]See David Scholer, "Women's Adornment: Some Historical and Hermeneutical Observations on the New Testament Passages," *Daughters of Sarah 6*, January/February, 1980, 3-6.

to be *in silence."* If Paul had commanded women to learn, someone might object, then he would be revolutionary. But since he commanded women to learn "in silence" then indeed he is treating women as adolescents. In the United States, "to learn in silence" has derogatory connotations since it suggests the type of rebuke an adult might address regrettably to a child or to the childlike: "Shut up and listen to what the teacher says!" However, what would "learning in silence" signify to a devout Pharisaic Jew such as Paul? Silence, first of all, was a positive attribute for adults, male as well as female. Second, silence was, as well, a positive attribute for rabbinic students. Paul's words were declaring to his Jewish friends that at this time women were to be learning in the same manner as did rabbinic students.

Several Greek words can be translated by the noun or verb form of "silence." *Epistomizo* and *phimoo* can mean to silence someone as a punishment or rebuke. For instance, Paul tells Titus that it is necessary to silence *(epistomizein)* the many disorderly people, empty talkers, and deceivers, especially those from the circumcision party, since they are ruining whole houses, teaching what is not necessary for the sake of dishonest gain. He continues: "Therefore rebuke them sharply in order that they may be sound in faith, not giving heed to Jewish myths and commands of people who reject the truth" (Titus 1:13-14). Similarly, Peter says, "it is God's will that by doing right you should put *to silence (phimoo)* the ignorance of unlearned or foolish people" (1 Peter 2:15). Further, when the king in Jesus' parable asked how the person without a wedding garment got in, "he was silenced *(phimoo)*" (Matt. 22:12). *The Mishnah,* also mentions several heresies for which a person is "put to silence" *(m. Meg.* 4:9; *m. Ber.* 5:3). Although such "silence" in the long run will edify both the deceiver and the deceived, Paul does not speak of such silence in 1 Timothy 2.[9]

In 1 Timothy 2:11-12 Paul employs the noun *hesuchia.* The

---

[9]Cf. *m. Sanh.* 8:5.

adjective is perhaps akin to *hemai,* "to sit."[10] The verb *hesuchazo* means "I am silent, I rest, or I cease from labor." In every instance in the New Testament this silence is an appropriate or, usually, an ideal response or state. In 1 Timothy 2:2, 1 Thessalonians 4:11, and 2 Thessalonians 3:12 all people are exhorted to lead a "quiet and *peaceful* life in all godliness and proper conduct" (1 Tim. 2:2). Paul exhorts the Thessalonians to work "with quietness." "Working with quietness" apparently is not being a gossip. As the second-century BC Jesus, son of Sirach, explained, whoever pays heed to the talk of a third party "will never again find rest or live in *silence*" (Ecclus. 28:16). The goal of all such "silent living" was not to decrease the noise pollution of the ancient world. The goal of "silent living" was to increase the respect of outsiders and thereby encourage them to become Christians.

Silence might or might not have anything to do with not speaking. *Hesuchia* connotes respect on the part of an audience. As well, it connotes lack of disagreement. An audience in "silence" is a convinced audience. It is true that because people are silenced, they are not necessarily won over. Luke's use of "silence" to describe the religious leaders in Luke 14:4-6 refers to persons who are silent merely because they are not *able* to disagree. They would disagree if they could.[11] Other than this reference to the verb form of *hesuchia,* this word connotes in the New Testament not only being unable to disagree but also not wanting to disagree. For instance, after hearing Peter's defense, the circumcision party was "silenced" and glorified God saying, "Then also to the Gentiles God has given the repentance into life" (Acts 11:18). They were convinced—at least some were. Moreover, their "silence" had nothing to do with lack of speech. As well, when Paul could not be persuaded from going to Jerusalem, Luke says, "We were silent saying 'let the Lord's will be' " (Acts 21:14). Paul's associates no longer disagreed with his plans.

---

[10]Thayer, p. 281.

[11]Mark employs the more neutral synonym *siopao* in Mark 3:4.

Their "silence" was demonstrated by their words of agreement. Luke employs two different words for "silence" in Acts 21:40-22:2. First, Paul motioned with his hand and the crowd was "silent." Luke uses *sige*. The people stopped speaking so as to hear Paul's words. Then, when Paul addressed them in Hebrew, they became "silent" (*hesuchia*). Now to quietness was added respect.

Silence is a state of being and way of living which is of great value to God. Proverbs 15:15 says in the Septuagint translation, "The eyes of the wicked are always looking for evil things; but the good are always *quiet*." Moreover, the Lord declares to Isaiah: "Who is the person I respect? It is: The one who is humble and *quiet*, and trembles at my word" (66:2). No wonder Moses tells the people: "The Lord will fight for you and you have only to be still (*sigao*)" (Exod. 14:14). Peter uses the adjective *hesuchios* to describe a woman's inward adornment, which is preferable to an outward adornment (1 Pet. 3:4). The respect and sense of conviction in the word is most apparent in Luke 23:56. The women disciples of Jesus prepared the ointments for his body but did not use them because they "were silent on the Sabbath." "Silence" is a synonym for "rest."

Consequently, when Paul commands that women learn in silence he is commanding them to be students who respect and affirm their teacher's convictions. "In all submission" is a synonym for "silence" here. Paul does not exhort women always to be submissive to men. Rather, "in all submission," as "in silence" modifies the manner of *learning* women should do. The women have not been silenced out of punishment but silenced out of conviction because their teachers are worthy of respect.

Such behavior was appropriate for all rabbinical students and all wise persons. Simon, the son of Rabbi Gamaliel (Paul's teacher), comments:

All my days have I grown up among the Sages and I have found naught better for a man than silence; and not the expounding [of Law] is the chief thing but the doing [of it]; and he that multiplies words occasions sin (*m. 'Abot* 1:17).

Rabbi Akiba, who was born around AD 50 said, "The tradition is a fence around the Law; Tithes are a fence around riches; vows are a fence around abstinence; a fence around wisdom is silence" (*m. 'Abot* 3:14). What did he mean by a "fence"? As oral traditions were supposed to protect the purity of God's law, so, too, silence can protect wisdom. The same tractate in the *The Mishnah* records that greater is learning in the law than the priesthood or kingship because learning in the law necessitates more positive attributes, forty-eight "excellences." Learners were to "make a fence around their words" (*m. 'Abot* 6:6), or guard what they say. Paul, too, knew the positive attributes of learning the law. Since they were biblical ones (e.g., Ps. 119), he was commending them to the women because now they, too, were in the position of rabbinical students.

Learners were to be silent. Teachers and all wise persons were to be silent as well. All the seven marks of the wise have to do with the use of words. Two of those characteristics are that the wise person "is not hasty in making answer" and "asks what is relevant" (*m. 'Abot* 5:7). Rabbi Shammai, a contemporary of Hillel, said, "Make thy [study of the] Law a fixed habit; say little and do much, and receive all with a cheerful countenance" (*m. 'Abot* 1:15). Rabbi Judah used to ask:

What is meant by the verse, "For thee silence is praise"? The best medicine of all is silence. When Rabbi Dimi came, he said: "In the West they say: A word is worth a *sela'*, silence two *sela's*" (*b. Meg.* 18a).

Rabbi Isaac would ask:

What is the meaning of the verse, "Indeed in silence speak righteousness; judge uprightly the sons of men?" What should be a man's pursuit in this world? He should be silent. Perhaps he should be so with regard to the words of the Torah? It says therefore, "Speak righteousness" (*b. Hul.* 89a).

Rabbi Huna used to repeat Rabbi Meir's saying:

A man's words should always be few in addressing the Holy One, blessed be He, since it says, "Be not rash with thy mouth and let not thy heart be hasty to utter a word before God; and for God is in heaven and thou upon earth; therefore let thy words be few" (*b. Ber.* 61a).

Before, throughout, and after Paul's time, the rabbis were agreed that silence was an admirable attribute for the pious scholar. As well, Rabbi Abbahu urges Rabbi Judah to find a wife for his son by going "after the peaceful," literally, "silence." He adds, "As the Palestinians make a test: When two quarrel, they see which becomes silent first and say, 'this one is of superior birth'" (*b. Kidd.* 71b). Even in the Qumran community, the preservation of silence was crucial. A person should be excommunicated rather than allowed to remain with the community, "for his silence (is invaded) by confusion of wickedness and defilements (are hidden) within his calm" (*The Scroll of the Rule* III. 2-3). Hellenistic Philo as well found silence valuable. When a Jew on trial is accused by a Roman judge, Philo said, he must needs be quiet (*siopao*):

For silence (*hesuchia*) too may in a way serve as a defence, particularly to us who could not answer any of the points which [Gaius] was investigating and wished to press, because our customs and laws muzzled the tongue and closed and stitched up the mouth (*The Embassy to Gaius* XLIV [360]).

The ancient Jews esteemed silence as a state of calm, restraint at the proper time, respect, and affirmation of a speaker because the Bible esteems such silence. They have alluded to several Old Testament passages. Proverbs 11:12, for example, says, "He who belittles his neighbor lacks sense, but a man of understanding remains silent." Proverbs 17:27-28 repeats that:

He who restrains his words has knowledge,
and he who has a cool spirit is a man of understanding.
Even a fool who keeps silent is considered wise;
when he closes his lips, he is deemed intelligent (rsv).

Consequently, the rabbis concluded, "Silence is better for the wise, and how much more so for fools" (*b. Pesah.* 99a). In the New Testament, the wise James, too, exhorts the Christians to "be slow to speak" (James 1:19).

Why have we moderns missed such overwhelming positive evidence for silence? And, why have we as well not regarded Paul's exhortations to women in 1 Timothy 2:11 as overwhelmingly positive? Paul was treating the women at Ephesus as wise students, persons of superior birth. We have missed those connotations because we have an un-biblical view of silence and we expect a negative view of women. We cannot perceive the Bible's radical demands to train men *and* women into the full knowledge of God's truth.

Were these connotations for "silence" missed too by the early church? *The Didache*, which is probably early second century, exhorts all believers to be "quiet" (*hesuchios*) and good (III.8). Ignatius, the third bishop of Antioch in Syria, who died around AD 108 during the reign of the Roman Emperor Trajan, had such a high view of silence that he told the Ephesians silence is a quality of a leader, a bishop, and a teacher, because silence emanates from Jesus:

And the more anyone sees that the bishop is silent (*sigao*), the more let him fear him (VI.1)....It is better to be silent (*siopao*) and be real, than to talk and to be unreal. Teaching is good, if the teacher does what he says. There is then one teacher who "spoke and it came to pass," and what he has done in silence is worthy of the Father. He who has the word of Jesus for a true possession can also hear his silence (*hesuchia*), that he may be perfect, that he may act through his speech, and be understood through his silence (*sige*) (XV.1-2, To the Ephesians).

Clement of Alexandria (*ca.*150-220) also sees silence as a virtue for men and women:

Woman and man are to go to church decently attired, with natural step, embracing silence, possessing unfeigned love, pure in body, pure in heart, fit to pray to God (*Paedagogus*, Bk III.11).

As Jesus, Paul assumed two radical presuppositions about women. First, rather than simply to hear, they were to learn formally and "in silence" as the men. Second, by implication, their role as homemakers did not fulfill the ultimate priority for which they were created. Paul's exhortations contradicted the first century Jewish practices which did not encourage women to become educated because then their homemaking would take a lower priority. Rather, Paul was equalizing the relationship between men and women. The women, as the men, were to learn. The men, as the women, were to be concerned for their children (1 Tim. 3:4-5, 12; 5:14; Tit. 1:6; 2:4). Paul does set a high priority on the management of the home. However, women are no longer to be restricted educationally because of their home responsibilities. People live a "silent" life and come to a knowledge of the truth by being taught correctly about the truth.

Clearly some kind of unorthodox teaching was occurring at Ephesus which consequently meant that there was also some kind of unorthodox learning. The main purpose Paul had in his letter was to assist a church which was suffering from unorthodox teachings. Before Paul was imprisoned in Jerusalem he warned the elders:

> I know that after my departure fierce wolves will come in among you, not sparing the flock; and from among your own selves will arise men speaking perverse things, to draw away the disciples after them (Acts 20:29-30 RSV).

And indeed Paul's knowledge is correct. Paul had urged Timothy to remain at Ephesus for this very reason:

> To charge certain persons not to teach any different doctrine (*heterodidaskalein*) nor to occupy themselves with myths and endless genealogies which promote speculation rather than the divine training that is in faith (1:3-4).

Certain persons already were wandering into "empty talk, desiring to be teachers of the law (*nomodidaskaloi*), without understanding either what they are saying nor the things concerning which they are confidently speaking" (1:6-7). Already, words for "teaching" (*didasko*) and "speaking" have occurred numerous times within the first paragraph.

The long list of unlawful practices in 1:8-10 Paul rephrases with the words "opposed to healthy or sound teaching" (*didaskalia*, 1:10). The church, Paul says, is the "foundation of the *truth*" (5:15) even as Timothy is Paul's "true" child in the faith (1:2). If Paul is delayed his letter should help people to know how to behave. In chapter 4 Paul repeats what he told the elders earlier: "The Spirit expressly says that in later times some will depart from the faith by giving heed to deceitful spirits and doctrines (*didaskalia*) of demons" (4:1 RSV). Good ministers, in contrast to these other people, feed on the words of the faith and the good teaching (*didaskalia*) which they have followed (4:6). A good minister has nothing to do with "vile and old-women's myths" (4:7). Paul concludes this brief exhortation to Timothy with the exhortation:

> Keep a close watch on yourself and to your teaching (*didaskalia*); continue with them; for while doing this also you will save yourself and the people hearing you (4:16).

The situation at Ephesus was clearly dangerous if even Paul's coworker, the evangelist Timothy, had to watch himself closely to keep from succumbing.

In chapter 6 Paul exhorts Timothy to "teach (*didasko*) these things and exhort." Paul thinks little of anyone who "teaches differently (*heterodidaskalo*) and does not agree with sound words, the ones of our Lord Jesus Christ, and the teaching (*didaskalia*) in accordance with godliness" (6:2-3). Paul concludes his letter repeating what he said in 4:16-17:

> O Timothy, guard what is entrusted to your care, avoiding the vile foolish talk and contradictions of the falsely-called knowledge, which by professing some have lost their way concerning the faith (6:20-21).

A form of the word "teaching" (*didasko*) occurs sixteen times in 1 Timothy and eight times in 2 Timothy.[12] Of the

---

[12]1 Timothy 1:3,7,10; 2:7,12; 3:2; 4:1,6,11,13,16; 5:17; 6:1-3; 2 Timothy 1:11; 2:2,24; 3:10,16; 4:2-3.

twenty-three occurrences of the noun form *didaskalia* ("teaching" or "doctrine") in the New Testament, two-thirds of them are in 1 and 2 Timothy.

The "different" or unorthodox doctrine at Ephesus has four main characteristics. Paul has highlighted its emphasis in word-battles, godlessness, law, and wealth. The teachings are not healthy or good. They are myths, endless genealogies, speculations, fruitless discussions, godless chatter, and contradictions. For instance, during prayer, the men were quarreling and disputing (2:8). The teachings were also demonic. "False knowledge" is an apt summary (6:20). These verbal battles result in envy, strife, blasphemy, evil conjectures, and constant irritations. Two areas of life in particular were affected, freedom and finances. The teachers were emphasizing legalism. They misused the law by applying it to everyone (1:7-8) while they themselves lived in wealth (6:3-10). Possibly the ascetic teachings forbidding marriage and abstaining from food mentioned in 4:1-4 are aspects of these legal teachings. At the same time, even as the Ephesians stressed ascetism, so too was excessive wealth a problem.

Women were clearly involved in all aspects of the problems at Ephesus. In 1 and 2 Timothy the persons who do the deceiving are described by generic terms: "some" (1 Tim. 1:6), "those" (2 Tim. 3:5), or "people" (2 Tim. 3:8). Young widows were participating in unnecessary and unhealthy gossip, indulging in wealth and turning to the demonic (1 Tim. 5:6, 13, 15; 2 Tim. 3:6). Women were clearly using adornments only the rich could afford (2:9). Even the myths themselves were called myths of "old-women" (*graodes* 4:7). Probably the women were passing on these unorthodox doctrines as they visited from home to home when they could have been teaching sound doctrines or been praying for the advance of God's reign. Unorthodox or different teaching was a prominent part of the particular problems at Ephesus. Consequently, orthodox teaching was necessary for their correction.

Yet women were the learners not the instructors of the sound teaching. Paul commands: "Let a woman in silence learn in all submission; but I am not allowing a woman to teach or to domineer over a man, but to be in silence" (2:11-12). To learn in silence was a privilege and a radical change for the women. They needed such knowledge because previously they had not been encouraged to pursue theological training. Since the women were less prepared to withstand heretical teaching, Paul was treating them at the time as less responsible. They were disobedient because they were deceived. Paul explains how he himself had persecuted the church because of his own ignorance (1 Tim. 1:13). The women needed to be taught as rabbinic students (*manthano*). In contrast, men such as Hymenaeus and Alexander were to be taught and disciplined (*paideuo*) by Satan as rebellious children (1:20)! Philo of Alexander, in discussing Genesis 30:36, explains the principle Paul seems to be using with the women. Error can come from "sinful wickedness" or "untutored ignorance":

Ignorance is an involuntary state, a light matter, and its treatment through teaching is not hopeless. But wickedness is a wilful malady of the soul, and its action is such that to remove it is hard, if indeed it is not hopeless (*The Sacrifices of Abel and Cain* XI [48]. See also *On Rewards and Punishments* VIII [49], "to educate a disbeliever is difficult or rather impossible.")

The women were being deceived because of their "untutored ignorance." They were enmeshed in a destructive situation surrounded with different doctrines somehow very appealing yet very dangerous. Women were learning unorthodox doctrines and probably also propagating unorthodox teachings. No wonder Paul commands they learn while not allowing them to teach.

Paul does not command the women not to teach. He employs the present active indicative for "allow." The present tense in Greek principally denotes continuous present action. It can refer to present necessity and obligation and to potential action.[13] Greek has its own imperative mood which is not here employed. Commands can also be phrased in the aorist or the future indicative. Neither of these tenses is here used. Nor does Paul use the perfect tense to denote an action in the past which has changed the state of affairs. Paul is saying: "I am not presently allowing a woman to teach." Somehow the usual English translation "I do not permit" appears to readers to be the same or more forceful than "let a woman learn." However, in reality, "let her learn" is the command; "I do not allow" is the present action.

Why is "learning" a command, but "allowing to teach" a present action? Verses 11 and 12 are one sentence in the original Greek text joined together with the adversative particle *de*, which signifies "but, however, yet, on the other hand." Paul was saying in effect, "I command a woman learn, however, I do not permit her to teach." The *de* indicates that the two instructions are somewhat contradictory. If anyone is taught, eventually they will teach. Paul assumes this reality in 2 Timothy 2:2: "these things entrust to faithful people (not men!), who will be able to teach also others." The author of Hebrews reprimands the listeners by saying:

> For though by this time you ought to be teachers, you need some one to teach you again the first principles of God's word. You need milk, not solid food; for every one who lives on milk is unskilled in the word of righteousness, for he is a child. But solid food is for the mature, for those who have their faculties trained by practice to distinguish good from evil (Heb. 5:12-14 RSV).

The rabbis also taught that one of the qualifications to be a good learner was to be someone who "learns in order to teach and that learns in order to practice" (*m. 'Abot* 6:6). Rab Judah said, commenting on *Mishnah Kiddushin* 1:7, "Our Rabbis taught: The father is bound in respect of his son, to circumcise, redeem, teach him Torah, take a wife for

---

[13]Paul uses the present indicative similarly in Rom. 16:17, Phil. 4:2, and 1 Tim. 2:1,8.

him, and teach him a craft." Mothers are exempt and have no such obligation. He goes on to ask:

> How do we know that [the mother] has no duty [to teach her children]?...whoever is commanded to study is commanded to teach; whoever is not commanded to study, is not commanded to teach. And how do we know that she is not bound to teach herself?—...the one whom others are commanded to teach is commanded to teach oneself; and the one whom others are not commanded to teach, is not commanded to teach oneself. How then do we know that others are not commanded to teach her?— Because it is written, 'And ye shall teach them your sons' (Deut. 11:19)—but not your daughters (*b. Kidd.* 29a-b).

In other words, learning and teaching are intertwined activities.

The noun *didaskalos* implies a teacher who is qualified. Such a teacher's primary effect is on the intellect. In contrast, the verb *noutheteo* implies a teaching which affects the will and disposition. The women at Ephesus had to learn, consequently, they were not ready to teach. Paul wanted to restrain the women from teaching until they themselves were well instructed.

The women were also not to domineer over men (or, literally, a woman over a man). The verb *authentein* occurs only here in the New Testament. In contemporary Greek society it signified "to commit a murder," "to kill with one's own hand either others or oneself." It also signified in a derivative sense "to have full power or authority over."[14] Josephus employs the noun form *authentes* to render "assasins," murderers of a Galilean Jew(s) on their way to a festival in Jerusalem (*War* BK.II.XII.5 [240]). Moreover, in the Wisdom of Solomon in the Apocrypha, which was written anywhere from 100 BC to AD40, the noun is used to modify parents ("slaughtering parents") who wish to kill defenseless souls by their own hands (12:6). Josephus similarly uses the noun to describe Antipater, Herod's son, accused of killing his two

---

[14]Liddell and Scott, p. 275; Thayer, p. 84.

brothers and attempting to kill his father (*War* BK.I.XXX.1 [582]). Philo uses the word metaphorically. The person who has tried to destroy the virtues has become his "own *murderer*" (*The Worse Attacks the Better XXI*[78]).[15] The verb *authentein*, as all verbs of ruling, takes the genitive case of the person who is murdered or over whom the destructive domination is executed. In contrast, *didaskein* takes the accusative case for the person and topic taught. Consequently, grammatically "man" is most likely to be the object only of *authentein*. Elsewhere, Paul employs a more common word for "authority," *exousia* (e.g., 1 Cor. 11:10; 15:24). Thus *authentein* signifies "to domineer" or "to have absolute power over" persons in such a way as to destroy them.

Authentein is similar in concept to the negative type of leadership Jesus portrays by the persons ruling over the Gentiles. Their leadership is described in two words *katakurieuo* and *katexousiazo* (Matt. 20:25). Both words are formed from the root preposition "under" (*kata*) which vividly describes the position of the person being ruled. *Katakurieuo* signifies "to exercise complete dominion." *Katakurieuo* literally means to make oneself "lord over." *Katexousiazo* literally means to wield "authority over." Both verbs, as does *authento*, take the genitive case for the person "over" whom one rules. *Katakurieuo* is used of the demons who "overpower" the Jewish exorcists so that they are left naked and wounded (Acts 19:16). Peter admonishes elders not "to domineer over" the flock but be examples to them (1 Pet. 5:3). Leadership which overpowers and destroys is never approved by Christ for either men or women.[16]

"To domineer" is in the same tense and mood (present ac-

---

[15]Catherine C. Kroeger has the interesting idea that *authentein* has sexual connotations as well. Paul was exhorting the woman not to "involve a man in the heretical kind of Christianity which taught licentious behavior as one of its doctrines. Such a female heretic did indeed 'teach to fornicate' in the Thyatiran church mentioned in Revelation 2:20." "Ancient Heresies and a Strange Greek Verb," *The Reformed Journal* 29 (March, 1979): 14.

[16]See also Mark 10:42; Luke 22:25-6; Acts 10:38 (devil); 2 Cor. 1:24; James 2:6 (rich). Liddell and Scott, p. 896.

tive infinitive) as "to be" in silence which follows it. Consequently they are antithetic parallel verbs. To domineer over a man here, then, opposes to be in silence.

Women are to become part of the entire educational process—one of "silence." Women are to be calm and to have restraint and respect and affirm their teachers rather than to engage in an autocratic authority which destroys its subjects. Paul here is *not* prohibiting women from preaching nor praying nor having an edifying authority nor pastoring. He is simply prohibiting them from teaching and using their authority in a destructive way. The overall purpose of the letter to remedy the teaching of different doctrines, the positive connotations for "silence," the use of the present active indicative for "I am not allowing," the use of the adversative particle "but," and the underlying principle that learning results in teaching—all imply that Paul's injunction was temporary. A "temporary" injunction is not solely relevant to the first century. Rather, it is applicable whenever, but only whenever, women who have not been theologically trained are succumbing to false teachings.

Verses 13-14 begin with the conjunction *gar* which expresses cause, inference, continuation, or explanation. They are one sentence and thereby cannot be separated in thought, literally: "For Adam first was formed, then Eve; and Adam was not deceived, but the woman having been deceived in transgression she had become." Paul is correct in reminding the reader that Adam was formed first. Being formed first is not necessarily proof of superiority. Philo said about the order of creation of animals to humans that:

Now in things which exist in part, the principle of order is this, to begin with that which is most inferior in its nature, and to end with that which is the most excellent of all (*On the Account of the Creation of the World* XXII [67]).

However, he later has to explain why: "It is no proof because man was the last created animal that he is the lowest in rank" (*On the Creation*, XXIX[87]). Since neither Genesis 1 nor 2 has any implication of hierarchy and we are positing that Paul's words do not contradict Genesis, the best way to understand Paul's words are in light of the situation he addresses. Adam was formed first, but Eve was the first to become a transgressor. She herself admitted it: "The serpent beguiled me and I ate." Although Adam was created first, Eve was deceived before Adam was.

The woman was not more evil inherently than Adam. Paul says the women "became in transgression because of her deception." "Became" (*ginomai*) is the perfect indicative. The perfect is a past action which affects the present state. Eve became a transgressor and thereby no longer could return to her former state.

Paul is citing Adam's and Eve's experience as an explanation or analogy for his readers. An analogy is a controlled comparison of one thing with another in some aspect under certain circumstances. Rabbis often sought to show the Old Testament's relevance to present circumstances and to ongoing situations through analogy. They would use Scripture as an illustration for everyday practices. An event in Scripture might serve as a type or an analogy for a certain practice in contemporary society. For instance, earlier, Rabbi Hisda was quoted as he interpreted "And the Lord God *builded*" Eve to mean that God "*built* Eve in the shape of a storehouse." Rabbi Simeon ben Menassia interpreted the verb "builded" differently:

"And the Lord God builded the side" teaches that the Holy One, blessed be He, plaited Eve's hair and then brought her to Adam, for in the sea-towns a plait is called "building" (*b. Erub.* 18a-b, *b. Ber.* 61a).

Both rabbis were explaining the verb 'build" with contemporary illustrations.

Paul too makes another analogy in Galatians 4:22-31 with Hagar and Sarah. He employs the deception of Eve also as an analogy for the Corinthians own deception in 2 Corinthians 11:3 and he also uses Adam as an analogy of one who allows sin and death to reign.[17] Paul employs the Israelites in the wilderness as an analogy for the Corinthians. They were "types" (*tupos*) of us." *Tupos* can signify "archetype, pattern, model, capable of exact repetition in numerous instances."[18] The Israelites are a negative example to the Corinthians in that the Israelites were believers who received God's blessings and saw visible signs of God's presence yet they came to desire evil. Likewise, the Corinthians who were believers were desiring to be idolatrous and immoral and to grumble and test God (1 Cor. 10:1-13). The Corinthians were not like the Israelites in all respects nor did the Corinthians have always to be like them. For instance, the Corinthians were Gentiles localized in one place. They were not Jews punished to wander in the desert. Elsewhere in 1 Timothy Paul employs himself as an illustration and synecdoche of all sinners. He repeats and afirms the saying the Christians were passing around: "Christ Jesus came into the world to save sinners." The Paul goes on to describe himself as an example (*hupotuposis*) of a great sinner who received mercy so that future sinners could also expect to receive mercy and life eternal if they believed in Christ Jesus (1 Tim. 1:15-16). As a "first" sinner Paul is a synecdoche of all sinners. In other words, if God was merciful to as great a sinner as was Paul, God could (and would) be merciful to any other sinner. Because Paul is a vivid illustration[19] of a great sinner, that does not mean he must always continue to be a blaspheming, persecuting, insulting sinner. Nor is Paul saying that Christ redeems all sinners, which would be universalism. Paul's illustration serves only to the extent that Paul intends it to serve.

---

[17]Romans 5:12-14; 1 Cor. 15:22. David Robinson, "Is Eve's Deception a Feminine Fear?" Unpublished paper, Gordon-Cornwell Theological Seminary (Jan. 18, 1983), pp. 7-8.

[18]Liddell and Scott, p. 1835.

[19]*Hupotuposis* was even a figure of speech: "any representation of facts which is made in such vivid language that they appeal to the eye rather than the ear" (Quintilian, *The Institutes*, Bk. IX.2.40).

What then would be the analogy that Paul was indicating between Adam and Eve and the Ephesians? The women of Ephesus were reminiscent of the woman (Eve) in Eden. The Ephesian women were learning and teaching a body of heretical beliefs to others in an authoritative manner, while submitting themselves to unorthodox teachers. Eve too had in her time been deceived into believing certain false teachings: "If she touched the fruit of the tree of knowledge of good and evil, she would become like God yet she would not die" (Gen. 3:3-4). God never had forbidden touching the fruit, only eating it. Moreover, Eve did die. Eve authoritatively taught these teachings to Adam. Unfortunately he learned. The entire state of humanity and nature was affected by their actions, enslaved to sin and death. Paul wants to break a similar sequence of events at Ephesus. The church at Ephesus could destroy itself just as Adam and Eve destroyed themselves in Eden. If the women at Ephesus continued in learning different doctrines, they too would be deceived and become transgressors.

Paul was slowing down the process which was leading to a genuine full and equal participation between women and men. Before people are "liberated" in Christ they need to recognize and understand the nature of that liberation. Otherwise they might strive after a pseudo-liberation which would terminate as slavery. Instruction in the faith has to precede the living out of that faith. Women were not prepared to withstand unorthodox learning since they were not required to learn the Torah. Probably they were among those who desired to be teachers of the law without understanding what they were saying (1 Tim. 1:7). However, Jesus and Paul were making it possible for them to understand.

Paul is employing a principle similar to that suggested by Genesis 3. What was Eve's sin? She wanted to be like God. Such an aspiration might be good, of course. Does not Paul challenge his readers to mature into the image of Christ (Col. 1:28)? But Eve's *means* of attaining wisdom was wrong. Her desire for nutrition, aesthetics, and wisdom were excuses for her to seize her wisdom rather than to receive her wisdom from God. Eve took the foolish way to wisdom. Wisdom or knowledge in itself is never as important as truly God-given knowledge received through obedience. Consequently, the best means of attaining true knowledge is more important than knowledge in itself.

Paul's pericope on teaching women ends with verse fifteen: "But she will be saved through the childbearing if they may continue in faith and love and holiness with self-control." If Paul had followed *dia* with the accusative case, the verse could have been translated: "she will be saved *because of*" the childbearing. A woman could not be saved if she did not bear children. However, Paul uses the genitive case which means "through" the midst of an intermediate or inanimate agent.[20] If women were saved through childbearing, believing women would not die from childbirth. Such a promise would certainly entice many women into Christianity. Rachel, however, did die from the birth of her child, Benjamin (Gen. 35:16-20). More advisable is the traditional understanding that Paul's use of the singular article to modify "childbearing" suggests the one most significant birth for Christians, the Child born to Mary.

The difficulty with understanding "the childbearing" to refer to the Child born to Mary is that the reference is vague. However, Ignatius who lived in the first century employs a similar synonym for childbirth (*ho toketos*) also to refer to Jesus:

"And the virginity of Mary, and her childbirth were hidden from the Prince of this world, as was also the death of the Lord. Three mysteries of a cry which were wrought in the stillness (*hesuchia*) of God" (*To the Ephesians* XIX.1).

And Paul himself has several other comparable references. For instance, God's son, Paul says, was "born of woman" (Gal. 4:4) and, "the man comes through the woman" (1 Cor. 11:12). Which women? Paul's argument in Galatians 3:16,29

---

[20]Robertson, pp. 582-84.

rests on the difference between the singular and the plural of "seed." So in 1 Timothy 2:15 Paul could very well be alluding back to Genesis 3:15, to the child who fulfilled that final victory over Satan. The protevangelium, that Genesis 3:15 refers to Jesus, is mentioned at least as early as Irenaeus in the second century who also frequently compares Eve and Mary. For instance in *Against Heresies* Irenaeus writes:

> And thus also it was that the knot of Eve's disobedience was loosed by the obedience of Mary. For what the virgin Eve had bound fast through unbelief, this did the virgin Mary set free through faith.[21]

Paul would then be declaring in these verses that in light of their similarity to Eve, the women at Ephesus should not teach nor dominate men, but they should learn in submission to sound teachers. However, he declares, so that no one would misunderstand, that the salvation of women is not here at stake. It was through disobedient Eve that transgression entered earth. It was through obedient Mary, giving birth, that salvation came. Paul consequently reminds and reassures "them," the male instructor and the female student, that if the women at Ephesus were properly instructed they will be saved if the male instructor and female student "continue in faith and love and holiness with self-control."

Paul's statement is in sharp contrast to the teaching in the *Mishnah* tractate on the Sabbath:

> For three transgressions do women die in childbirth: for heedlessness of the laws of the menstruant, the Dough-offering, and the lighting of the [Sabbath]lamp (*m. Sabb.* 2:6).

Possibly Paul was disagreeing with such a tradition when he wrote 1 Timothy 2:15. Although the later rabbis understood this Sabbath tradition to reflect negatively on women (e.g.,

---

[21]Bk. III. XXII. 4. See also *Against Heresies* Bk III. XXIII.7; Bk IV.XL.3; Bk V. XIX, XXI.1 and *Proof of the Apostolic Preaching* 33. See also Luke 1:35.

Midrash Rabbah on Genesis XVII.8), in its context these practices are positive and highly esteemed. In the tractate women do die in childbirth. However, Paul focuses on the positive—women will be saved through The Childbirth. In the tractate the lack of observance of a legalistic duty can cause death. In contrast, Paul highlights three attributes which bring life. Faith, love, and holiness bring eternal salvation not only to women but also to men.

The verses following 2:15 in chapter 3 confirm the possibility that women could teach in the future. Although some translations render 1 Timothy 3:1 "If a *man* desire the office of a bishop" (KJV), the Greek is more accurately rendered "If someone longs for an office of bishop." The pronoun *tis* refers either to a male or a female. A bishop in contrast to a deacon had to be an "apt teacher" (3:2). Women at Ephesus could not yet teach but they could learn to be teaching bishops, as did the women we shall meet in the next chapter.

In summary, in 1 Timothy 2:13-14 Paul has employed an analogy between Eve and the women at Ephesus, both of whom were misled. When women anywhere, including Ephesus, grow beyond a resemblance to Eve in this respect, then the analogy is no longer valid. Ultimately Paul was teaching equality through Christ who humbles all. The difficulty has been that women everywhere have been compared with the women at Ephesus. Are women to be students who never graduate? The next chapter will show how Paul himself did not make this generalization.

A young man once explained that his ancestors prior to his grandfather were in the mining business. His great-grandfather recognized that mining as an occupation was very dangerous and consequently oppressive. Even though he himself could no longer leave the mines, he made it possible for his son to learn to become a carpenter. And for the son, carpentry signified liberation and freedom from the dangers of mining. The next son remained in the business because it was all he knew. It was a decision from habit and routine, one about which he gave little thought. Yet when the fourth generation, the young man with whom I spoke, was forced to enter the carpentry trade, for him carpentry had come to symbolize oppression. The norm which the great-grandfather wished to foster was not carpentry but freedom. It was misunderstood to be carpentry. Likewise, the norm which Paul wished to foster was liberation in Jesus. For the first-century women at Ephesus, learning the knowledge of God's truth from the appropriate persons was liberating. But more than 1900 years later simply learning in submission and never teaching men still is the norm to follow with many persons. The passage of 1 Timothy 2:11-15 does not suggest opposition by Paul to the ordination of women. If anything, the development of Paul's work at Ephesus should culminate in the authoritative leadership of schooled orthodox women today. Paul never meant for women to remain at the beginning stage of growth exemplified by women at Ephesus. It was his design to have them mature as heirs according to God's promise (Gal.3:26-29). Thus, he would rejoice to see Galatians 3:28 become a reality in our actions:

There is neither Jew nor Greek, there is neither slave nor free, there is neither male and female; for all of you are one in Christ Jesus.

4

First Apostles, Second Prophets, Third Teachers: Examples of Women in Authority in the New Testament

While I was still with the police authorities my father out of love for me tried to dissuade me from my resolution.

"Father," I said, "do you see here, for example, this vase, or pitcher, or whatever it is?"

"I see it," he said.

"Can it be named anything else than what it really is?" I asked, and he said, "No."

"So I also cannot be called anything else than what I am, a Christian" (Vibia Perpetua, AD 202-03, *The Martyrdom of Perpetua* 3).

Even in the first century not all Christian women were affected by Paul's directions to Ephesus. Women were doing things which were unusual for their time. They were learning religious truths, speaking in public, and speaking authoritatively. Some were teaching. In fact, the New Testament provides overwhelming proof, first, that women held and were approved in positions considered authoritative in the first century, and second, that women were given gifts from God to fill positions for which churches now ordain people.

As Paul exhorts the Corinthians:

But you (pl) are [the] body of Christ and a member of a part. And God appointed in the church first apostles, second prophets, third teachers, then miracle workers, then gifts of healing, helpers, directors, kinds of languages (1 Cor. 12:27).

What characteristics distinguish apostles, prophets, and teachers from all other gifts? Many persons would affirm that the use of "first, second, and third" suggests sequence of rank and degree, those positions with the highest authority, honor and status. Christian authority, of course, is not authority for its own benefit. Paul may simply have used numbers to indicate that these positions are most important for the establishing of a church. "First, second, and third" may also indicate foundational priority. If a city has no apostle to testify personally to the resurrection, how can people go on to teach? Paul does seem to be indicating that these positions are crucial and they do include authority. The New Testament records women who are both called to and described as holding each of these three top positions: apostle, prophet, and teacher. These are the positions considered authoritative and crucial by the New Testament church. And these are the positions women held and in which they were affirmed.

Women were also given gifts from God for positions for which churches now ordain people. Ordination or the laying on of hands in itself does not bestow spiritual authority. God commands a specific calling. Ordination is the church's assent to God's command. Hands are an ancient and a biblical symbol of strength and might. Even today hands can symbolize power as is seen in such metaphors as "putting a heavy hand on," "the iron fist within the velvet glove," or "heavy-handed methods." The laying on of hands was a symbol of the transfer of power or giving of blessing (Mark 10:16).

Ordination is symbolic. When Simon Magus saw Peter and John place hands on persons, who being baptized in the name of Jesus, received the Holy Spirit, he too wanted that same power. He wanted to pay to receive the same powerful hands that Peter and John had: "Give also to me this power (or authority) so that to whomever I place my hands may receive the Holy Spirit" (Acts 8:19). He confused the symbol with the source.

The laying on of hands represents what God has already commanded. The Lord told Moses: "Take Joshua, a person in whom is the Spirit, and lay your hand upon him" (Num. 27:18). Joshua was chosen by God to replace Moses because the Spirit dwelt already in him. Moses was to ordain Joshua before Eleazar the priest and all the congregation because they would need to accept God's calling of Joshua. Similarly in New Testament times, the church in Antioch had prophets and teachers. Possibly they were "ordained," possibly not. The reader is not told. Timothy, who was an evangelist and a coworker was ordained, as well as the seven men who distributed food to the widows (Acts 6:6; 1 Tim. 4:14, 2 Tim. 1:6; 4:5; Rom. 16:21). Elders probably also were ordained (1 Tim. 5:17-22). Nevertheless, Luke does clearly record that at Antioch, while the Christians were worshipping, the Holy Spirit said, "Separate to me Barnabas and Saul for the work to which I have summoned them" (Acts 13:2). Then, after the church fasted, prayed, and placed their hands on Paul and Barnabas, they sent them off. Clearly their ordination included the laying on of hands and prayer, the church's symbolic earthly obedience to God's specific command.

Consequently, the truly biblical question is *not* should women be ordained but rather does God command women to preach, to teach, and to have authority? Then the church can symbolically affirm and pray for what God has already commanded. Ordination is frequently mentioned in the Bible. It is not as easy, however, to determine exactly who was then ordained. Nevertheless, one common denominator in churches today is to ordain persons who labor "as pastors, teachers, administrators, prophets and evangelists, and in such other works as may be needful to the Church, according to the gifts in which they excel."[1] What unites those positions?

According to Paul, Christ gave apostles, prophets, evangelists, pastors, and teachers "for the equipping of the saints for a work of ministry, for the upbuilding of the body of Christ" (Eph. 4:12). The phrase "equipping of the saints" is a synonymous phrase for "upbuilding of the body." *Katartismos* or "equipping" has the basic sense of "repair, mend," as to mend a net (Matt. 4:21) or set a limb. It also signifies "instruct, or train." *Oikodomen* or "upbuilding" has more a sense of building as of a house or, in the context of the verse, a body. Christ gave the people as "gifts," people who would focus on Christ's own body, the church, mending, repairing, instructing, upbuilding, and strengthening that body in order that it might mature. Maturity includes obedience to God, unity, knowledge, truthfulness, and love (Eph. 4:13-16). Now, too, we ordain persons whose calling is to equip other Christians for ministry.

Consequently, we should ask whether the Lord gives gifts of apostleship, prophecy, evangelism, teaching, and pastoring to women. And did Paul approve of women employing those gifts in the church? And if so would not the God who gives gifts and heartily reproves not developing such gifts (e.g., Luke 19:11-27) want women to develop their leadership gifts and be publically approved for doing so? Indeed, if even one woman could be found who was affirmed as an apostle, a prophet, an evangelist, a pastor, or a teacher, then one could—one must—conclude that women have been given gifts from God for positions to which we now ordain people and for positions considered authoritative in the first cen-

---

[1]United Presbyterian *Book of Order* VIII.1; VI.2 in Presbyterian *Book of Order*. See also Paul O. Madsen, ed., *Leaven: An Interpretive Volume Originating in the American Baptist Convocation on The Mission of the Church* (Valley Forge: American Baptist Home Mission Societies, 1962), pp. 70-3; *The Book of Discipline of the United Methodist Church 1980* (432) wherein: "Ordination is a public act of the Church which indicates acceptance by an individual of God's call to the upbuilding of the Church."

tury church.[2] However, Bible students can and have found creative ways to water down or obliterate every reference to a woman leader. Not everyone who claims the Bible is authoritative allows the Bible to speak authoritatively.

First Apostles

What is an apostle? *Apostolos* literally is someone sent forth with orders. An *apostolos* could simply be an invoice or a passport. The Jews had apostles (*shalah*) or "messengers" who were dispatched from a city by the rulers on a foreign mission, often to collect the tribute paid to the temple. In the New Testament an apostle could be one of the Twelve (Luke 6:13) or a larger group. For instance, Paul says in 1 Corinthians 15 that Jesus appeared "to the twelve" in verse 5 and "to all the apostles" in verse 7. The Twelve represented the twelve tribes in Israel. Possibly Paul as the thirteenth represented the Levites who were not counted. Apostles by definition were broader than the symbol of the Twelve. An apostle was someone who had seen Jesus (1 Cor. 9:1, thus, Paul could be one) or more specifically, someone who had accompanied the original twelve from the time that John baptized until Jesus ascended (Acts 1:21-22). Consequently Barnabas, Silvanus or Silas, James, the Lord's brother, and Andronicus were apostles although they were not of the Twelve.[3] With this definition of apostle, the women who accompanied Jesus could be called apostles: Mary Magdalene, Joana; Mary mother of Jesus, Mary mother of James, wife of Alphaeus; and Salome mother of James and John, wife of Zebedee. They were commissioned by the angel (Matt. 28:7; Mark 16:7).

---

[2]Synecdoche, wherein the one or the part represents the whole, is a consistent symbolism used by God. Adam and Eve represent all humans (e.g. Rom. 5:14). Jacob becomes and represents Israel (e.g., Gen. 35:9-12). Consequently, when Cornelius and his family and friends received the Holy Spirit the believers then concluded appropriately that God has also granted repentance to life to the Gentiles as a group (Acts 10-11). Similarly, even one woman leader affirmed by God signifies that all women leaders may be affirmed by God.

[3]Acts 14:14; Rom. 16:7; Gal. 1:19; 1 Thess. 1:1, 2:6.

Is any specific woman called an apostle? Paul ends his letter to the Romans by affirming Andronicus and Junia: "my fellow-citizens and my fellow-prisoners, who are prominent among the apostles, they also came before me in Christ" (16:7). Junia is a common Latin woman's name. Junius is the male counterpart, as Julius is the male counterpart of Julia and as Priscus is the male counterpart to Prisca. If a scholar were to posit or to assume that women cannot have authority, what could he do with Junia? What some scholars have done is to posit that Junias ("Junian" is in the text) was a shortened form of Junianus. However, Latin diminutives were formed by lengthening, not shortening a name, as, for example, Priscilla which is the diminutive of Prisca. Understandable then, the form "Junias" has yet to be found in extrabiblical sources.[4]

How did early commentators understand "Junia"? Origen, who lived toward the end of the second century, assumed Junia was a woman in his *Epistolam ad Romanos Commentariorum* 10, 26; 39. John Chrysostrom, living in the fourth century praised her:

> Oh! how great is the devotion of this woman, that she should be even counted worthy of the appellation of apostle! (*Homily on the Epistle of St. Paul the Apostle to the Romans* XXXI).

Jerome, who lived in the latter half of the fourth century, also assumed Junia was a woman (*Liber Interpretationis Hebraicorum Nominum* 72, 15). Commentators throughout the years have assumed Junia was a woman until Aegidus of Rome (AD 1245-1316) simply referred to the two persons Andronicus and Junia as "men" (*Opera Exegetica*, Opuscula I). Ironically, he preferred the variant "Julian," which modern

---

[4]James Hope Moulton and George Milligan, *The Vocabulary of the Greek Testament: Illustrated from the Papyri and Other Non-Literary Sources* (Grand Rapids: Eerdmans, 1930), p. 306. One Junia is described as "the daughter" and another one as "mother" in *Corpus Inscriptionum, Graecarum* (I.448; III.3927). If anything, *Iounianos* is the diminutive of *Iounios* as in the instance of "*Iounianon* a child" (III.4118). Ed. Augustus Boeckhius (Berolini: Academica, 1828).

scholars would understand to be clearly feminine.[5]

Some writers have posited that if Junia were a woman, she was admired *by* or well known *to* the apostles, not prominent *among* the apostles. *Episemos* properly means "a sign or mark upon," such as a mark or inscription on money.[6] It implies selection *from* a group.[7] Furthermore, the preposition *en* always has the idea of "within." In the plural *en* is translated "among" although it still has the basic idea of "within." *En* signifying "among" is a common idiom in the ancient Greek.[8] Consequently, Paul explains that Andronicus and Junia are *notable* from *among* the apostles. The meaning "by" would be rendered by prepositions signifying "with" such as *para* or *pros* (Luke 2:52; Acts 2:47).

Junia (and her male colleague Andronicus) would be Paul's counterpart in Rome. As an apostle, sent by God as an eyewitness to the resurrection of Jesus, Paul would lay the foundation for a church.[9] Certainly authoritative preaching would have to be part of such a testimony. Junia, along with Andronicus, apparently laid the foundation for the churches at Rome: "they came before me in Christ" (Rom. 16:7). The churches they helped establish have lasted to this day. No wonder Junia and Andronicus were *notable* apostles.

---

[5]Bernadette Brooten, "Junia...Outstanding Among the Apostles" (Romans 16:7), *Women Priests: A Catholic Commentary on the Vatican Declaration*, eds. Leonard Swidler and Arlene Swidler (New York: Paulist, 1977), pp. 141-55. James Hope Moulton and Wilbert Francis Howard cite Junia as a Latin woman's name. *A Grammar of New Testament Greek*, Vol. II (Edinburgh: T. & T. Clark, 1920), p. 155.

[6]Liddell and Scott, p. 656.

[7]William Sanday and Arthur C. Headlam, *A Critical and Exegetical Commentary on The Epistle to the Romans,* The International Critical Commentary (5th ed.; Edinburgh: T. & T. Clark, 1902), p. 423.

[8]Robertson, p. 587.

[9]Luke 11:49; 1 Cor. 3:6-10; 2 Cor. 10:14; Eph. 2:20; 3:5; Rom. 15:18-23; Acts 14:21-3; 15:36; 18:23.

Second Prophets

A prophet is someone who receives and speaks forth a message from God. A prophet can both foretell as did Agabus (Acts 11:27-28; 21:10-11) or forth-tell in the manner of Silas and Judas (Acts 15:32). According to 1 Corinthians 14, a prophet speaks to people during worship for their upbuilding, encouragement, and consolation (v. 3).[10] In contrast to people who speak in an angelic language, prophets use their minds. Prophets convict the outsider and instruct the Christian (vv. 15-9). Everyone preaches (*kerusso*) the good news, but only some are prophets. The prophet functioned in the service as does a contemporary preacher. Then, of course, the service had preacher*s*.

In the Old Testament Miriam, Huldah, and the wife of Isaiah were called prophets.[11] Miriam was God's appointed leader over Israel along with Moses and Aaron (Micah 6:4). Only Huldah could interpret the significance of Deuteronomy to the devout King Josiah, to Hilkiah the high priest, and to Josiah's cabinet, Shaphan, Ahikam, Achbor, and Asaiah. Deborah was both a prophet and a judge (Judg. 4:4). As a judge, she was appointed by God to rule the government, direct the army, and judge legal matters. Deborah was so impressive as a military strategist and a prophetess that Barak refused to combat Sisera without her. Under this "mother of Israel," the land had rest for forty years.[12] Many Old Testament heroes, while devout, had major flaws, but Deborah and her contemporary Ruth stand out in the Scrip-

---

[10]*Oikodomen* or "upbuilding" is the same word used in Eph. 4:12.

[11]Exod. 15:20; 2 Kings 22:14-22; Isa. 8:3. Isaiah and his wife were a "clergy couple." Possibly, God employed so much feminine imagery to describe deity in the Book of Isaiah because of Isaiah's wife's participation in their joint ministry of prophecy. Since the same term "prophetess" is used of Miriam, Deborah, and Huldah, as of Isaiah's wife, she is also likely to be a prophetess rather than "the wife of a prophet" as G.B. Gray suggests. *A Critical and Exegetical Commentary on The Book of Isaiah I*, The International Critical Commentary (Edinburgh: T. & T. Clark, 1912), p. 144.

[12]Judg. 5:7, 31; 4:4, 6, 14; 2:16, 18. See also wise women, 2 Sam. 14:1-24; 20:14-23.

tures as totally pure. Joel proclaimed that God will afterwards pour out God's Spirit on all so that the daughters will
prophesy and so they did (2:28). Anna is called a prophetess
(Luke 2:36). Only Anna, together with Simeon, recognized
the youthful Savior and she preached about Jesus throughout Jerusalem. Phillip's four daughters were active prophets
who became well known in the ancient church.[13]

However, we understand the metaphor "head" in 1 Corinthians 11 and the "silence" in 1 Corinthians 14:34, they did
not mean that women could not participate in leadership at
worship.[14] Paul *assumes* in 11:5 that women are praying and
prophesying. The question in chapter 11 was simply their attire while doing so.[15] The women were not silent, they apparently were monopolizing the entire service! As Paul asks,
"Has the word of God reached *only* you" (14:36)? Three
groups of people are "silenced" in chapter 14: speakers in
tongues when there was no interpreter (14:27-28), one
prophet when a revelation was made to another prophet

---

[13]Acts 21:8-9; *Eusebius Church History,* Bk III.31,37.

[14]"Head" has become so synonymous with "boss" in the American culture
that people have often forgotten that it is a metaphor. As a metaphor, the
physical head is in some way analogous to some concept Paul wants to describe. "Head" was then used literally, as a synecdoche for hair (Acts 18:18),
to designate the chief leader or prince (Num. 1:4; 25:15; Judg. 10:18; 11:9-
11), source of life (Isa. 43:4, Acts 18:6), or beginning (Exod. 12:2, Judg.
l:19). The source or "head" of four tributaries was in Eden (Gen. 2:10). An-
cients would often use "head" as we today use the metaphor "heart." The
head was the source of life. Consequently, Jesus as our "head" nourishes
and causes growth to the body (Col. 2:19). God is the "head" of Christ because God gave life to the Messiah at the incarnation or appointed the Messiah as sovereign and priest (1 Cor. 11:3; John 1:14; 5:25-9; Matt. 1:20; Ps.
2:7). Man is the "head" of a woman because he was her source of life at creation. Paul describes the same concept with different language in verse 7.
"The woman is [the] glory of man" in the sense that she was taken "out of a
man" (v.8). In the Lord, however, the woman is also the source of life to man
(vv. 11-2). Paul alludes here probably to a woman, Mary, giving birth to the
Savior, or, less likely, to women giving birth to all children.

[15]When in the Apocryphal tale the disreputable elders ordered Susanna to
be unveiled, the act was so debased and dishonorable her family and all who
saw her were in tears (1:32).

(14:30-31), and women learning in a shameful manner (14:33-36), because God is a God of peace and not of disorder.[16] The Corinthians were boastful, arrogant, and quarrelsome, using knowledge and right as license and speaking in tongues in such a way as to create disorder and encourage arrogance. Paul's overriding purpose in 1 Corinthians is to explain to his readers that love or service to others for the sake of the gospel is greater than any other principle, such as knowledge or right.

Paul employs a different word for silence in 1 Corinthians 14 (*sigao*, vv. 28, 30, 34) than he does in 1 Timothy 2 (*hesuchia*, vv. 2, 11, 12). Both terms have positive connotations. *Sigao* is used in the New Testament to signify listening, not creating a disturbance or keeping a secret.[17] Paul's concern at Corinth would be similar to his concern for women at Ephesus expressed in the earlier verses of 1 Timothy 2 (vv. 9-10). In all the churches Paul wanted the women to pray in decorum. At Ephesus the women were flaunting their wealth by their attire, while at Corinth they were boisterous, flaunting their freedom in Christ. If indeed the unveiled or shaven woman had the same appearance as a cultic prostitute or an adulteress,[18] then Paul might have been alluding in 14:34 to laws of holiness against harlotry or adultery (e.g., Lev. 19:2, 29; Deut. 22:5; 23:17; Num. 5:18).

Recently, some writers have suggested that prophets have less authority than the judges of the prophetic message. Douglas J. Moo explains that in 14:34, "it is probably this questioning of the validity of the prophetic word that is forbidden women."[19] The ability to distinguish (or judge) be-

---

[16]See A.J. Gordon, "The Ministry of Women," *Missionary Review of the World* 7 (December, 1894): 910-21.

[17]Acts 12:17; 15:12-3; 21:40; Luke 9:36; 18:39; 20:26; Rom. 16:25; Rev. 8:1.

[18]Patricia Gundry, *Woman Be Free!* (Grand Rapids: Zondervan, 1977), pp. 65-66. The greatest institution of the cultic prostitutes or "sacred slaves" (*hierodules*) was the temple of Aphrodite-Melainis in Corinth.

[19]"I Timothy 2:11-15: Meaning and Significance," *Trinity Journal* 1 (Spring, 1980): 74.

tween spirits is one of the Spirit's gifts to the church (12:10). The gift in 12:10 is described by the same basic root of *krino* and follows mention of prophecy. Why would this one gift in the list of 12:8-10 not be given to women whereas all the other gifts listed are given to women? Moreover, although distinquishing between spirits is a different function than prophecy itself, the prophets are the ones who are challenged to evaluate the prophetic messages. "Let the others weigh"(v. 29), Paul says, and "spirits of prophets are subject to prophets" (v. 33). Spirits need to be tested to see if the prophets are genuine, even as doctrines need to be evaluated to see if the teachers are orthodox.[20] The context of 1 Corinthians 12-14 does not in any way acccentuate judgement over preaching. Judgement cannot occur without prophecy; nor prophecy without evaluation.

The New Testament provides clear examples of women who are called prophets and described as prophesying. Prophets come second in Paul's list of the priority of gifts and second in his list of persons given to the church.

Third Teachers

Wisdom personified as a woman takes her stand by the gates where judgements are made and calls to all:

> Take my instruction and not silver,
> and knowledge rather than choice gold;
> for wisdom is better than jewels,
> and all that you may desire cannot compare with her
> (Prov. 8:10-11).

Few, however, were the women in the first century that were trained to educate. Understandably then the New Testament has fewer examples of women teachers than it has of women prophets. Yet, even though Paul calls himself a teacher,[21] he always mentions prophets before teachers. The New Testa-

---

[20]E.g., 1 John 4:1-6; 1 Thess. 5:19-21; Rom. 16:17-20; 1 Tim. 4:1; 6:3; John 7:14-9; Heb. 13:9.

[21]1 Tim. 2:7; 2 Tim. 1:11-2; Acts 11:26.

ment does, however, record some significant women teachers.

Priscilla, who was present at Ephesus early in Paul's ministry there and at the time of his last imprisonment,[22] was herself an able teacher. In Acts 18:26 Luke records, "Having heard [Apollos], Priscilla and Aquila took him aside and more accurately expounded to him the way of God." Is "expounding" the same as teaching? *Ektithemai* means "I expound, set forth, declare, exhibit publicly, explain by means of abstraction." The basic root of the word signifies "to place outside."[23] The word does not connote a simple explanation. Rather, it connotes a public declaration and exposition. Luke employs the same word to describe Peter's defense before the circumcision party and Paul's daily exposition before the Jews in Rome (Acts 11:4; 28:23). Since Priscilla is mentioned first in all of the best manuscripts, she herself certainly would have expounded the teachings. Moreover, she along with Aquila not only expounded the way of God to Apollos, they also more "accurately" did so. The same care Luke employed in his gospel (Luke 1:3), Priscilla and Aquila employed in their teaching.

Often little attention is given to the "old women" at Crete mentioned by Paul in Titus 2:3. However, the word "old" is the word *presbutis* or "female elder."[24] The women could as easily be understood as "women elders" rather than "old women," especially in light of the fact that they are called "teachers" (*didaskalos*), "teachers of the good." The contrast between bishops and deacons (or ministers) in 1 Timothy 3:1-8 rests primarily on the ability bishops must have to teach

---

[22]Acts 18:18, *ca.* AD 52; 2 Tim. 4:19, *ca.* 67-68. Priscilla and Aquila were in Rome *ca.* 57, Rom. 16:3. When 1 Timothy was written they could have been in Rome or in Ephesus or elsewhere.

[23]Liddell and Scott, p. 522.

[24]*Presbutis* is the feminine of *presbutes.* Both are prose forms of *presbus,* which can signify an "old man, most important, ambassador, president, elder" (Liddell and Scott, p. 1462). People had to be sixty to be fit to be a Jewish elder (*m. 'Abot* 5:21).

ably.[25] The women elders at Crete had the ability and were told to use it.

Evangelists and Pastors

Although many churches feel free to send women to the mission field as evangelists, the New Testament does not describe women with such a title. Only two men are given the title "evangelist": Timothy and Philip (2 Tim. 4:5; Acts 21:8). Evangelists baptized and instructed people concerning Christian salvation. (Philip baptized in Acts 8:12. Paul who traveled with Timothy claims he usually did not baptize [1 Cor. 1:14-17]. Consequently, possibly Timothy did.) However, women did bring the good news to others; for example, the women who witnessed the empty tomb and the present body, and the Samaritan woman at the well.

Similarly, the New Testament also does not record any example of a woman pastor. Yet, neither does it record any example of an individual male pastor. The only individual called a "pastor" or "shepherd" (*poimen*) is Jesus. The pastor is the one who protects. (*Poimen* comes from *poia*, "to protect.") The pastor has a personal knowledge of the people, has compassion for them, sets examples, protects, and judges as a sovereign would.[26] Shepherds were used as metaphors for sovereigns by Jews. Philo says about the Roman emperor that he should "always and everywhere" remember "his sovereignty, that he is a shepherd and master of a flock" (*Embassy to Gaius* VII [44]). A guardian he describes as "a shepherd of the civilized flock" (*Embassy to Gaius* III [20]). Outside of Peter, only the elders as a group are called "to pastor." Neither 1 Peter 5:1-4 nor Acts 20:28 record their sexes, yet as we have seen Titus 2 does indicate that women could be elders.

When examining the New Testament to decide whether

---

[25]See also Titus 1:9. Elder and bishop are used synonymously in vv. 5-7.

[26]E.g., John 10; Matt. 9:36; 25:32.

women should become active acknowledged leaders in ministry, one notices that present church practices and first-century church practices often jar against one another. The presence of women apostles, prophets, and teachers indicates that women had and were approved in positions considered authoritative in the first-century church. Those positions did equip the body of Christ for the work of ministry, a common contemporary criterion for a "Minister." Probably the functional equivalents of today's "head" pastor was yesterday's oveseer of church communities.

Church Overseers

The New Testament records many women overseers, yet often they have been overlooked: the Elect Lady, the Elect Sister, Phoebe, Euodia, Syntyche, Prisca, and possibly also Stephana, Tryphaena, Tryphosa, Chloe, Lydia, Mark's mother, Nympha, and Apphia.

The Elect Lady

John addresses his second letter to the "elect lady and her children" (v. 1). Today a "lady" can refer to a woman with manners, although usually it is simply a more polite version of "woman." *Kuria* is the feminine of *kurios*, "lord" or "master." The feminine *kuria* occurs only in 2 John (vv. 1, 5) in the New Testament. Paul calls *kurios* the person who owns an entire estate and is not under guardians and trustees (Gal. 4:1). The *kurios* is a guardian, master of a house, or head of a family. The person owning and overseeing a slave is a *kurios* (e.g. Eph. 6:5, 9). Of course, "the Lord" is primarily, in the New Testament, a name for Jesus, the Lord over all lords (John 4:1; 1 Tim. 6:15). The noun *kuria* simply means "authority" or "power." The vocative, which is *not* used in 2 John, in the first century as in contemporary practice, can simply mean "madam." Moreover, the context of the letter makes such a possibility unlikely.

This woman addressed in 2 John was not only an authority. She also is chosen. John calls her "the woman chosen to be master" (v. 1). However, this woman has often been dis-

missed when considering the possibility of a woman leader
of a church. A. E. Brooke, in his commentary on the Johannine Epistles, says: "Perhaps it would be better to regard [la-
dy's] use as rather playful, or not to be taken too seriously."[27]
Often Bible students will say that "elect lady" is a metaphor
for a congregation. So, literally, John has addressed his letter to an entire church. However, such an interpretation is
unlikely. If "elect lady" stands for a church, then who are
"her children"? John calls the recipients of 1 John "my little
children" (e.g. 2:1). A church would have to be called *either*
elect lady *or* children in John's language scheme, not both.

All the data is best understood if John were writing the
letter to a woman who was the person in authority over a
congregation. He uses for her the singular metaphor *kuria*[28]
and for the congregation the plural metaphor "children."
Consequently, the children are "hers," just as the children of
1 John are "his" (John's). John uses both the singular and
plural pronouns for "you" in 2 John. As the King James Version clearly indicates, John uses the singular "thy" in verses
4 and 5 and in 13. He uses the plural "ye" in the body, verses
6-12. The "children" belong to one person (v. 4). John addresses that same one person as *kuria* (v.5), but he also
writes "ye" (v. 12). The "children" have all to be adult believers (not literal minors) because they are challenged to "look
to yourselves, in order that you may not lose that for which
you have worked but receive a full reward" (v. 8). Also the
"children" are commanded to receive into the house (singular) anyone who does not believe that Jesus came in the flesh
(vv.7-10). Clearly John has in mind a church meeting in a
house, probably the house of the elect lady. She is addressed
as the person having authority. Moreover, in the last verse

---

[27]A. E. Brooke, *A Critical and Exegetical Commentary on the Johannine
Epistles,* The International Critical Commentary (Edinburgh: T. & T. Clark,
1912), p. 167.

[28]Possibly in the same manner Paul uses a military metaphor, "true com-
rade," to address an unknown person in Philippi (4:3). Clement of Alexandria, too, thought 2 John was written to "a Babylonian lady" (*Fragments* of
Cassiodorus IV).

John indicates that there was another such woman who also was an overseer over a church community. She, too, was an "elect sister," probably a sister in Christ.

Joan Morris in *The Lady was a Bishop* notes in addition that *kuria* is nowhere employed as a metaphor for a congregation, although "elect" sometimes denotes a clerically ordained person. In the New Testament Rufus is another individual believer called "elect" (Rom. 16:13).[29] "Elect persons" can refer to clergy such as presbyters, bishops, ministers (or deacons), and widows.[30] For instance, Clement of Alexandria, who was born around AD 150, concludes the *Pedagogus*:

Innumerable commands such as these are written in the holy Bible appertaining to *chosen* persons, some to presbyters, some to bishops, some to deacons, others to widows (Bk. III.12).

Moreover, 2 John is most likely to be addressed to an individual since the letter heading is so similar to 3 John. 3 John reads literally, "The elder to Gaius the beloved one, whom I love in truth." 2 John reads "The elder to elect lady and to her children, whom I love in the truth." 3 John is clearly ad-

---

[29] Although "the elect" (masculine) by itself or a feminine metaphor can refer to the church in the New Testament, in 2 John "elect," in contrast, modifies "lady" and "lady" is not used for a church. The "elect" refers to the church in Matt. 24:22,24,31; Luke 18:7; Rom. 8:33; 2 Tim. 2:10; Col. 3:12; Tit. 1:1; and Rev. 17:14. Peter uses the feminine article by itself apparently to stand for the feminine noun *ekklesia:* "The *one* in Babylon *chosen* along with you greets you as well as Mark my son" (1 Pet. 5:13). Peter's ending seems to hearken back to the introduction of his letter. The church is chosen for suffering in behalf of its testimony to Jesus Christ (1 Pet. 1:1-2). Since both 1 Peter and 2 John are probably later letters, the use of "elect" to modify the lady of 2 John may also suggest the woman has had to suffer in behalf of her love of truth.

[30] *Testamentum Domini* (ca. 475) I.35,40 describes the ordination and office of widow. The feminine "elder" *(presbyterae)* was used in Egypt probably as a synonym for the widow. *Testamentum Domini* is cited by Mary Lawrence McKenna, *Women of the Church: Role and Renewal* (New York: P.J. Kenedy, 1967), pp. 54-62.

dressed to Gaius.[31] Apparently John is writing Gaius since Diotrephes, the proper person over that church, did not acknowledge John's authority (v. 9). John did not have any such difficulty with the two elect sisters.

Readers today should not be at all surprised that "the elect lady" was a woman overseeing a church in her house. Of course, all churches met in homes until the third century. Even the earliest church buildings were built to imitate guest rooms in homes.[32] Almost all Christian assemblies mentioned in Acts and in Paul's letters are in houses of women or, if not, of couples: Chloe (1 Cor. 1:11), Lydia (Acts 16:40), the mother of John Mark (Acts 12:12), Nympha (Col. 4:15), Prisca and Aquila (Rom. 16:3-5; 1 Cor. 16:19), Philemon, Apphia, Archippus (Philem. 1-2) and possibly Stephana (1 Cor. 16:15, 17). Chloe's congregation or Chloe's appointed leaders had reported to Paul the quarreling occurring at Corinth.

Lydia, as well as being the head of her household (Acts 16:15) and hosting the church, was a successful career woman. The purple dye she sold was the most valued of ancient dyes since it was expensive and a symbol of power and honor. A considerable amount of capital was needed to trade in purple cloth. Thyatira, Lydia's home city, was renowned for the dying of purple cloth. Mary Mooyart therefore concludes: "Her business had prospered so much that she had found it necessary to establish a depot at Philippi, where her bales could be stored for overland transport to the towns of Greece."[33] Probably, as well, the Roman officials in Philippi would buy her goods. Paul, Luke, Silas, and Timothy did not hesitate to accept Lydia's hospitality and, moreover, to allow her to take a leadership role in the Philippian church.

---

[31]Joan Morris, *The Lady Was a Bishop: The Hidden History of Women with Clerical Ordination and the Jurisdiction of Bishops* (New York: Macmillan, 1973), pp. 1-2.

[32]Robert Banks, *Paul's Idea of Community: The Early House Churches in Their Historical Setting* (Grand Rapids: Eerdmans 1980), p. 41.

[33]Mary Mooyart, *In the Days of the Apostles.*

Phoebe

Paul commends Phoebe to the church at Rome (Rom. 16:1-2). Since he calls her "our sister," she is clearly a woman. He describes her with two remarkable titles. She is a minister and a leader.

Diakonos literally signifies "servant." *Diakonos* became an especially important metaphor for the Christian church to render personal service in obedience to Christ and for the edification of others. The first-century secular uses of the word developed in the church into two general types of "personal service." When the noun *diakonos* by itself refers to an individual Christian, it is used synonymously with "ministry of the word" or "ministry to equip the saints." This metaphorical use of "minister" appears to derive from the literal use of a "Servant or Minister of a Sovereign."[34] Such a servant would be comparable to today's "minister" of government, as the Minister of Interior. A minister would personally assist the sovereign by making suggestions and implementing and delivering orders. In effect, this servant was a "messenger" for the sovereign.[35]

When the noun *diakonos* is reduplicated as in a "ministry of ministry or service" it comes from the literal use of *diakonos* to signify the meeting of physical needs. A servant could be the person who serves food and drink, pays for food and drink, or supplies more general external needs such as food, drink, shelter, and clothing.[36] For instance, Peter describes "ministry" (*diakonia*) as having two types: "If any speaks, [let that person speak] as a word from God; if any *serve*, [let that person serve] as out of the strength which God provides" (1 Pet. 4:10). The first ministry is a verbal one; the second is one which is physically exhausting. God is the source for both types of work, both of which are ministry

---

[34]E.g., Matt. 22:13; Rom. 13:4; Esther 1:10; 2:2; 6:3,5;

[35]Liddell and Scott, p. 398.

[36]E.g. John 2:5-9; Luke 8:3; 10:40; 12:37-38; 17:7-8; 1 Macc. 11:58; Acts 6:1-4; 9:36-42; Matt. 25:44; 2 Tim. 1:18; 4:11, 19; Philem. 13. In Rom. 15:25, 31 and 2 Cor. 8:4, 19 the monetary offering is a *diakonos*.

(or personal service) "in order that in everything God may be glorified through Jesus Christ, to whom is the glory and the power forever and ever; Amen!" (1 Pet. 4:11).

The twelve apostles employed similar categories in Jerusalem. The daily distribution (probably of food) to the widows would be the "ministry of service" which was contrasted to the "ministry of the word" (Acts 6:1-6). Clearly Stephen and Dorcas served as ministers of external need. The "disciple" Dorcas is a remarkable "minister of service." She was so effective that the church at Joppa could not allow her to die (Acts 9:36-42). Paul's listing of those who "equip the saints" in Ephesians 4:11-12 are apostles, prophets, evangelists, pastors, and teachers, persons who are verbally oriented. The order of widows is an order of prayer; however, its prerequisites include a ministry of service. A true widow must be an elder well attested for her good deeds and hospitable, having washed the feet of the saints and relieved the afflicted (1 Tim. 5:5-10). All Christians are enjoined to participate in both types of ministries, but particular people devote themselves to one or another.

When the noun *diakonos* refers to an individual male it is always translated "minister" by the King James Version and usually translated "minister" by other versions. Paul, Timothy, and Epaphras are always called "minister."[37] Tychicus is called "minister" at least once (Eph. 6:21; Col. 4:7 NIV). However, to some scholars, simply because Phoebe is a woman she cannot be called a "minister." As James Hurley writes: "If the name in the text were Timothy or Judas, ninety-nine per cent of the scholars would presume that diakonos meant "deacon."[38] If Timothy or Judas were called a *diakonos* one hundred percent of the scholars would presume diakonos meant "minister"! For example, Kenneth Taylor describes Phoebe as a "dear Christian woman" whereas Timothy is a "worthy pastor" (1 Tim. 4:6 *The Liv-*

---

[37]E.g. Eph. 3:7; Col. 1:7,23,25; 1 Tim. 4:6.

[38]James B. Hurley, *Man and Woman in Biblical Perspective* (Grand Rapids: Zondervan, 1981), p. 124.

ing Bible). Again, each Bible text is not allowed to speak for itself. Since Phoebe is described by Paul as a *diakonos* of a specific church, the church in Cenchreae, that is all the more reason to translate *diakonos* as "minister" rather than "servant." Helen Barrett Montgomery's *New Testament in Modern English* reads: "I commend to you our sister Phoebe, who is a minister of the church at Cencreae."[39] The position she takes as a "minister" of a particular congregation was the model for many women later. Two women ministers at Bithynia-Pontus in Asia Minor were tortured during Emperor Trajan's reign (AD 98-117) as the leaders and most knowledgeable persons in their congregation. After Pliny describes a report of an apparently innocuous service he decides, "it was all the more necessary to extract the truth by torture from the slave-women, whom they called ministers" (*The Letters of Pliny*, Bk.X.96).

Phoebe is not only a minister, she is also a minister who should be welcomed as worthy by the saints at Rome and assisted (*paristemi*) in anything she requires, for Paul explains "she herself has been a *prostatis* over many and even of myself (16:2)." *Prostatis* has been translated "helper, help, succorer, and good friend." Such translations are more appropriate to the earlier verb *paristemi*. *Paristemi* literally signifies "to stand, place, or set beside or near," whereas the verb form of *prostatis*, which is *proistemi*, literally signifies "to stand, place before or over." *Paristemi* and *proistemi* have the same basic verb (*istemi*) plus a preposition (*par* or *pro*). The different prepositions give different connotations for "help." In one, you "help by presenting," in the other, you "help by ruling." The Romans are asked to place themselves at Phoebe's disposal and thus "help" her. Phoebe on the other hand is "a woman set over others" or "one who stands before." No other person is called a *prostatis* in the New Tes-

---

[39]Also E. Earle Ellis, concluding that *diakonoi* are "a special class of co-workers, those who are active in preaching and teaching," goes on to include Phoebe as a preacher and teacher in a local congregation. "Paul and His Co-Workers," *New Testament Studies* 17 (July, 1971), 442-43.

tament. The Romans are to be at Phoebe's disposal because she has been a leader over many and even over Paul!

The verb form *proistemi*, though, occurs a few times. The verb with the genitive signifies "I am set over, I am the head of," especially in reference to being chief or leader of a party, "I govern, direct," and "I stand before so as to guard," hence a champion or protector.[40] The noun *prostatis* takes the genitive case of "many" and "me" to indicate these are the persons over whom Phoebe has been set. Phoebe is an explicit, commendable example of a woman set in authority over a man, in this case, the great apostle Paul. One of the gifts of the Spirit is this kind of "leading," which Paul commands to be done with diligence (Rom. 12:8). Furthermore, Paul exhorts the Thessalonians:

> To pay proper respect to the ones working among you and *chosen as your leaders* in [the] Lord and instructing you and regard them very highly indeed in love because of their work" (1 Thess. 5:12-13).

Both the bishop and the minister (or deacon) are to *govern* their own houses well. As Paul adds, "If people do not know how to govern their own house, how can they look after the church of God?" (1 Tim. 3:4-5, 12). The elder who also "*directs* well" is worthy of double honor (1 Tim. 5:17). Paul consequently employs the verb form with persons as direct objects [41] to signify "set before others as a leader." Therefore, the most likely significance of *prostatis* is its common meaning of a leader and ruler.

Josephus consistently uses the word *prostates* to refer to the leader of a nation, a tribe, and a region, or the leader of all, God. *Prostates* always has positive connotations. Moses and Joseph are called *prostates* of the people as are Herod, Agrippa, and Hyrcanus. Solomon was made *prostates* of the temple by David. Agrippa pledges to be a good *prostates* as opposed to a tyrant (*turannos*). Hyrcanus would be a *prostates*, king, and ruler as opposed to a master (*despoten*), ty-

---

[40] Liddell and Scott, pp. 1482-83, 1526; Thayer, pp. 539-40; 549.
[41] Cf. Titus 3:8, 14 "to *manage* good deeds."

rant, and enemy. Herod is hailed as a savior and protector after he won a battle. Josephus as "governor" is a *prostates.* Gadalius would be the *prostates* because if anyone molested his people he would protect them. Antipater calls Caesar the *prostates* of the world. God is *prostates* over all.[42]

In the later church the term was used of civil rulers, ecclesiastical rulers, and bishops.[43] Clement calls Jesus Christ the *prostates,* the leader who champions his followers, "the high priest and *guardian* of our souls" and "the high priest of our offerings, the defender and *guardian* of our weakness" (1 Clement XXXVI.1; LXI.3). In the Old Testament and Apocrypha *prostates* can refer to stewards of King David's property, chief officers over the people, the governor of Judea, and the ruler of the temple.[44] The Septuagint rendering *prostates* translates the Hebrew *paqid,* which signifies a commanding officer such as a "commissioner, deputy, overseer."[45]

Thus, can Phoebe simply be dismissed as a "good friend" or a "help"? Phoebe is praised by Paul as a responsible leader in authority, in contrast to women such as those at Ephesus who were using their authority to destroy men.

Coworkers

Although we often envision Paul as a lone evangelist walking across deserts from city to city, he very much enjoyed and encouraged team ministry. Coworkers (*sunergon*) in-

---

[42]Moses *Ant.* Bk III [98]; Joseph *Ant.* Bk I [87]; Herod *War* Bk I. XIX.6 [385]; *Ant.* Bk XIV.XV.8 [444]; XV [159]; Agrippa *War* Bk II.XI.2 [208]; Hyrcanus *Ant.* Bk XIV.IX.2 [157]; Gadalius *Ant.* Bk X.IX.2 [161]; Caesar *War* Bk I.XXXII.3 [633]; Josephus *Life* 48 [205]; Solomon *Ant.* Bk VII.XIV.10 [376]; God *Ant.* Bk II [122]; Bk IV [185]; Bk VII.XIV.2,11 [340, 380].

[43]G.W.H. Lampe, ed. *A Patristic Greek Lexicon,* (Oxford: Clarendon, 1961), p. 1182.

[44]Sanabassar, the *governor* of Judea (1 Esd. 2:12) Phinehas, the *chief* of the sanctuary and of his people (Ecclus. 45:24); Simon, *governor* of the temple (2 Macc. 3:4); chief officers for kings (1 Chron. 27:31; 29:6; 2 Chron. 8:10; 24:11).

[45]Francis Brown, S.R. Driver, and Charles A. Briggs, *A Hebrew and English Lexicon of the Old Testament,* p. 824.

clude Paul, Timothy the evangelist, Silas the prophet, Apollos, Tychicus, Titus, Epaphroditus, Epaphras, Luke, Onesiphorus, Mark, Philemon, Demas, Jesus Justus, Aquila, and Aristarchus.[46] Paul calls several women "coworkers" as well. Prisca, Euodia, Syntyche, and maybe Stephana. Tryphaena and Tryphosa he calls "workers."[47]

"Coworkers" comes from two words signifying "to work together." It can simply signify a "helper," if in the dative case. But in the genitive case, which Paul always employs for these people, it signifies "a person of the same trade, a colleague."[48] In 1 Corinthians 16:15-16 Paul describes one such household, the household of Stephana, which devoted itself to ministry. Therefore, Paul exhorts, "be subject to such people and to every coworker and worker" (v. 16). And he repeats, "therefore give recognition to such people" (v. 18). Paul employs the generic masculine pronoun as a noun. He does not use the sex-specific term *aner* for "male." In Paul's team ministry coworkers and workers were persons to whom the churches were to be subject.

Paul employs the same term for "workers" in 1 Thessalonians 5:12. There, too, he exhorts the church to pay proper respect to such people and regard them very highly. Moreover, many ministers of the word, apostles, prophets, evangelists, pastors, and teachers (Eph. 4:12), are also coworkers. The term "minister" may be seen as a synonym, since *diakonos* is one variant in ancient manuscripts for *sunergon* in 1 Thessalonians 3:2. Consequently, because of its meaning as "colleague" and Paul's use of the word, "coworker" in the New Testament is more than "a helping person." Rather, a "coworker" and possibly "worker" is someone whom Paul considers a colleague placed in a position of au-

---

[46]"Coworkers" are limited to persons described as such by the term *sunergon* or, if specified, by the term *kopiao* "workers." Rom. 16:3, 21; 1 Cor. 3:9; 2 Cor. 8:23; Phil. 2:25; 4:3; Col. 4:10-14; Philem. 1, 23-24.

[47]Mary and Persis have "worked" among the Romans; Rom. 16:6, 12.

[48]Liddell and Scott, pp. 1711-12.

thority similar to his own position.[49] Women certainly were called "coworkers."

Euodia and Syntyche clearly were colleagues, since Paul calls them not only "my coworkers" but also women who "labored side by side" with him in the gospel (Phil. 4:2-3). The phrase literally reads "fought at my side," since Paul pictures ministry as combat. Euodia and Syntyche were important enough at Philippi that their disagreement could affect the entire church and thus warrant a personal entreaty. Priscilla oversaw several churches in her home, taught, and served as Paul's colleague whenever she travelled. Stephana might very well have been a woman (1 Cor. 16:15). Stephana is a woman's name. The male counterpart of course is Stephanos (e.g.Acts 6:8). *Stephana* might possibly be a diminutive of *Stephanos* (e.g., *Loukas*, 2 Tim. 4:11) or *Stephanephoros*.[50] The genitive case of any name ending in -*as* can take the unusual -*ân* ending. Consequently, the name "Stephana" could be a woman's or a man's name. Unfortunately, since "Stephana" has had authority, commentators and translators have assumed Stephana was a man and not a woman. Either is possible.

Summary

In conclusion, the New Testament records many women leaders. But more than that, the New Testament writers have left for us examples of women in significant positions, positions considered authoritative in the first century

---

[49]E. Earle Ellis not only writes about "coworkers" as colleagues and itinerant workers whose work entitles them to the Christian community's esteem but he also develops a convincing case for "the brothers" to be an official title to refer to a limited group of workers, some of whom have the Christian mission as their primary occupation. Epaphroditus, Titus, Timothy, Tychicus, and Apollos were all "brothers" as well as "co-workers." Ellis, 437-52.

[50]F. Blass and A. DeBrunner, *A Greek Grammar of the New Testament and Other Early Christian Literature*, trans. R.W. Funk (9th ed.; Chicago: University of Chicago, 1961), p. 68.

and positions considered authoritative today. Junia is called an apostle. Mary Magdalene, Joanna, Mary mother of Jesus, Mary mother of James, and Salome mother of James and John were "apostles" by definition. Anna is called a prophet, as were Miriam, Huldah, the wife of Isaiah, and Deborah. Philip's four daughters prophesied as did the women at Corinth. Priscilla and the women at Crete were teachers. The women at Crete were elders. Priscilla as well was a coworker and church overseer. The Elect Lady and Elect Sister were church overseers. Phoebe was a church overseer and a minister. Stephana, possibly a woman, was clearly a person in authority and a coworker. Lydia and Chloe were probably church overseers and perhaps, as well, were the mother of Mark, Nympha, and Apphia. Euodia, Syntyche, Tryphaena, Tryphosa, and possibly Mary and Persis were Paul's colleagues, having each their own positions of authority.

Why have Bible scholars not highlighted these women for us? Have some translators and commentators refused to allow or never even posited the possibility that women could be in authority? The reasoning goes somewhat like this:

Phoebe could not be a minister because she was a woman. Junia could not be a woman because she was an apostle. The Elect Lady must be a church because she could not be a lady. Stephana could not be a woman because people were subjected to her.[51]

Or, does the lack of recognizing these ancient authoritative women exist because modern women have not always been encouraged to study the Bible formally so that they, too, can authoritatively contribute their perspectives? Study opens our eyes to the truth. As our biblical sisters once were called, God still calls women to minister.

---

[51]W.D. Spencer and A. Besançon Spencer, "In Defense of the First Church of Tootsie," *The Wittenburg Door,* April/May, 1983, 27.

5

The Full Vision: Feminine Images of God for Ministry

When Rabbi Joseph heard his mother's footsteps he would say: "Let me arise before the approach of the Shekhinah" (*b. Kidd.* 31b).

God may have said, " I am God and not man" (Hos. 11:9),[1] however humans do not always act as if that were true. Deep within their psyche many people do feel that God is male. However, since God is a Spirit, no one or nothing on earth is totally comparable to God (Isa. 40:25; 46:9). Yet, out of love, God wants to reveal God's nature. God has three major ways of self-revelation: descriptive adjectives ("a God merciful and gracious, slow to anger, and abounding in steadfast love and faithfulness" Exod. 34:6 RSV); acts in history ("the Lord brought us out of Egypt" Deut. 6:21); and images. God must use metaphors and similes and other images to help

---

[1]The term for "male" *('ish)* is employed in Hosea 11:9. Since *'ish* is sometimes used generically for "human," God may simply be saying God is not human and therefore is compassionate. However, *'ish* has to include at least "male." Yet, the images God employs preceeding and following verse 9 are feminine. See also Num. 23:19; 1 Sam. 15:29; Isa. 44:9-13; Deut. 4:15-16.

humans understand what God is like.[2] If indeed males and females reflect God's image, then conversely God must use the characteristics and roles of both males and females to help people understand God's nature. As well, women and men are needed as models to help other humans understand God's image. Therefore, if we want people to mature in God's image, it is *imperative* that we have women and men to model all aspects of God's nature. Women and men are needed to participate at every level of theological practice and discussion so that God's full counsel can become apparent.

Roles do not always delineate men from women. God "sews," clothes, cooks, and provides food.[3] In theory those practices are common for women in the Americas. However, such may not be true for Bible times, when these practices occurred. Moreover, in many countries as in the United States such practices are only theoretically women's duties. In reality, many men barbecue, cook regular meals, tailor, repair clothing, and farm, and then they do not consider themselves in any way unusual. However, only women can conceive, become pregnant, bear children, nurse, and be mothers. Only a female can be called a "woman," or a "lioness."

---

[2]All images God employs are in some way like God, but none of them is totally like God. As Charles Williams says: "This also is thou; neither is this Thou." To envision God as all male (or masculine) or all female (or feminine) is blasphemy. See on "The Ways of the Images," Mary McDermott Shideler, *The Theology of Romantic Love: A Study in the Writings of Charles Williams* (Grand Rapids: Eerdmans, 1962), pp. 11-28. An image is something that represents something else. It includes figurative expressions such as metaphor, simile, personification, and, sometimes, synecdoche. In effect, images are types of analogies. Two things of unlike nature that yet have something in common are compared so that one or more properties of the first thing are attributed to the second thing. For specific definitions see Appendix II Aida Besançon Spencer, *Paul's Literary Style: A Stylistic and Historical Comparison of II Corinthians 11:16-12:13, Romans 8:9-39, and Philippians 3:2-4:13*, Evangelical Theological Society Monograph Series (Winona Lake: Eisenbrauns, 1984), pp. 280-313.

[3]E.g., Gen. 3:21; Exod. 16:4; Neh. 9:21; John 21:9-12.

God as Mother (Human)

God uses every aspect of childbirth as a metaphor to help God's children conceive of their relationship to their Maker. In order to disparage the idols Bel and Nebo, which must be borne upon weary beasts and cannot save anyone, even the weary beasts, from captivity, God declares:

> Hear me, house of Jacob,
> and all the remnant of the house of Israel,
> those being carried from the womb,
> those being lifted up from the womb;
> and until old age I myself am the One,
> and until grey hairs I myself will bear,
> I myself have made and I myself will lift up,
> and I myself will bear and I will deliver (Isa. 46:3-4).

God is Super-Mother. While the idols must be borne, the living God bears. The idols cannot produce, but the living God can bear children. But even greater than any woman, the living God makes and delivers children, not for a few hours but for a lifetime. The children are borne and then lifted high, safe from all danger. Our God is as great as that! In addition God can do what every woman dreams. God can cause conception and birth without labor (Isa. 66:7-9; John 3:5-8). God is the perfect midwife (Ps. 71:6; 22:9). God is well worth trusting!

God, too, is like a woman suddenly in travail. One moment God is silent and does not act; at the next moment God destroys and creates with the same commotion and suddenness of a woman beginning labor (Isa. 42:14-16). Moreover, God says, a human should not bother asking questions of God which are as futile as asking a woman why she is in labor (Isa. 45:9-10).

As well as labor, God uses the image of a nursing mother. The Israelites in exile think God has forgotten them and has no mercy for them. However, God asks, "Can a woman forget her nursing child, that she should have no compassion on the child of her womb?" (Isa. 49:15). God's reliability and compassion are like that of a nursing mother. Even her body reminds her it is time to feed the child. God is even more constant. Even if a forgetful mother might exist, God will never forget. David uses similar imagery in Psalm 131. He describes God as One who nurses. But this time David emphasizes the calmness and quietness he experiences when he trusts God "like a child quieted at its mother's breast; like a child that is quieted is my soul" (Ps. 131:2 RSV). God also uses the imagery of nursing and the satisfaction of being fed as images to describe what Jerusalem may expect in the future. Even more than satisfied, the Hebrews will be consoled: "As a boy whom his mother comforts, just so I myself will comfort you and you will be comforted in Jerusalem" (Isa. 66:13). God does not always use masculine imagery for God and feminine imagery for God's people or the church. Sometimes God reverses the imagery to feminine for God, and masculine for people. (The church is masculine in Eph. 4:13.) Isaiah 40-66 are replete with images of mothering because mothering is a very appropriate metaphor for understanding future fulfillment: the capacity to bear burdens, to produce, to save, to perform the inexplicable, and to be decisive, constant, calming, and compassionate.

God as Educator of Small Children (or Eagle)

God does not stop with pregnancy, labor, or nursing. The mother and young child relationship can mirror God and God's people. A parent who loves a child and consequently constantly educates, heals, and feeds that child will be deeply hurt if someone else, someone destructive, receives the credit for all such care. Israel's political alliances with Egypt and Assyria are similar rejections of trust in God's power. So, God says:

> And I myself taught Ephraim to walk,
> taking them by their arms;
> but they did not know that I helped them.
> With cords of a man I led them,
> with bands of love,
> and I became to them as one

who eases the yoke on their jaws
and I bent down to them and fed them (Hosea 11:3-4).

God does not relegate the training of God's children to a
slave or nurse but personally and lovingly oversees it.

Moses' song records again God's constant care for the people. He, too, reiterates that we, God's people, must acknowledge it is God and no foreign god who cares for us. He
develops his song by comparing God's solicitation to an eagle's care of its young, a recurring biblical image, first used
by God to describe the way the Israelites were saved from
Egypt: "I bore you on eagle's wings and brought you to myself" (Exod. 19:4). The eagle:

found it in a desert land
and in the howling waste of the wilderness
and it encircled it, it cared for it,
it kept it as the center of its eye. As an eagle that stirs up its nest,
that broods over its young birds,
it spreads out its wings, it catches them,
it bears them upon its wings. The Lord alone did lead it
and no foreign god was with it;
[the eagle] caused it to ride upon the heights of the earth,
and it ate the fruit of the field; and it made it suck honey out of the
rock,
and oil out of the flinty rock.
Butter from cows, and milk from goats,
with marrow of lambs and rams
children of Basham and goats
with the finest of the wheat
and of the blood of the grape you drank wine (Deut. 32:10-4).[*]

God finds us abandoned, rescues us, makes us a home, educates us, cares for us by giving us the very best sustenance,
comparable to an eagle's care of its newly found young. The
care is not given without constant love. As the Spirit at creation, the eagle, too, "broods over" its young birds (Gen. 1:2).
It shares with its young the beauty and majesty of the

---

[*]The masculine pronoun is used in Hebrew in this passage for the eagle and
its young although the eagle is clearly female.

earth. The eagle's sight is keen enough to find the abandoned bird. Its strength is great enough to catch the young bird. Its nest is high enough to keep the bird safe (Job 39:27).

Boaz describes Ruth's choice to follow God as taking refuge under God's "wings" (Ruth 2:12). David alludes to Moses' song when he asks to be kept as "the center or apple of the eye," hidden in the protection of God's wings, safe from all his enemies (Ps. 17:8-9). God's wings symbolize God's care, protection, safety, loving kindness, and help and they are consequently a place of joy.[5]

No wonder Jesus, God incarnate, uses the image of a bird with wings to express both his deepest desire to nurture and to protect his people and his anguish because his people would not respond:

> Jerusalem, Jerusalem, the one killing the prophets and stoning those having been sent to her, how often would I have gathered your children, in the same way as a hen gathers her brood under her wings, and you would not (Matt. 23:37).

Jerusalem was about to kill the very Sender, the eagle come to earth as a hen. However, the people who reject God's care and protection then receive God's condemnation. "Behold," Jesus now adds, "your house is forsaken and desolate." The other side of care, protection, safety, loving kindness, help, and joy is judgment, desolation, and misery.

God as Guardian (or Lioness and Bear)

A lioness and a mother bear can also serve to teach us about God. The lioness has a roar that commands fear and response. In the same way, "the Lord God speaks, who will not prophesy?" (Amos 3:8). Although the Israelites are scattered in exile throughout the Earth, the Lord will roar like a lioness: "Yea it will roar and the children will come trembling from the west" (Hosea 11:10). The lioness' roar is great

---

[5]Pss. 17:8; 36:7; 57:1; 61:4; 63:7; 91:4.

enough to command all her young to return. God will not leave God's people lost without guidance, punished forever.

The Lord also told Isaiah:

As the lioness roars and the young lion over its torn beast,
when a multitude of shepherds are called forth against it,
it is not terrified by their voice and it is not humbled by their noise,
thus the Lord of hosts will come down to fight upon Mount
Zion and upon its hill (Isa. 31:4).

The lioness who has just torn apart some animal it has captured wants to eat and to bring the meal to its young. Even a multitude of shepherds cannot intimidate it now. So, too, the Lord can protect Israel so much more than any competing human armies.

The lioness and the mother bear, unlike the mother eagle, are symbols as well of God's judgment. A dog with newly born puppies might snap at some stranger's toe who dares to come near. But imagine the response a bear would have when robbed of its cubs. When people become secure and forget the One who has made them secure, then God says:

I will meet them as a bear that is bereaved of her whelps,
And will rend the enclosure of their heart;
And there will I devour them like a lioness,
The wild beast shall tear them
(Hos. 13:8, Jewish Publication Society).

Where are Israel's false securities to help her now? No one can help her should she fall into God's judgment. When Jeremiah looks around at the fallen Jerusalem, he feels as if God does not answer his prayers. He feels desolate. God is as "a bear lying in wait, as a lioness in hiding, it led me off my way and tore me to pieces" (Lam. 3:10-11).

The lioness and the bear teach us both about the feminine and about God. The female can also command response and fear and can cause intimidation. When the female must protect and care for its young, as God, it may need to destroy in order to do so. Again, the other side of comfort and protection and salvation is destruction.

Ministry as Woman's Work

No wonder when Moses complains to God about the burden of leadership, he uses the imagery of a mother to express that the burden is too great:

Did I conceive all this people?
Did I bring them forth,
that though shouldst say to me,
"Carry them in your bosom,
as a nurse carries the sucking child,
to the land which thou didst
swear to give their fathers?"
Where am I to get meat to give to all this people?
For they weep before me and say, "Give us meat, that we may eat."
I am not able to carry all this people alone, the
burden is too heavy for me (Num. 11:12-14 RSV).

Only a true mother could care for her young in such a way as to sustain the Israelites. God is such a mother and has such care. Moses, though, is given seventy elders to help him lead so that the seventy-one can carry a mother's burden.

Paul, too, employs the analogy of father and mother to describe the excellence of his, Silvanus', and Timothy's ministry among the Thessalonians. As a father with his children, Paul exhorts, encourages, and charges the Thessalonians to lead a life worthy of God (1 Thess. 2:11). As mothers or nurses, Paul and his coworkers do not try to flatter them. Like mothers taking care of their children, they share not only the good news but also their very selves because they love the Thessalonians (1 Thess. 2:5-8).

Paul also describes the return of the Lord with the imagery of motherhood. Even as a woman cannot know when to plan for labor, so is the day of the Lord unexpected. Moreover, even as labor is a time of pain, distress, and rush, so too the day of the Lord brings destruction to those people who are relying on the peace and security of the moment (1 Thess. 5:2-3). Appropriately Paul expresses his chagrin at the Galatians' abandonment of the faith by saying he again "suffers birth-pains until Christ be formed" in them (Gal. 4:19). Will the Galatians arrive still-born? Paul displays as well his dismay with the Corinthians by saying he is feeding them with milk and not solid food because they are not ready for the second (1 Cor. 3:1-2).

A mother as one who aids growth and development is an apt metaphor for ministry. Children bring with them a burden. But as God's ambassadors, we, too, carry God's concern for the rearing of the children.

The feminine metaphor is as appropriate to describe God as is the masculine. The feminine is consequently appropriate to describe leadership of those who serve God. Ministry entails care, difficulties, challenges, the giving of self, love, purposefulness, education, growth, and development. Motherhood in all its aspects can mirror the process of enabling maturity. Women are needed! Given such a basis in Scripture and practice, how can women not be appropriate as ministers, educators, and theologians? Whole dimensions of God, ministry, education and theology are being obscured and ignored if women are not properly trained, then invited, even more so welcomed, to participate as significant leaders. They should be heard, respected, and affirmed once they do lead.

God as Household Manager

Although this chapter primarily has highlighted motherhood to distinguish the feminine, we did not do so because motherhood and feminine are necessary correlaries to one another. Motherhood is simply one clear-cut role which only a woman can perform. Jesus, though, uses the image of a woman to describe one characteristic God has which one woman and many other women also evidence, carefulness and thoroughness. He tells a parable:

> Or what woman having ten drachmas, if she loses one drachma, does not light a lamp and sweep the house and seek thoroughly until she finds? And having found she calls together her friends and neighbors, saying, "Rejoice with me, since I have found the drachma which I lost" (Luke 15:8-9).

Why did Jesus use the imagery of a woman? Was it because the woman oversaw the financial accounts of the house? A drachma is about one day's wage for a laborer. Or was it because her own allowance was small? Either way, she knew her financial need and she valued every part of her total budget. She was willing to work hard, carefully, and thoroughly until she found what she sought. And she celebrated her hard work with those persons closest to her. God is like that.

God as Sovereign

As the Israelites would climb to the temple they sang:

> To thee I lift up my eyes,
> the One enthroned in the heavens.
> Behold, as the eyes of subjects
> to the hand of their lord,
> as the eyes of a female servant
> to the hand of her queen,
> thus our eyes to the Lord our God
> until God have mercy on us (Ps. 123:1-2).

Since God is called here "the One enthroned," the similes which follow develop the image of a sovereign, one who rules. The Sovereign in heaven is comparable to the sovereigns on earth. "As the eyes of subjects to the hand of their lord" and "as the eyes of a female servant to the hand of her queen" are synonymous parallels, indicating that neither image by itself is sufficient to understand the Lord "in the heavens." As well as like a king, God is like a queen. *Gebereth* may signify "queen" or "mistress." The word *'ebed* can be translated "subject" or "slave, servant, worker." The basic verb *gabar* signifies "be strong, mighty." "Queen" is a possible translation of *gebereth* since elsewhere the word is used to signify *Babylon*, queen of all kingdoms (Isa. 47:5,7). *Gebirah* refers to Tahpenes, the queen of Egypt and Pharaoh's wife (1 Kings 11:19) and Maacah, the queen of Judah, King Asa's mother (1 Kings 15:13). In Jeremiah 13:18 *gebirah* or "queen" is paired with "king." If *gebereth* is translated "mistress" and *'ebed* as "servant," still the psalmist has in mind one who rules over someone else, as Sarah ruled over Hagar (Gen. 16:4; Isa. 24:2).

The worshippers have known the fear they have as subjects. Their sovereign has all power over their lives. So, they ask for mercy. For too long their proud enemies have scorned them. The sovereign has power to reward and to elevate. The king or lord has power over the subjects or slaves. The queen or lady has immediate power over her female servants. But she can be merciful. Be merciful with us today all-powerful Sovereign!

Conclusion

Women and men need not hesitate to allow women to model themselves after the Wise Woman in Proverbs (ch. 8). Wisdom itself is one aspect of God that is personified by a woman. The Wise Woman stands at the gates of the town with the elders making judgments. She calls out, she preaches, she teaches. She is strong, wealthy, powerful. She is righteous and true and knowledgeable. She decisively rewards and she decisively punishes. She gives life and death. "All you desire cannot compare with her," she says (8:11). Is it not time for the church to encourage and affirm women to begin and continue to personify that wisdom of God in their very own lives? The church needs strong, wise women to preach and to teach. If the Bible uses feminine imagery to mirror certain aspects of God, should not the church allow women leaders to reflect God similarly? For God is like mothers and like all females in that God has the capacity to bear burdens, to produce life, to save, to perform the inexplicable, to be decisive, to be thorough and careful, to be constant, to be compassionate, to calm, to comfort, to care, to protect, to help, to love, to bring joy, to command fear and immediate response, to intimidate, to destroy, to guide, to educate, to feed, to persevere, to develop, to rule, and to be merciful. Women can be images of strength and care. The church indeed will be "happy" if it follows our God, freeing woman from the curse of the evil tree to become the fruitful tree of life God intends her to be.

6

Conclusion

"Greet Mary, who bestowed much labor on us."
How is this? A woman again is honored and proclaimed victorious! Again are we men put to shame. Or rather, we are not put to shame only, but have even an honor conferred upon us. For an honor we have, in that there are such women amongst us, but we are put to shame, in that we men are left so far behind by them (Chrysostom, *The Epistle to the Romans* XXXI).

When Jesus saw the crowds of people worried and dejected, he was moved from his very depths to compassion. So, Jesus commanded the disciples to pray to the Owner of the harvest to drive out workers into the harvest (Matt. 9:36-37). Even when the seventy (or seventy-two) more were commissioned, Jesus continued to command the disciples to pray for more workers (Luke 10:2). God has often surprised the church by the workers sent out. And, many times the church has waited in pleasant expectation. However, at other times, the church has not been pleased. Women often respond to God's drive.[1] Yet, to serve effectively they need to employ the gifts God has given them to testify to the presence of the living Jesus, to preach to people about God's message today, to teach and explain all God commands, to

---

[1]For examples see Ruth Tucker, *From Jerusalem to Irian Jaya: A Biographical History of Christian Missions,* Academie Books (Grand Rapids: Zondervan, 1983).

lead in worship, to provide food, housing, and clothing, and to bring the reign of God to earth even as it is in heaven.

Summary

We have learned from Genesis 1-2 that one reason women so eagerly respond to God's call to work to reap the harvest is that they were created to rule the earth, to till and guard the garden, jointly with the men, as their friends and equals. The harvest was plentiful even in Eden, as it was in the years of God's incarnate ministry, and as it is today. God intended men and women to share tasks and to share authority in order to reflect God's full image and better to reach God's goals. Eve was quite intellectual and aesthetic. Unfortunately, she, together with Adam, sought to be wise by attempting to become God. She took the foolish way to wisdom.

Each of the punishments Eve and Adam received reflected their pre-fall state and their sins. Obedience to God's tasks now would entail hard work. Moreover, the loving relationship between source and derivation was broken. As the ground comes to rule Adam, so too the man comes to rule his woman. Even the curse does not allow any man to rule any woman. After the fruit is eaten Eve and Adam begin to take on the semblance of the tempter: shame, independence, and irresponsibility. God's immediate response in Eden and later response at the cross are both models and effective agents to show and empower us to go beyond the curse, to live lives affected by redemption.

Jesus by his example and teachings harkened back to God's original intention at creation for women's full participation in the public tasks of life. He also liberated them from the entrenched male domination caused by the fall. In contrast to contemporary Jewish teachings and practice, Jesus changed what women could do and their priorities. He encouraged women to seek religious training challenging the traditions which exempted a woman from learning the Torah because woman's role as homemaker was primary. Again,

Jesus would challenge the teachings today which are restricting women from full participation in Christian service for the very same reasons the rabbis employed in the first century. Jesus wanted women redeemed from the curse to learn so that they too would be ready to testify as apostles at the resurrection. Jesus also spoke with women in public so that the fear of unchastity would never limit education nor genuine communication.

Paul, like Jesus his teacher, similarly challenged the foundation of his Jewish traditions, both in his teachings and practice. To be "one" biblically always has spiritual and social ramifications. When Paul includes women with men as heirs, he too shows that because of the Messiah they now again, jointly with males, are to be sovereign over the earth under the direction of the Sovereign over all. Women are to be reigning heirs who fully receive God's blessings. In order to make such leadership possible, Paul commanded the women to learn in a rabbinic manner so that they might have full knowledge of God's truth. Although Paul exhorted married men and women to treat their family as their ministry, he assumed that women's religious education was more important than their homemaking. However, Paul did restrain women from teaching until they were well instructed and from using authority in a destructive manner. The women at Ephesus were like Eve in that both were deceived by unorthodox teaching. Like Eve, their search for knowledge led them down a destructive path. Paul was slowing the process which led to freedom and full rights so that women might be genuine and equal participants in ministry. Unfortunately, Paul's words to Ephesus, like the serpent's rephrasing of God's command in Eden, have been made much more extensive than the words literally signify. Moreover, Paul's means have become ends in themselves. Women have been kept under the law, the schoolmaster. The intention of the law has been ignored. Whenever the analogy between Eve and a formerly misled and now enlightened woman is no longer valid, then the restriction no longer applies.

Paul's own affirmation of women in leadership positions

shows that his restriction of women at Ephesus had to be limited. The New Testament testifies to women being given gifts from God for authoritative positions. Women were apostles, prophets, teachers, coworkers, ministers, and church overseers. Paul affirms Junia, Priscilla, and Phoebe. Phoebe and Priscilla are clearly teaching and leading men. The Bible also records the leadership roles of Mary Magdalene, Joana, Mary, Mary, Salome, Anna, Miriam, Huldah, Deborah, Philip's four daughters, Lydia, Chloe, the elect lady, and her elect sister. A multitude of women testify to God's call to women to lead the church.

What we have seen in examples and teachings, we have also seen in images. God uses the roles and characteristics of both males and females to help humans understand God's nature since both females and males reflect God's image. God uses every aspect of childbirth and motherhood, primary education, household management, and female sovereignty to teach humans what God is like. God even uses the lioness and she-bear as illustrations. Ministry itself is explained through female images. In the process, many so-called truisms about femininity are shown to be false. Rather than women being passive and subservient,[2] they, like their Maker, can be strong, persevering, reliable, compassionate, comforting, bountiful, and decisive mothers. Women can personally care, love, provide, share, protect, give joy, and be rightfully jealous. Females can powerfully command, judge, and intimidate. Women can be careful and thorough (which are key scholarly traits).

Are women called by God to ministry? I have shown that, in the texts that describe the times before and after the fall and the teachings and practice of Jesus and Paul, the Bible's answer is a resounding, "Yes!" But the curse has become license for oppression. The law has become a never-promoting schoolmaster. Serious Christians who love their Creator and

---

[2]E.g., Donald G. Bloesch defines "femininity" as "receptivity and loving obedience" while "masculinity" is "initiative and power." *Is the Bible Sexist? Beyond Feminism and Patriarchalism* (Westchester: Crossway, 1982).

honor the Scriptures should affirm, encourage, and listen to
women who desire to mirror and celebrate God and to lead
and teach others about the One God, the Savior who, as
Mary sings "has noticed the low estate of the handmaiden"
(Luke 1:48).

Some Consequences

As women begin and continue to take their parts as leaders in promoting God's reign, the church can see with a fuller
vision God's intentions. Although understandably women
feel ambivalent about subservience,[3] I nevertheless find it remarkable that all the current evangelical women promoting
the full participation of women in ministry in book form
have reminded the church of Jesus' continued use of volun-
tary slavery as an image to understand his own leadership
style, a leadership style which we are to emulate. Letha
Scanzoni and Nancy Hardesty wrote in 1974 that in "the
new life in Christ" all persons are mutually interdependent
with one another.[4] Three years later Virginia Ramey Mollenkott organized her study of *Women, Men and the Bible*
around the thesis: "the Christian way of relating is mutual
submission and mutual service," not "the worldly principle
of dominance and submission."[5] In the same year Patricia
Gundry concluded: "You need no pope, bishop, synod, or
council to tell you what you may believe or how you may
serve Him. We are all priests and kings before God."[6] In 1982
E. Margaret Howe defended the need for creative ecclesiasti-

---

[3]Judith Plaskow, for example, eloquently posits the possibility that wom-
en's experiences have tended to encourage women to be sinful in ways less
usual in men. Self-sacrifice in a woman, she says, "can represent a subtle
bid for power or become a tool through which to manipulate a family." *Sex,
Sin and Grace: Women's Experience and the Theologies of Reinhold
Niebuhr and Paul Tillich* (New York: University Press of America, 1980), p.
152.

[4]*All We're Meant to Be: A Biblical Approach to Women's Liberation,* p. 205.

[5]*Women, Men and the Bible* (Nashville: Abingdon, 1977), pp. 20, 138.

[6]*Woman Be Free!* (Grand Rapids: Zondervan, 1977), p. 111.

cal structures and leadership based on spiritual gifts. The office of church leadership "is a service-centered office which must always remain flexible enough to adapt to changing needs and changing opportunities."[7] Mary J. Evans, as well, reminds her readers "that leadership in the New Testament is always seen in terms of service rather than of status." She concludes that "we need a drastic reappraisal of our whole outlook" if men and women are "to live out their diversity, unity and complementarity."[8]

Who is the greatest among us? Jesus says "If anyone wishes to be first, let that person be last of all and servant of all" (Mark 9:35). When Jesus, who is the Lord of lords and Teacher of teachers, stoops down to serve us, we are awestruck. However, when we women, who already have been treated and who perceive ourselves as servants of society, stoop down to serve others, we merely appear to be "in our place." Very few are impressed. Yet, these evangelical feminists have embraced their heritage to perceive anew Jesus' disturbing call to all of us. We are to be servants of the Sovereign. First, we serve the Sovereign. Second, as Christ's ambassadors, we serve others. The more women have power, the more meaningful will be their service.

What new insights will we receive into the deep, ever-gushing streams of living water if we look for the full participation of all Christian women and men? Together we can look forward to a stronger, fuller vision, holding hands as we try to keep each other on the narrow path, a runner going forward to the heavenly sanctuary where a great gathering proclaims the majesty and the reign of God the Almighty (Rev. 19:6). Women have much to teach the church about how the Bride can make herself ready.

---

[7]*Women and Church Leadership,* p. 69. See also ch. 11.

[8]*Woman in the Bible: An Overview of all the Crucial Passages on Women's Roles* (Downers Grove: InterVarsity, 1983), pp. 109. 132.

Equaling Eden:
A Practical Male Afterword
William David Spencer

Doctor:	(very seriously) Yes, I trust women.
Smith:	You trust a woman with the practical issues of life and death, through sleepless hours when a shaking hand or an extra grain would kill.
Doctor:	Yes.
Smith:	But if the woman gets up to go to early service at my church, you call her weak-minded and say that nobody but women can believe in religion.
	G.K. Chesteron, *Magic: A Fantastic Comedy*, Act II.

Usually males are accused of being the head (the theorizing, coldly reasonable, abstract head of male/female partnership) as opposed to women's warm, earthy, emotion-centered, right side of the brain, heart approach to issues. Therefore, it would seem an anomaly for a male to write an experiential response to this closely reasoned exegetical tour de force that has just preceded.

Shared History

My reasons for writing a practical response are twofold. First, because whenever Aida has presented findings like these to sincere male Christians in the past, the questions have seldom been exegetical or logical; they have always been emotional. Second, I wonder if the traditional archetype has us pegged correctly? Are all we males really the cold, relentless, and reasoning machos who sacrifice our grandmothers for truth, or are most of us, instead, more accurately P.G. Wodehousian heroes who love to enjoy life, play with words, and avoid sticky scenes until fiercely serious women force us to deal seriously with issues? The enormous truth came to me forcefully in 1974 at a leading evangelical seminary when that brave student body, in conjunction with the Evangelical Theological Society, invited Aida to present the first of her findings on women's leadership, at the time just published in the *Journal of the Evangelical Theological Society*. When she finished we were amazed to find that I was as bombarded by questions as she was. The men were all asking me, "What is it like to have a wife who is a minister? Do you find it threatening? What happens when you have to make a decision? Who has the final decisive power?" Strangely all her careful reasoning and scholarship in the final analysis seemed secondary. Of course, men did appreciate her careful exegesis. During the coffeebreak, I circulated among the seminarians—ironically incognito because of my maleness—and was delighted to hear them greeting newcomers, "Hey, you just missed a great talk!" But the essential impact of her presentation apparently had not stopped in their reason, it had hurtled deeper in and scored in their emotions. In point of fact, since that eyeopening day we have noted that most questions people ask us pertaining to the ordained leadership of women (however couched in theological terms or deftly disguised to appear objectively biblical) actually proceed from their personal histories. One minister even asked us what he considered to be the final stumper, "If you two see yourselves as equal, at the end of a day, who talks about their day first?" Honest.

The irony of this predicament is further underscored because, when she first began to study in 1971 the issue of the role of women leaders in the church, Aida attempted to be as objective as possible. Not reared in an evangelical family, she had gone blithely off to seminary to learn more about Jesus. Like most new Christians who have not discovered that we are supposed to be timid about Jesus, both of us had been ministering naturally since our commitments during college thanks to the Rutgers/Douglass Inter-Varsity Christian Fellowship.

Aida at graduation had gone on to become a community organizer in Plainfield while I soon did street work door to door in Newark, New Jersey. All of us who remember the riots that swept the United States in the late 1960s remember those stunned stumbling recovery attempts when people within and without the city sought to discover why the critical urban mass had detonated and how to keep such explosions from recurring. Through 1969 and 1970 Aida worked with Community Action Program and Model Cities, first as secretary of the Spanish office and later as the Spanish community organizer. Increasingly, the ultimate futility of making lower class people simply middle class frustrated her. She saw that such a task, necessary as it is, did not address the ultimate malady; only its symptoms. Watching the oppressed become the oppressors drove her at last to seminary on a quest to find the diagnosis that would dictate true therapeutics. It was in this context one day in the Princeton Seminary cafeteria that a table full of evangelical brothers, who—by my guess—had overeaten so that the blood drained out of their brains, momentarily leaving them without empathy and courtesy, verbally accosted her with the challenge, "What are you doing in seminary when women aren't supposed to speak?" All she had said was "Hello." They laughed it off and went on to other topics, but she was stunned. Aida had never before heard that passage applied in her five years as a Christian.

In a quiet moment she assessed the significance of the challenge. Ordination was not a problem for her. She did not have the least intention of being ordained. Who, in the late 1960s and early 1970s, had even met one of those will-of-the-wisp female ministers? Besides, in these rebellious times, who in their right mind would want to be a minister anyway? Certainly not a Spanish community organizer who was taking a three year hiatus to learn how to make lower class people something more than middle class. What troubled her was the implied challenge that women had no right to learn in seminary. Such a conclusion seemed to strike at the very core of all that Christianity had revealed itself to be to her. Was not Jesus engaged in making all believers his disciples? Her professors were of little help to her. One mentor merely advised, "Don't worry about it, it doesn't apply to you." "Why not?" she asked. When he had no adequate answer, she set forth on a three year study that culminated in that 1974 article which has become one of the stepping stones on the way to the forging of a sensible evangelical position on women. Looking at it again, and its essence has been woven into the fabric of Chapter 3 on Paul and his view in 1 Timothy 2 in the present volume, one can see how important the question of women's learning was and still is to female students. The by-product, however, was equally intriguing. As I have mentioned, Aida was not particularly interested in ordination at the time, since she had no precedents for it and had not considered it as a desireable state. Her sense of call was simply to serve God and learn more about God's nature and God's directions for the Christian life. But as she studied the question, she became increasingly struck by the anomaly present in the text. Paul, who had surrounded himself with women leaders, was appearing on the surface to forbid women's leadership. How could that be?

At issue here was nothing less than the reliability of the text itself. On most theological issues, as most of us know, there is healthy illuminating debate on the meaning of texts. This is one issue, however, where I believe there is not. The way the largely acrimonious debate on the issue has gone in recent years is such that either extreme has felt it necessary to jettison either Paul or his coworkers.

Faithful believers, however, ought not to tamper with the text. In the last analysis, an interpretive option such as the one Aida proposes is actually not an option at all. It is one of the only choices. The two opposing extremes are not actually exegetical options in the final analysis since they do surgery rather than exegesis. They pare away part of the text, leaving a mutilated limb hanging in space.

Some feminists, sadly pushed to the wall, have sought to mute the male imagery of God in reaction to the entrenched, classically conservative translators who have for centuries muted the female imagery of God. After all the good news is supposed to be a proclamation of freedom for the captives. Some theologians, however, have made it into a handbook for the guards. So the captives revolted and rejected the bad news that was presented to them in place of the good news. God, however, has employed both types of imagery, male and female, for self revelation, basing the New Testament presentation of the fatherhood of God on the Old Covenant context of the motherhood of God, as we saw so well delineated in the final chapter, "The Full Vision." Therefore, a true exegete would not tamper with the text but would do as Aida has done, ferret out the actual images and let the text speak. Otherwise, there is no real exegetical debate going on at all, there is simply pernicious mistranslation and sexual war with the text as battleground. What we need essentially is more obedience, responsible humility to the content, revelation, and counsel of the Scripture. Where the text leads we have to follow. Where else are the words of truth? Feminists have often asked us why we stay in an "arch-conservative" organization like the Evangelical Theological Society, where up until recently Aida was often the only female scholar presenting a paper. Not only have we stayed but Aida has served as chairperson of the Southeastern region and as first presiding chairperson of the reorganized New England region. That is out and out active support. The E.T.S. is totally misunderstood by most scholars outside it. The E.T.S. by definition is an organization of scholars who love the Scriptures and are sworn to study obediently the full revelation. As such, even while often hotly debating not simply her findings but all other colleagues on all other issues, the

E.T.S. warmly welcomes study that takes the full text seriously. Its goal is the same as those of any true exegete: to hear the text speak. This shared goal, then, was the starting point of Aida's first study. Unhampered by a desire to be ordained and therefore to have it come out "right," her concern ran much deeper. Should women learn in seminary? Should women preach the good news?

Pursuit of that question ushered her into the biblical gathering of Paul and his coworkers, and there she was surrounded by a host of articulate, revered women leaders. Her resulting list recorded in Chapter IV reads like a lost volume of *Who's Who?* "How could this be?" she asked in amazement. "Why haven't I ever heard of any of these women?" Obviously something was going on in this Timothy text at a level much deeper than the surface. No person, especially not one as astute and perspicacious as the Apostle Paul, hands out categorically exclusive advice while, in manifest contradiction, touring around in company with the exact antithesis of what he has been advising.

Why has Paul's consistency not been obvious to us? Why have we not recognized the existence of female coworkers and interpreted his writings in the context of a shared male and female ministry?

The fact is that in our culture, buried as we are in such a rubble of socialization as "be a man!" "boys don't cry," "the white man's burden," the inversely pedestaling "my better half," and so forth, we seem to have come to believe that God is solely a blond, blue-eyed Caucasian male, and Caucasian males as a result are the main if not sole custodians of true religion.

The point became obvious when Manhattan's St. John the Divine Cathedral displayed Edwina Sandy's sculpture of a female Jesus, "Christa." In the resulting fervor one woman put the objection into words for *Time Magazine*: "it's disgraceful. God and Christ are male. They're playing with a

symbol we've believed in for all our lives."[1] For many of us
God really is some kind of cosmic old man with a long white
beard, or for the more sophisticated, some reasonable spiritual facsimile.

The question raised here is an extremely significant one.
Can the Christ be portrayed symbolically as female? For
that matter, can Jesus be portrayed as black, as we once saw
in a Baptist church in New Jersey, as Oriental, as in Shusaku
Endo's novel *Silence*, as Eastern as in the many portraits
catalogued in such books as Masao Takenaka's *Christian
Art in Asia* or Arno Lehmann's *Christian Art in Africa and
Asia*, not to mention in the iconography of the Byzantine
Church? Can the Christ be portrayed as an American Indian? As an Eskimo? As an animal—as C.S. Lewis did in his
Narnia stories or as Robert Siegel did in his *Whale Song*?
More exactly to the point: Can Jesus really be portrayed as a
blond, blue-eyed Caucasian? From the Turin Shroud, British
artist Curtis Hooper has attempted to reconstruct for us as
closely as possible a portrait of Jesus from its image of a
first-century Jew.[2] His Jesus is certainly an ancient Semitic
Jew. When did God give us the right to make the sole exception, portraying the Christ as blond and blue-eyed while
branding the other portrayals heretical? Jesus of Nazareth
looked like a Semitic first-century Jew, but Matthew 25:40
tells us the Christ is in the faces of many who suffer. Have
we not been hiding our faces from the ugly, sorrowing, broken, suffering servant and seeking instead a golden, fair-
haired conquerer?

Confronted with this realization the natural inclination for
newly enlightened males is to pitch it all and go the "mea
culpa" route, turning all of us males into unisex supplicants,
seeing all of us males (and North Americans and middle
class whites) as the chief of all sinners. And sometimes we
are treated that way. There used to be such a reactant hostile

---

[1] *Time*, May 7, 1984, 94.

[2] See "Is This What Jesus *Really* Looked Like?" *Christianity Today*, March
16, 1984, 40.

fringe in the modern women's movement when it was first revived after Betty Friedan's epoch-making *The Feminine Mystique* of 1963, and the founding of NOW three years later relaunched it. I remember even in evangelical circles in the mid-1970s being one of a handful of men at the first Evangelical Women's Conference in Washington and being attacked when I tried to make a contribution. So, deciding to get smart quick and not speak at the next small group session that afternoon, I was roundly attacked again, this time for not speaking. Fortunately sensitive women defended me and kept me in the movement. Over the years I have noticed that this lunatic fringe has disappeared completely from the E.W.C.

In 1981 Betty Friedan on the secular front announced, according to a Knight-Ridder News Service article:

"Something really profound is happening to American men," Friedan said... "Our secret weapon, the new political force for the second stage is men."[3]

In 1982 and 1984 I noticed a similar mellowing out at the Evangelical Women's Caucus. All acrimonious hostility against men was absent. Most men, on the outside, of course, have missed this and are still acting as if we were living in 1963. Therefore, they are still reacting as if they were entrenched and embattled, and their pernicious defensive attitudes make consciousness-raised women retreat historically, forcing them to recreate again, as it were, the feminine/masculine Battle of Gettysburg.

As a result, many men I find are largely offering themselves but two options from which to choose, to be God or to be the devil. But neither is valid, of course. God has certainly created males with physical, spatial, emotional limitations in a limited span of years and has given us helpmates, families, communities, and the body of Christ to help sus-

---

[3]Mary Grossmann, "Beginning Round Two of the Battle of the Sexes...Friedan says Men are the Secret Weapon," *The Louisville Times,* May 7, 1981, B12.

tain us. Built into our definition is limitation. We are bordered by time, energy, fatigue, space, others, and eventually death. Rather than solely limiting, such a reality is in fact freeing. We males do not have to be God and despite Aleister Crowley's manic delusions, we are not the Devil. We are a significant part of the whole. We are one muscle in a strong torso. We can contribute fully to our task, a strong link, while allowing others to make their similar contributions. Men who do not learn this truth put their potential widows and dependent orphans in big trouble when they succumb to the stresses of overwork. In the church, on the job, in the town, they litter a trail of frustrated women behind them, itching to clobber the next poor guy who as much as blinks at their job.

Part of the camouflage here is that we read again and again the fallacious argument that all this participation of women in life outside the safe harem confines of the home is an all new phenomenon, a product of the last twenty or so years. Reuters reported that in 1977 archeologists near the Moldavian Village of Balabany dug up the remains of an "Amazonian" woman warrior from the fourth or fifth century BC buried complete with her warhorse, spears, arrows and, of course, gold earrings. She was a warrior of the Scythians, that ancient Nomadic tribe that roamed north of the Black Sea.

For all of us North Americans, women in the military has always been several notches below the bottom line. But so accomplished was this ancient woman that she was buried with full military honors.[4] Aida has shown us how the same kind of leadership, converted to the appropriate peaceful context of Christianity, was true of the women of the early church. The only real factor here is not the sudden present involvement of women today but the fact that, traditionally, we men have written the histories and have left women out of the story. Instead of telling the whole story, we have used

---

[4] "Old battleaxe," *The Star-Ledger,* December 2, 1977, 2.

historical writings largely as a means to celebrate ourselves and what we consider our accomplishments. I am sure that in many cases omitting women's contributions was not so much a malignant act as one of neglect. We men were just not interested.

Librarian Dee Brown has done a service for the American Indian (as in that sense has Ruth Beebe Hill and others), attempting to salvage out an Indian history of North America in his *Bury My Heart at Wounded Knee.* The previous expansionist histories were simply not interested in the whole truth but in that part of the truth that made palatable, and ever-glorious, our history. Therefore since the point was self-justification, self as corporate national justification, the part women, as Indians, played did not further that goal and as such was largely omitted.

When Japan's Misako Enoki gave up (she was the pharmacist who founded the Chupiren Association, often called the "Pink Panthers" for their pink-helmets, Japan's "Society to Fight for Women who Would Otherwise Grin and Bear It"), she lamented the low esteem with which women have traditionally been regarded in Japan. She was fighting a situation which forces women, as Tokyo television star Miki Ayuro explained, to deal with men in subterfuge, puffing husband up to feel like a Samurai, while dangling him on puppet strings.

In Africa, Ghanan justice of the appeals court of Accra, Annie R. Jiagge, elaborated, "Women themselves have accepted the inferior status imposed on them as an inescapable fact of life." Prakai Notawasee, a principal of a theological seminary in Thailand, lamented the traditional thinking of the old Thai proverb, "Men are the front legs of the elephant and women are the back legs." "This attitude, inwardly accepted, rules out the need for a conscience by women."[5] Even in the "everybody's-a-comrade" Soviet Union, historically the only full female member of the fifteen

---

[5]"Sexism Outcry: Women Rally for Rights at World Church Forum," *The Star-Ledger,* November 29, 1975, 5.

member Communist Party Politburo was Nikita Kruschev's girlfriend Yekaterina Furtseva, from 1957 to 1961. At that same time, of the ninety-nine ministers and government committee members not one was a woman, since few Soviet husbands lowered themselves to help with shopping, childrearing, or housework. Only 25 percent of Communist party members were even women, and, in place of power, trained women served at low pay, largely as doctors and secondary school teachers, without achieving key positions. When in July, 1984 Svetlana Savitskaya became the first woman cosmonaut to walk in space, one superior was still marveling, "women really can do everything."[6]

Men are continually astounded when women turn out to be accomplishing human beings. And as the rest of the world's secular society goes, so lamentably goes the United States church. When a United Methodist church in Connecticut hired a woman minister, the lay leader commented, "She soon proved that she could do the job as well as any man."[7] Women seem to be considered by men as inept until proven otherwise. Associate Professor of Pastoral Psychology at the Colgate Rochester Divinity School, Dr. Maxine Walaskay, reflected on the ambivalence with which her own preaching was greeted during her seminary training:

My hunch is that, even when they like what they hear, they feel ambiguous about what they see. As one of my male seminary professors said twittingly: "It was a very well done sermon though my own theological inclinations on this matter are somewhat different than yours....When you come right down to it, it's just that I don't want a woman to tell me what to do!"[8]

So, coming full circle, when, back in 1971, Aida worked to be as objective as possible about her study, praying that she

---

[6]"Soviet Is 1st Woman To Walk In Space!" *The Boston Herald,* July 26, 1984, 12.

[7]Pam Proctor, "Do Women Make Good Ministers?" *Parade,* December 22, 1974, 10.

[8]Maxine Walaskay, "Gender and Preaching," *Sharing Information By Women Clergy/Seminarians* 2 (October, 1982): 4.

would submit herself to its findings as a faithful servant (no matter how bitter these findings might be) and then found herself in a crowd of biblical female leaders who were somehow exempt from Paul's ruling, she was left baffled that she had not heard of them before.

The follow-through of our discovery was twofold. On the career front, when after seminary Aida began a prison ministry coupled eventually with a campus ministry, the Presbytery one day called her up offering ordination, a recognition she had not sought. Her study allowed her to feel comfortable in joining the ranks of those women leaders of the ancient church. After all, she was now trained, and what is a call? The scriptural doctrine of ordination, she had discovered, is human affirmation of divine endowment. Therefore, when the Presbytery telephones, that literally is a call in the fullest sense. So, unexpectedly, not least of all to ourselves, she became ordained.

The second part of the follow-through involved our life together, how we answered those questions the seminarians were asking. Now that I too was ordained (as a result of the same call) and I was married to a pastor, to my pastor, how did we flesh out our co-partnership in the gospel?

Shared Marriage

In 1978 after six years of marriage the brief but beautiful magazine *Free Indeed* immortalized our first fleeting answers to those last questions. Confronted with the data Aida had amassed to that point, I found myself asking these questions in response to an abbreviated form of Chapter 1, "Equal in Eden." What sort of lifestyle is the Scripture dictating to me? How will I get to it as a person? What will I have to bend in my personality or the onward progression of my history to reach it? What will I look like afterward? And how do I start?

First, I thought we had better assess exactly where we were in historical perspective. I figured that God's commands to Eve and Adam still exist. They are harder, but they still stand. We are to till and guard the garden together.

Perhaps now we must do it in the sweat of our brow, but we still must do it. So we ask, now that we Greeks, Jews, Scythians, slaves, and free have died and Christ has been raised and lives in us, how can we reach again to equal Eden, despite our fallen world? In what way can an Edenic lifestyle be re-approached today? And, since I must answer this personally, what kind of lifestyle have my wife and I been developing to fulfill this Scripture in our lives?[9]

Aida and I have begun by interpreting practically what "helpmeet" means. *Help* we have recognized means "to share the same tasks" and *meet* "to do it as equals." We have been asking: What are our tasks? And what are equal shares? You will note, as we did, that the first question entails a true evaluation of what is actually worthwhile and a paring away of what is not. The second demands an honest examination of 50/50 sharing, while appreciating and utilizing the individual talents God has given each of us. For us it was liberating to discover that, despite the traditional practice of the North American church and in light of the estrangement it causes, we need not join the lemming march to marital misery that appears obligatory to many ministers.

I noticed that, of all things, the way most of our churches are structured impedes rather than promotes familial solidarity, especially when the family is segregated into fragments, each meeting at a different time—the children on one night, the mothers on another night, the fathers at breakfast, and men's fellowship on a third night. What is the point of having festivals that focus on the family when we are fragmenting and dividing up the family all through the week in the structural style of the worst secular diversions? Churches that are doing this are doing their families a disservice. The church is literally helping these families to dis-

---

[9]At this point a qualification is in order. I note that up to now the philosophy expressed, this changing of biblical mandates into principles for implementation, has been uniform for single and married people. At this point, however, each of us must flesh out the answer in her or his own experience.

integrate. If your church is like this you need to change the church or change churches.

Another pitfall, particularly for assistant and associate ministers, is the deadly retreat malady—that wet rot that eats away at so many ministerial marriages. If we would allow, engagements, conferences, and talks would take one or both of us away every weekend. One couple we knew in seminary was so responsive to calls that they wound up spending a year in different countries on separate calls. At the end of the year they decided it was hardly worth being married. So they no longer are. If the apostles brought their spouses, should we not? Clement tells us Peter parted with his wife when she was led to death. How many of our ministers and their spouses are parted all through their lives? Thus we take only joint retreats, and we attempt to control their number so that we can work on our own relationship—keeping our own home in order before we presume to affect God's.

Now that we have been in educational ministry for the last decade, we notice this same pox is true of scholarly meetings. A mark of a well-rounded scholar is membership in scholarly associations. Well and good. But four days here and five days there for meetings, speaking engagements, lecture series, and workshops can chip away at time spent with the family just as thoroughly as pastoral duties. The American Academy of Religion, Society of Biblical Literature and that other host of organizations that get together jointly in one great gala week of scholarship each year has just begun to include a babysitting service in their huge meetings. Evangelical Women's Caucus does the same and the Evangelical Theological Society regionals in which we have been involved have proved more than amenable to this need. But babysitting is not simply the answer.

Scholarship is at the core of our "religion of the book," and we have found that good programs for children at the E.W.C. and at the E.T.S. regionals are most welcomed by the children. Further, when we scheduled the 1981 Southeastern regional of the E.T.S. at lovely and welcoming Toccoa Falls College in Georgia, we noticed that spouses were not only attending the "spouse programs" we had scheduled but the scholarly ones as well. Scholars' spouses are among the most theologically astute and enlightened (and forgotten) component of the church, having not only agonized with their spouses over studies but also often themselves audited courses, typed papers, corrected grammar, and attended programs schools regularly open to the public. By 1985 in the New England regional we had dropped the spouse program and were paralleling scholarly sections with practical ministry sections for all the scholars, spouses, pastors, evangelists, and other thinking Christians who work to balance reflection with actions. And we added planned activities for children. As a result, families are encouraged to come reason together. Our houses and God's house are kept orderly as the Word directs.

Addressing Together The Small Killing Duties

Christian lawyer Bruce I. McDaniel, who won the Bronze Star for his service as a medic, told us the soldiers in combat in Vietnam had this motto: "It's the little things that are killing us." We all know that sometimes it seems easier to be a Christian in the great battles, the big decisions, than in the day to day routine, the Monday through Saturday ones. But if we concentrate on them, interestingly, the big things seem automatically to fall into place. So here are three examples: first, a day-to-day task that needs to be done; second, a division of a task by talent; and third, assigning a task that nobody wants.

Task No. 1. We need to eat at least three times a day. A convenient schedule for me is to make breakfast and dinner. Aida prefers to make supper and take on another household task to balance the schedule. Naturally, we plug in for each other's duties when necessary, trying to ease the other's burden. Both of us have noted that a marriage can seem either to be a battle for supremacy, a rivalry between strong opponents, or a cooperative symbiotic venture where what is done for one is seen as done for the whole. An achievement of my wife is an achievement for us all; an honor for our son is an honor for the whole family; an opportunity for dad is a cooperative opportunity for the whole. When one of us has guests the others serve. This is just common sense (not to mention courtesy), a concrete application of the "one flesh" theology of marriage, and a reflection of the body of Christ. That is how one's body works by protecting, nurturing, and strengthening itself—unless it is sick.

Task No. 2. This is all fine for pleasant regular tasks, but what of those that neither of us wants to do? What about something homely like sticky phone calls or obnoxious personal contacts? Misery for each of us is as varied as common cold bacteria. It might be reprimanding somebody for the seventeenth time to wipe the table after eating when we lived in community or contacting our former nasty landlady about the howls of her pathetic dog again or taking back opened unsales-slipped defective merchandise to the store. Some men would rather drive five miles in the wrong direction than ask directions from a stranger. We have found that for me it is easier to deal with sticky situations among people I know. For Aida it is easier to handle difficult communications with people we do not know.

Task No. 3. But what happens when we cannot decide? What happens when there is no true division by convenience or talent or less aversion? What happens when neither of us wants to do it equally? When Reverend Troublemaker, who wants to lay some guilt upon us which is his way, calls and specifies either one of us will do, who will go? Here you will recognize a great existential question that will divide up any family or any model, whether egalitarian, hierarchical, or undecided. "As the head of this house I order you to... " or "As the head of this house you have to.... " What we do is apply Proverbs 18:18, "The lot puts an end to disputes and decides between powerful contenders" (RSV). Taking a cue from the disciples in Acts 1:26, benefiting from our collective history, we "choose it out," odds or evens, and the decision is binding. We have noted that God chooses most wisely, as the case of Jonah will bear out.

Now, these are three practical and homely day to day problems. Small and humdrum though they may appear, nevertheless they are the true things that preoccupy us.

What of the Big Tasks?

As the servants with the talents learned, when one is faithful in the little things, the big things follow. For instance, whose job or call does a dually ordained couple pack up and follow: his or hers? What couple on any marital model ordained or otherwise has not experienced resentment on this account? In our case we began by taking turns. I graduated first from seminary and developed a chaplaincy position. Aida accompanied me and, with effort, found work in a maximum security prison and eventually in a neighboring teaching/college chaplaincy position. Both of us were called to Newark to do educational ministry among adults. Then following that assignment it was her turn to choose, and she sensed a call to complete her education at the Southern Baptist Theological Seminary in Lousville, Kentucky, so I accompanied her, finding a ministry setting up and supervising adult literacy centers. The Gordon-Conwell position completed her transition. Were we to move again it would be my turn. Such were my thoughts in 1978.

Now, however, I am growing to the point where I would like to see all future decisions jointly beneficial. Of course, that benefit has to extend now past the two of us to a new member.

Shared Parenting

The saddest prospect imaginable for any true minister is to stand before God clutching a handful of other people when his or her own children are missing. Parenting as God intended so that children grow up to love God is the chief duty of parents, and there are plenty of resources cached away in the supposedly "bad old traditional" days if one only has eyes to see them. Like the proverbial woman, who says, "I'm not a women's libber, but..." we know many couples who would not tolerate being called "equal parents" who, by force or necessity, have practiced some form of it.

For example, if he was studying and she was at work, he might be forced to feed the kid and change the diapers. Our difference was that we both felt called by God to share equally in the nurturing of this precious life entrusted to us. So, instead of grumbling about our fate, we set about to enjoy this little life and build out of our family a trinity of love that might in some faint way mirror that great love that is the Godhead.

When we began looking for a paradigm for shared parenting in the Scriptures, we experienced a series of shocks. What we found was great advice juxtaposed against mainly negative examples.

Proverbs 1:8-9 counsels us to, "Hear my son, your father's instruction, and reject not your mother's teaching; for they are a fair garland for you head, and pendants for your neck." As you may recall, the theme of Proverbs is stated in 1:7, the verse immediately preceding, where we are told, "The fear of the Lord is the beginning of knowledge; fools despise wisdom and instruction." So it strikes us with the fact that God's wisdom is transmitted through both parents—a weighty and holy task indeed!

If we agree that Solomon was the one who collected these proverbs, we certainly are given pause to think about the example offered by his parents. His mother, Bathsheba, was an adulteress; his father, David, an adulterer and a murderer. Like Isaac, David apparently did not expend much effort in rearing his children. And both men saw their gray hairs go down in sorrow to the grave as a result. Isaac was deceived and robbed of his blessing; David was hounded across the countryside in open warfare against filial revolt when he should have been relaxing in his palace, his sons gathered jovially about him.

God praises the Rechabites in Jeremiah 35 solely because they obeyed their father's instruction not to make or drink wine, or take up permanent residence. As a result of their obedience he holds them up as an example to Israel and showers blessings upon them. God apparently approves the close-knit family group. Only a special situation like Hannah's, perhaps, where a child was entrusted to God's care by pre-arrangement, allows any sort of relaxation of continual parental responsibility.

Paul's advice in the pastoral letters to bishops, and to young widows as well, is that they must be able to manage their own households, "having children in obedience with all respect. But if someone does not know how to manage that one's own household, how will such a one take care of God's church?" (1 Tim. 3:4-5). Those men, then, who leave the child rearing and the family management to the "womenfolk" move under the curse—not the praise—of God. Sadly, they read like a "who's who" in the Bible.

But what are the principles they and we should be following?

1. The Golden Rule, recorded in Matthew 7:12 (which, incidentally, is addressed to believers plurally, as a group, not singularly as we usually take it), is Christ's basis for all human interaction. Literally rendered it counsels, "Everything that all of you may wish that people do to you, in the same way also you do to them. For this is the law and the prophets."

2. Genesis 1:27 informs us that both female and male are needed to express the full image of God. Therefore, Proverbs 1:8-9 points out that both father's and mother's input are needed equally in childrearing.

3. Psalm 127:3 assures us that children are indeed a gift from God. "Lo, children are a heritage from the Lord, the fruit of the womb a reward." Psalm 128:3-4 tells us God's blessing is indicated by many children around one's table. Both of these are psalms of Solomon, who certainly enjoyed God's blessings before he began to overdo it, going after foreign wives and eventually collecting seven hundred official ones and three hundred stand-bys. His principle was right. He erred in methodology.

4. The biblical understanding of masculinity and femininity is not always our culture's. Jesus cooked (John 21:9-14) and wept (Luke 19:41, John 11:35). Our society's permissions and limitations on what men and women may do are

not God's. Tasks need to be shared between helpmeets. Any truly shared marriage needs to apply these scriptural principles. The way we attempt to flesh them out and open ourselves for God's Word to live through us is by making sure we are in control of our lives and not enslaved by society, its expectations, our careers, and others' opinions.

Both of us happen to feel called to careers, and we both want to be full participants in our family. So, we adjust our schedule to enable us to share equally, and we demand that our careers adjust themselves to fit these goals. In our case, one of us has pursued a career in the morning primarily; the other in the evening.

Before Aida took the call at Gordon-Conwell Theological Seminary she received the school's blessings to make family life a priority. As a result, she attempts to perform the majority of her teaching duties between the hours of 8:00 A.M. and 3:00 P.M. After 3:00 she grades papers and prepares lectures at home until 5:00, available for Steve if he needs her. I have retained preparation of breakfast and the noon meals. I do the clothes, pick up the house in odd moments, make up the shopping list, and played with our son during the morning when he was younger and get him ready and off now he is in school. Aida shops and does the errands one morning. She shops only once a week, which saves an enormous amount of time. In the afternoon when Aida returns home, I take a nap and Steve plays. These days inside he tends to write stories or papers like his parents, draw pictures, or build forts out of the sofa pillows. Outside he has a treehouse fort under construction, or he plays and bikes with friends. Aida cooks the evening meal. She also cooks the holiday meals and a great cook she is, too. Despite one of society's cherished myths, accomplished people, I have noticed, often work well in many areas just as lazy or disorganized people tend to be lax or create chaos in whatever they touch. In fact in Louisville she won a recipe contest for an excellent delicious original chicken recipe. I for the previous years would then go off to work at 5:00, for most of that time setting up and running adult literacy and high school equivalency centers in urban areas. In the evening Aida plays with Steve, helps him bathe and puts him to bed. We all clean the house on Thursday evening from 6:00-8:30. As a practical, efficient team we can hit the place in one night and leave it shining; so as a team we expend just one night for cleaning, one morning for shopping. Saturday is our family day.

One cannot conceive of the sheer constant battle the family has to wage to ensure this last point. Saturdays, since they are the day that most people are automatically free, are continually being scheduled for crucial meetings. Presbytery meets on Saturday. One-day conferences are often scheduled on Saturdays. Breakfast meetings are followed by dinner meetings. We try to hold the line at limiting our violation of the family day to once a month at the very most. In the same way with our nights, though not necessarily inviolable, we do try to hold off the greedy schedule consumers.

My wife has a reputation in her teaching for being unusually open to students. She is constantly hosting them at her home, attending their major events, scheduling on-campus lunches with them, or having them over collectively and individually. One group, however, became so enmeshed in the artificial "in loco parentis" atmosphere of one of the institutions we served that they demanded my wife schedule in a second Saturday every month and come to a meeting scheduled "at student's convenience" to demonstrate her commitment to the group. She refused. No truly loving mother of a six year old will regularly trade the one day her child is home from secular or Sunday school to meet with adult students. As a result the students complained loudly that their needs were not being met. Opposition can come for the most incredible reasons from the most unlikely sources. In this case it was overindulged students themselves supposedly training to be ministers to others!

People often want a minister at their constant disposal. The logical tendency when people invade our schedule is to give in or knuckle under in the name of peace. But the price is too high if at stake is our family or our own sanity. Putting our family or sanity as a priority will cost us elsewhere in the expressed discontent of the chronically malcontent. So many pastors have given in to people whose own skewed values and familial emptiness has allowed them to become selfish predators; there is often a high cost in our popularity, especially when people let themselves go and demand our total service to them as their minister. But what we pay in maintaining our own discipline we reap bountifully in familial dividends. And we also enable these people to regain a more salutary and accurate glimpse of their rights and their proper place in our life and service to them.

The same reminder must be delivered as well to the world of work, as our society itself has defined it. Only part of the problem of putting our families first resides in other people and their expectations for us and plans to utilize us for their ends. Another major part, of course, lies in our own ambivalence toward our family, our desire to get ahead, and our guilt to fulfill those expectations of others. A third great part lies in the way work has come to be structured now that the tight apprentice structure of the home business has disintegrated into separate work places. Certainly God commended the Adam, male and female, to till the garden. But how did our particular divisive definition of the world of work become a given premise? Large blocks of time are dedicated to the work place with the unspoken, pressuring expectation that a truly dedicated worker will give extra hours gratuitously, if that worker is *truly* dedicated and of any real worth at all. (Job sharing is implicitly if not explicitly frowned upon in so many high-powered companies.) This commitment impedes the kind of balance that makes familial life a truly shared experience. Spare time is consumed by the job, and exclusive hobbies sometimes get the crumbs; hobbies needed to recover from the stress of over working! Instead work places need to evaluate workers on forty hours of work as contracted (rather than sixty or eighty hours worth of work) and the quality of that work, in other words, the goals accomplished rather than the distribution of hours that a worker can schedule. If the job is covered and done with quality, that is the fair trade a work place should expect; not a visible head count from 9:00-9:00. We believe in working hard in contracted limits but not in over or under working.

In fact, we have noticed that by maintaining tight scheduling we are enabled to get an enormous amount accomplished, more than those whose loose schedule deludes them into thinking that they have plenty of time to spare and there is no need not to procrastinate. Our schedule does not allow the unnecessary luxury of procrastination. As a result we continually find ourselves enabled by working hard to produce much more in a limited time than those who "take their time" and work lightly in an unlimited time. A job should then honor the quality, if true quality it is, that a disciplined worker produces. If it does not, to change the job or to change jobs is certainly the answer. This, of course, implies that our family priorities truly are our priorities, that we are not actually stepping on the backs of our family to succeed, oppressing the people who love us in order to impress other people who frankly do not care if we live or die. It also demands of us something that the often uncompromising world of work sometimes does not value in a worker: individual courage to act lovingly but firmly on our convictions rather than simply goose-step in line to the company's familial death march.

So, in solidifying the bulwark of our family against the world, these adaptations work for us. Time period division works well if you determine to do it *before* you accept a job. It also calls upon you as a participant to face unpleasant tasks and do them if they fall within your period, bar none, to stay out of your partner's way if it's your partner's time to be in charge, and to keep the lines of communication open. Regular dates for parents are also essential if the husband-wife relationship is to keep pace with the child-parent ones.

Traditional Parenting vs. Shared Parenting

When we were asked to give the parenting seminar at the E.W.C. conference in Seattle, we wrote in the promotional blurb, "Equal Parenting—is it possible? Will it just confuse your child?" When couples who, on a continuum, practice some kind of shared parenting recoil at the term "Equal Parenting," they are expressing a fear that any tampering with the tried-and-true traditional model will send their child into role confusion. Their little one will not know whether it is a boy or a girl. It will be sexually confused, out of phase with society, unable to relate normally to other children. The child will develop hatred for the parents who put it in this position. It will exhibit antisocial behavior. Its values will be skewed. It will go into spiritual revolt, turn out to be criminal. Eventually, because of its confusion about who it is and who God is, it will reject the parents and the parents' belief in God, and perhaps end up committing patricide, matricide, suicide, or all three. All this will occur because its foolish parents dared to stray from the traditional model.

And what is this wonderful traditional model? It is Dad going off to work, being absent all day. It is Mom locked in the home with the children every day of her life until she stands chagrined before an empty nest, her earthly reason for living suddenly gone.

We had the opportunity to examine the traditional model, flip-flopped, in a unique laboratory when we lived with some 240 other families in Southern Seminary Village in Louisville, Kentucky. There dads studied; moms worked. So when one four-year-old boy asked Aida, "Whatcha doin'?" and she replied, "Studying," he said, "Oh no you're not."

"Well, feast your eyes," she said, showing him the book.

"You can't be studying," he ruled with assurance. "Boys study; girls go to work." In a world turned around, all the traditional model provided for this child was rigidity. When his dad finally finishes and goes to work, this little fellow will have his whole world turned topsy-turvy because he is convinced—some things boys do, some things girls do, and that is God's universe. *There* is role confusion if it exists anywhere!

Traditional fathers are absent all day, but this is not enough to cause their offspring to reject them thoroughly. Still, it does cause problems, and Dr. Benjamin Spock identifies two periods, at five months and two and a half to three years, when children hate strangers as they learn to differentiate between people. Father, the stranger in the house, soon finds himself persona non grata as his child rejects the unfamiliar. Spock counsels:

It's more often the father who is particularly unpopular at this period, and he sometimes gets the feeling he's pure poison. He shouldn't take it too seriously. It will help the child to play with his father alone, at times, so that he can know him as an enjoyable and loving person, not just an intruder.

Don't worry, writes Dr. Spock, it's only natural. Father will be remembered in a while.[10]

Spending so many hours every day with my son, I happily skipped these stages. At five months Steve snuggled into Daddy's arms at the approach of outsiders, and at two and a half to three years Steve refused to drink milk because Daddy could not drink it and Stevie wanted to be like Daddy. There were no strangers in our house. Only true outsiders suffered.

In the years I have done city ministry each suicide or social aberrant I have seen was directly traceable to a home marred by alienation, neglect, or cruelty. None came as a result of equally shared parental care.

An equally strong loving mother matched with an equally strong *present* loving father are a safeguard against such alienation. And what about spiritual revolt? Studies show that the most likely children to attend church in adulthood are those whose parents both attended. If we actually put Proverbs into practice and fathers and mothers together shared equally in the total nurture of the child, the world might look less like the cursed, divorce-plagued, suicide-ridden, warmongering sludge hole sin often makes it and more like the Eden God first and always intended for us. Shared parenting

---

[10]Dr. Benjamin Spock, *Baby and Child Care* (2d ed.; New York: Pocket Books, 1968) pp. 357-58.

seems to me to be a step in the direction of God's intention. And taking that step and reaping from it the warm love of our children is worth more than any career achievement, any compliment or display of envy by other people, any other inducement that the mere world has to offer. Perhaps two things, at least from the male side, that keep this often counterproductive model going are male fears and role expectation, self-limitations left over from childhood.

I remember as a little kid wondering, what if my mommy died? What would happen to me? I could not see my dad doing much. Now, however, when I review my childhood I see that whenever there was a real emergency my dad was magnificent. He was the one who cared for the terminally ill grandparent and who nursed me when there were big injuries or hospitalization. He could cook and my grandfather could sew. Yet I was not trained to expect these capabilities, and my dad was so rugged and self-assured that his easy assumption or rejection of the homemaker role never seemed out of the ordinary. Therefore, I never noticed it or looked to him for that kind of nurturing, no matter how many times he provided it. Instead, like so many boys, I believed what my playmates believed, that what one does, rather than who one is, ultimately defines one's identity. While there is a great truth in the former when applied to Christian social action, it does not mean, for example, that crawling on all fours under our own children makes us a real horse. And it does not mean that sharing in the work that goes into making a home somehow mystically threatens to annul our maleness. Yet these childish fears and limitations never seem to leave many men. Instead, they transfer from fears centered in mothers' care-taking to the locus of wives' care-taking, tied in with fears about the authenticity of males' masculinity. Since males do not cook or care for a house—will I starve if I do not keep my wife in line? Our child as a toddler used to roar like a monster then become authentically terrified at the imaginary monster he had created. Like this, self-created fear becomes a motivating determiner: if I go in for this sharing stuff, I will lose my masculinity! I will become a—

God forbid—effete "househusband"! And I will be the only man in the playground, out of phase with the rest of the guys, condemned to soap operas forever. And how will that look on my résumé? Unemployed for a year, that's how. And what about my wife, if I help out? Will she start shirking her part? And will I get stuck with it? And then will my family break up? Will my wife be caught up in the career swirl and be swept away if I do not keep her safely chained here at home? After all, I find her desirable. Everybody else out there might respond that way, too. And I will not be there to control what happens; to see how she responds. In essence, work, other men, and a new life of interests might take her away from me. And what have I given her here in our life together to make her reject any such irresistible temptations of escape?

All these fears flow from a lack of trust, a low self-image, and a few good reasons due to women's lot. If I do not make sure she stays here, I will never be able to keep her. God knows, she would never stay here on her own. Essentially, all these fears drain into this central sink-hole of insecurity: if I do not keep things as they are, I will lose control. My life will spin wildly into chaos. In addition I will lose my masculinity and fritter away my energy on insignificant, drudging odd jobs. I will have to cook. I will have to clean. I will have to take care of these rotten little uncivilized kids. What if one of them throws up? In essence, I will lose the fruit of oppression for which my forefathers struggled through the battle of the sexes to pass on to me as a sacred trust.

Why *do* men oppress women constantly year after year, generation after generation, and why is the oppression so hard to correct? And we should make no mistake about that, it *is* hard to correct.

Rigidity in the home is the personal microcosm of the societal macrocosm. Just as society has assigned to adult men the role of superior and to adult women that of inferior, so the roles of husband and wife in the home are defined as oppressor and oppressed. At the very least, society demands, there must be one partner who is boss and one who is servant. Therefore, there is a continued competition for power together with reactant sedition by whichever becomes the oppressed spouse, whether it be the unsuccessful man whose wife "really wears the pants in the family" or the wife whose husband squelches all her creativity and maturity. Where there is not overt rebellion, there is sublimated manipulation wherein the oppressed lives life through the figurehead oppressor, usually with the child against both, or worse, taking sides regularly against one of the parents. This is the equivalent external expression of that dreaded physical syndrome wherein the body acts against itself to its own detriment. Tension repressed to the boiling point, particularly in women forced to remain home as some kind of honorary older sibling to their children, eventually reaches critical mass. No fully matured, gifted adult can withstand a life-time of suppression. And God help the man whose wife fulfills herself by channeling her energies through him, for he will have no rest. He will have to live out the lives, desires, and ambitions of two people while God has equipped him physically and emotionally to satisfy only those of one. The alternative extreme is that of missionary child Pearl Buck's grandmother, as described in her biographic diatribe about her ancestors, *The Exile.* One day her grandmother simply stopped cooking, doing housework, and caring for her family and primarily sat in a rocking chair from then on. The usual option for the masses, however, is to live lives of quiet rebellion and lifelong nagging discontent.

This is not to say that no women should remain at home. Not at all. To say all women must express themselves outside is equally oppressive. Women who choose homemaking as a career should be seen, in the model of Proverbs 31:10-31, as fully employed, skilled homemakers. This is an occupational choice and should be seen in that light. The World Priorites survey estimates the economic value of women's home labor at $4 trillion and speculates that, if women were paid for housework, they would supply nearly one-third of the world's annual economic product. Dorcas chose home labor as a primary occupation and was approved. Deborah did not choose it and was also approved. As for making the home work, however, the Scriptures clearly decree that is the duty of both spouses, for *no one* whose children are out of control is qualified to lead the church. Men are not exempted. If men are not exempted, then the home cannot be solely the responsibility of women. It must be the responsibility of both.

A shared marriage and ministry can take all the pressure to manipulate and control the success of wives and children off husbands. Control is not and never was solely the concern of the male. No normal family depends on the male keeping order lest the wife wander off and chaos rule. Normal women, especially Christian ones, are the very soul of responsibility. Males who try to exercise control over them as if their wives were one of the kids will precipitate in their own home the sexist version of that old racist image we have been so ready to apply to other cultures, the harried dictator of the proverbial banana republic. They will barely be keeping a lid on reactant rebellion.

Between mature adults, control is the concern of both. Love cannot be coerced: neither can control. God does not try to coerce it; why should we? Coercion will not work with children; what makes us think it will work with spouses? If women, then, are not irresponsible adult adolescents who need control to keep them from wandering, if that is ridiculous and insulting, men should consider them for what they are—co-equal partners, helpmeets.

Any male who operates on any other model will produce tension in his wife, tension in their relationship, tension in the home, and, indubitably, inherited tension in the kids. He will be constantly quelling a rebellion which will ultimately get out of hand. And until it does he will endure a life of continual manipulation. Who needs to live like that? He will end by fostering the very fragmentation, embarrassment, estrangement, and disaster he was seeking to avoid.

Far better for males to serve our wives as Christ did the church and as Ephesians 5 counsels, enabling her to become that lovely shaped and polished jewel glorious with lustrous good works in the human bracelet that adorns the hand of God. And women, who seem to have inculcated in them more of a constant sense of responsibility than many men, will turn back a great appreciation on their husbands, who will live a life a Sultan would envy. That has certainly been my experience. Aida does not try to live her life through me. Instead, freed, she looks for chances to please me and serve me. She knows what irritates me and makes a special kind effort to deflect it and handle it herself, as I do for her. In work she looks out for opportunities for me to prosper in my career as she prospers in hers. She treats me with the same love and respect in private as she does in public.

Such an approach works beautifully for us and eliminates much of the tension between my wife and myself and my child and myself that I read and heard and thought was inevitable. Will the approach work for you as well, improving your relationships and lessening your tensions? "Shared marriage" as a concept, of course, will not assure you of a good marriage or an equally shared ministry. Shared practice, however, will. Unlike some religionist career mongers who run around talking about social action without practicing it, thinking the right thoughts in a proper Judeo-Christian mode is tantamount to doing them. Lack of action is lack of true belief in the Hebraic manner of thinking which our faith entails. Faith without work is essentially dead, because there is no real Christian faith that does not work. We are not, then, arguing here for a political principle. We are talking about an intentional style of living. Both partners need to work hard at serving the other to make a marriage work. Any marriage that works, traditionally or non-traditionally structured, is ultimately based on mutual service, on loving, serving, intentional, mutually beneficial interdependence.

Essentially a shared approach of respect, a partnership with your marital partner can make your home a relaxed glimpse of paradise. By the same token it should develop into a shared ministry that can make your service to others multiply like loaves and fishes.

Shared Ministry

When I was writing songs in college I noticed that writing with another does not make a song twice as good, it makes it four times as good. For some reason co-effort done properly tends to have the effect not of addition but of multiplication, of squaring one's effort, raising it to the nth power. This is obviously the sphere of God's activity, since the triune God delights in working through positive community.

Ministry in parallel should ultimately reflect the acting nature of God. Since God chose to reveal Christ as a servant, ministry is styled on servanthood and ought to flow from our familial service to each other. Waiting on tables is good practice for higher forms of service, as we see in the effects of the diaconate of the New Testament Church of Acts. Done rightly, joint service in the home flows out in cooperative ministry to others.

What practical advice can we offer to couples wishing to minister together? We are convinced that a couple's relationship sets a tone for ministry. After all, ministry itself is simply a series of relationships begun in the divine relationship among the persons of the trinity and extended by God through Jesus to human beings. Webster's has defined our term "minister" as a person acting on behalf of another, as another's agent, carrying out that other's orders or designs. We are agents not simply for some business or some government, but we are agents for no less than the Great God of the Universe. We are emissaries of the great government of heaven. Throughout the New Testament we can see that understanding fleshed out in Jesus' acting on his Father's business, in Paul fulfilling his calling from Jesus. That is why practicing servanthood in the home on behalf of one another prepares a couple to live a servant-life of ministering to others.

To insist then that one member of the couple's "ministry" should take precedence over the other's is to misunderstand the nature of ministry. It is a contradiction in terms. This attitude produced the ludicrous situation of the Corinthians berating Paul for serving them rather than lording it over them as did the false apostles. What Paul did was ministry. What the false apostles did was tyranny. Unfortunately, what many couples do is practice a form of tyranny in the name of ministry. And usually it is the tyranny of the male's activity at the expense of the female's. Thus, the means for ministry contradict the ends. The male or the female sets out to do something on behalf of God in service to others and winds up tyrannizing his or her own spouse. So ministry is lost. But Ephesians 5 calls us males to love our families as Christ did the church.

What did Jesus do? Jesus built up his disciples, washed their feet, healed them, patiently taught them, and sent them out as leaders to do greater works than even he had done, as John 14:12 notes. So how can we build a life of mutual servanthood that will establish a climate in which will grow a co-operative ministering style as a family? Interestingly, these principles apply to all endeavors where Christian men and women work together, not just in ministry by the nuclear family but also in activities of the entire extended Christian family. What are our foundational suggestions?

Beginning a Ministry

1. Mutual respect is paramount. We need to assess a true appraisal and develop a true appreciation of our own and our partner's gifts. One helpful exercise is to list ten things that you admire most in your spouse. Once, when counseling an engaged couple, we noticed they were constantly bickering, so we suggested this exercise. Though the aspiring groom came up with a list of qualities which, after preparing, caused him to look more adoringly at his prospective bride, to our chagrin and his mortification the bride could not think of one compliment to pay her intended. The minutes began ticking by as she struggled and the tension and embarrassment in the room began to mount. We ordered the bride to go home and come back in several months with a list of ten items. When she returned six months later they were both glowing happily and she had a list of many more than

ten entries. As it turned out, God called them to a particularly difficult life behind the Iron Curtain but their family, which now numbers four, is living and ministering happily ever after.

2. Help make that list come about: build each other up. When we were doing prison ministry our motto was: treat a person the way you want that person to be and he or she will become that. We need to help each other develop our gifts, realize the full potentiality we have. Each of us then can rise together.

3. To do these two things we need a sense of community. The whole family ought to become our self-identity. That is what "one flesh" really means. No longer are we you or me, now we are you *and* me, us. We need to build a lifestyle good for both of us, and, if God grants it, eventually all of us. That is why scheduling is so crucial to make these principles practical. A family schedule that works and to which all are truly committed will allot family time and energy for achieving every member's goals and filling every member's needs.

4. Inversely, we allow no destructive criticism or humor in our house. Those "Hi, ugly" or "Here's my wife, my ball and chain..." and those jokes that prey on weight, physical defects, or mental failings destroy relationships and kill a home's spirit. The home, after all, is supposed to be the oasis, the fortress, not the desert, not the battleground. Therefore, we outlaw that type of humor. Our house is full of jokes, full of humor. We notice all city ministers who have been able to stick it out have well developed senses of irony and humor. Ironic humor that helps interpret life and upbuilding humor are the spice of relationships. Destructive humor is their cancer. Often intolerance is the virus that causes that disease.

5. Tolerance is foundational. We try to allow the others freedom to act their way and fail. God permits us to fail. We in the church fail all the time. To allow another person to do things their own way when they are in charge of a job is a simple act of courtesy. That is doing to others what we want others to do to us. And when they no longer feel threatened that we are going to take over their leadership, when they

feel affirmed in our support, then we can offer gentle criticism, the kind of criticism we ourselves would wish to receive.

6. A helpful rule to follow, especially for us strong leader types, is, "I should change myself, not my partner." Do you know why so many Christians get into husband and wife problems? They read the wrong Scriptures. We males may not dwell very much on the covenantal laws for the man who owns an ox, but we certainly do spend an inordinate amount of time in lectures and sermons and books reading and interpreting our wives' mail from God. And our wives read and write and talk about God's mail to us. But if we were busy concentrating on changing ourselves into what we understand God directing us to be, we might free our partner to change, too.

7. With this kind of attitude goes a simple rule that even our secular courts of law have realized, while many of us in the faith who should know better have not. We need to give our partners the benefit of the doubt when we hear accusations against them or when things go wrong. We need to treat them as innocent until proven guilty.

8. The whole point of all this advice is to enjoy each other as Proverbs 5:18-19 so beautifully describes:

Let your fountain be blessed, and rejoice in the wife of your youth, a lovely hind, a graceful doe. Let her affection fill you at all times with delight. Be infatuated always with her love.

9. What is our final foundational suggestion for how a couple can jointly minister without destroying each other's individuality? It is our primal foundation. If God is at the head, each of us is freed to be simply a part. In submitting to God we are freed to submit to one another.

Thus, in a joint ministry each can exercise his and her gifts. If one has a project, the other can take an assisting role. And this kind of productive humility encourages good spiritual growth. So, living a life of mutual servanthood on behalf of one another encourages a life of ministry to flow out to others.

Maintaining a Ministry

Now, once that life of ministry is flowing, what are some of the ways we can aid its continuance? What are some of the ways we can keep that ministry joint and happy?

1. First we have to know how to measure our ministries. Often books I have read on the subject we are discussing stop at the end of the last set of guidelines. But once we put them into practice we gain a whole new set of problems for which we are unprepared and we have to wait for another volume to come out to tell us what to do now. What to do now begins with learning to measure your ministry in order to decide whether or not it is adequate.

Ezekiel 3:16-21 tells us that our job is to warn people, describe their problems, prescribe a therapeutic, and, if we are capable and qualified, help supply it or, if we are not, refer to someone who is prepared and qualified to help. We are not, however, responsible for making people respond, or, as the old adage may be adapted, leading the horse to water and tripping it into it. 1 Corinthians 3:5-15 advises us that God gives the growth, not us. We are responsible to till and sow and tend, but we are not responsible for the growth. God gives the growth. And each of us workers has a part in the process. We may be tillers or sowers or pruners or de-weeders or waterers or the person who stirs together the plant food or the one who applies it. None of us is responsible, or should be responsible, for the entire process. What often confuses us is the fact that all of us need approval and we look to our work or the people we serve to gain it. But 2 Corinthians 10:17-18 tells us that approval comes from God. We are never going to get full approval from the people to whom we minister. Jesus certainly did not get it. Are we greater than our Master? We have God as the source of our approval as well as the human who, on earth, is closest to us and through whom God often ministers to us, our beloved, our partner, the one with whom we are one flesh. Often we can be more edified and reproved by our little children than by a hundred dollar session with the local psychiatrist. Sometimes we might need the psychiatrist, of course, but, as often, that professional will send us back to our families to clean up our relationships anyway.

2. Once we learn how to measure our ministries, we will know when to continue and when we have done our work. Some of us ministers never seem to know when to quit work. We seem to think the Holy Spirit and the rest of the body of Christ cannot survive our rest breaks. Like the evangelist who has delivered the good news and does not know when to stop the commercials and let the Spirit work and the other respond, we need to know when to stop ministering, when to quit work. God rested on the seventh day. Ecclesiastes 3, as sung everywhere on the secular radio, tells us there is a time for everything. Why should we not rest when our Creator does? We need to remember that, as the old saying has been adapted, absence makes the heart go wander. So many Christian superstars are having marital problems that the prospect should scare any sensible active Christian. Encouragingly, the Evangelical Fellowship of Canada's *Faith Alive* magazine found in a survey on Christian marriage that,

answers from "A" marriages included a Christ-centered life, personal maturity, teamwork, and a willingness to change....Shared leadership marriages on the average rated a grade of "A-minus", with husband-led marriages ranking an average "B-plus" and wife-led marriages a "C-plus."[12]

Interestingly, wives who work outside the home ranked the satisfaction of their marriages two categories above wives who stayed at home. Sadly, while pastors gave their marriages high grades, pastors' wives as a group gave theirs the lowest grades of the survey, ranking pastors' wives as the group whose marriages were the least satisfying. While often-absent working wives and pastors' wives with absent husbands headed the list in considering divorce or separa-

---

[12]In a survey, most Canadian evangelicals grade their marriages with high marks. *Christianity Today,* April 19, 1985, 59.

tion, *none* of the missionary couples queried answered yes or even maybe. Missionary marriages ranked "among the happiest." And, for the most successful Christian marriages, "Those who claim a shared spiritual leadership or mission seem to be happiest and most fulfilled in life." We do need to live and work and minister and rest and enjoy ourselves together as a couple as much as possible.

3. To become a Christian we learn how to say Yes. To be a good lasting minister we need to learn how to say No. People will often make us feel guilt when we do not accede to all their requests. But we need only to do for others as much as we would want done for us. We ought only to feel guilt when we ought to feel guilt. God knows, there are plenty of real opportunities for that!

4. When we have become more adept at separating true guilt which we accept and for which we seek forgiveness from false guilt and similar annoyances, we need to learn to develop ways to deal with those regular irritations which inevitably arise in everyone's ministry. In our first full ministry together we noticed we were beginning to fight. That was a situation we had generally avoided in our first few years of marriage and its occurrence disturbed us greatly. After one particularly bitter disagreement we sat down together to figure out what was going wrong. Finally, we traced the source to another minister with whom we worked who was dividing us and putting an incredible amount of pressure on each of us to perform in the way he wanted. The next time we got together with him we confronted him jointly. It was good for him, it was good for us. This was a great man of God. He thanked us. Irritation needs to be traced to its source. We need to deal with that source. We do not need to take out our tension on each other. We do not need to kick the dog. We do not need to take it out on the mail carrier. You know how that chain of command operates. Dad, who gets blamed by his boss (who has been blamed by his boss), yells at Mom. Mom bawls out Junior. Junior kicks the dog. The dog bites the mail carrier. Instead, we need to attack the source of our irritation and, of course, in as gentle and loving a way as we can manage.

5. What we want to preserve and develop is our family as a united front. We need to discuss our familial differences privately. Society says, "Be honest! Be painfully honest, if necessary." But 1 Corinthians 13 teaches us that love is greater than knowledge. Truth is a treasure not a weapon. Each of us tries never to gang up with another person on the other. If we cannot defend our partner's position we usually stay out of the discussion unless our partner asks our advice. If we must speak we try once gently to give our correcting point and if our partner rejects it in the heat of disagreement we step back out. All ministers who have done a lot of ministry learn that we do not have to correct everybody all the time. We can become like a spiritual version of those incredibly annoying people who go around correcting everyone's speech. God does not do this to us. Why should we do it to each other? Truth is not a weapon with which to bludgeon others into submission, it is a treasure to share, it is pearls to display in appropriate settings.

6. Finally, when we have our own house together, we must then make sure our church is in order, too. We must make sure our church encourages joint ministry.

The family unit, we realize, is a microcosm of the whole extended family of Christ. While all of us strive for effectiveness in our ministry, we should recall that we are created in the image of God. It takes both male and female to express that image, and since most problems touch not only individuals but also all those with whom each of us has contact, a shared approach by both male and female Christians serves the full gamut of personality(ies) involved in any difficulty. Having both the male and female perspective turned on a problem examines it from all angles. There are perspectives which only one or the other sex can supply. In regards to clergy couples, for example, how much bad advice that pastors of one sex hand out not only to the other sex but also at times to their same sex about the other sex could be annulled or at least deflected if an ordained partner were sitting there available to blow the whistle when knowledge yields to ignorance.

Pastors of each sex, too, can be called in on referral for specialized problems. Not always but sometimes only a member of the same sex or age or similar background can actually understand a person's problems.

Ministry, however, is not the sole province of the ordained, if our Protestant reclamation in the Reformation has recaptured anything of the early church practice. And by the same token it is not the sole province of the married. Those who are lay Christians are called to full, ministering servanthood. Those who are single wield a power to minister and serve as fully, and as the case of Paul teaches, often, if not usually, surpassing that of the married. Finally, it is not the sole province of us males. What robs us of this realization is the age-old prejudice that those who are different from us must be inferior. A tragedy we see enacted these days among seminary students is the rush by third year male students to marry so that churches will not turn them down as inferior because they are single. If this has always been the practice, and we have only just realized it, perhaps we have an explanation for why some clergy marriages are breaking up in this more accepting age. They are built not on the rock of sound relationship but on the sand of job anxiety. We who have been liberated by Christ are freed to abandon this bleak terrain. Particularly in the church the Holy Spirit has not gone the Deism route and left us unsupported by God or women with some kind of theological white man's burden. Why should we, then, arrogantly assume one? This is bigotry and blasphemy. Instead, why should we not take full advantage of the mutually supplementary gifts God has given to us as we minister two-by-two in the New Testament mode or best of all, perhaps, in full community. When I ministered in Philadelphia I discovered the advantage of partnership with an older mature church woman and insisted upon that arrangement when ministering back in Newark later on. Two young white males approaching a city dwelling look suspiciously like bill collectors, two ragged blue-jeaned ones look like derelicts. A nicely dressed white adult with a child looks like a Jehovah's Witness. But a young adult male and a mature woman (or vice versa) transcend the categories. Really, there is nothing like the participation of mature Christian seniors to enhance any enterprise.

We are all called to minister. The plural yet single God has so constructed us, and the New Testament has further demonstrated to us that we do it better in twos. Single or married, lay or ordained ministers though we may be, why should we not take advantage of all our plurality as we seek to serve fully those to whom we are called to serve, to evangelize, to counsel, to feed and shelter? Our goal in all of this is still the Edenic goal: to till and enjoy the earth and care for its inhabitants as God directed, with the hope of heaven as its end.

Conclusion

If we males are to assume our God-given responsibility to enable our wives to reach full splendor in the gifts God has given them as they will help us reach ours, we ought to go out of our way to provide them with the time, encouragement, and opportunity to discover and exercise those gifts. If we are to take our family responsibility seriously, we have to make our home, our spouses, our children, and at times our extended family, along with ourselves, the earthly priority for our concerns and action.

Ministry, if it is done correctly, should flow from our relationships. Evangelism and social service should be done by ourselves, our spouses, and our children together, and probably should be done separately only when absolutely necessary. And, in any case, every action should be understood to flow out of the familial whole.

Necessary household duties ought to be divided by scheduling. After all, how many men whose wives have heart conditions do the vacuuming? Essentially, all of them who are good husbands and cannot afford professional domestic help. Naturally few people, if any, like a lifetime of day-after-day drudgery, so duties should be divided across the board to both spouses and to the children. All professionals usually need good assistance, even professional homemakers.

After all, making the home work benefits all, so it is in actuality the responsibility of all. Ideally, the domestic chore most suited to one's recognized gifts should be assigned, and the sheer drudgery should fall equally on all.

Every act we choose to do or to omit is dictated by our priorities in life. After one workshop I was asked to conduct on sharing home responsibilities, one tall, irate, young, upwardly-mobile executive with wife in tow towered over me with, "That's all well and good if you are in teaching, but in the business world you can't do all that kind of stuff. I'd love to do it, but...." His wife commented that he was, indeed, never home before 7:00 P.M. each night. "How much do you need to live on?" I asked. "Have you considered job sharing?" Was I kidding? In his line of work, which was computers, that was frowned upon. Yes, he was in every aspect a young, upwardly-mobile future executive with a corporation president's office as the heaven that was on his mind.

"That all sounds good, but...," he kept saying and deflected every suggestion I made. Finally I asked on a venture, "Tell me something. If we could envision a perfect job for you where you worked only four hours a day, would you do it?" He paused. "No!" shouted his wife suddenly, and we both jumped as the first rosy-fingered blush of enlightenment dawned in her face.

"You wouldn't!" she bellowed.

The husband turned beet red and stuttered.

"You hate being home with the baby," she insisted.

"No, I don't."

"Yes, you do. That one Saturday you couldn't wait to get away."

"Well," I said, "I was just going to tell you about a friend of mine in Kentucky who has three kids and is buying his own home. He works four hours a day at home as a music engraver, but I guess that's irrelevant because that's not the real issue for you, is it? Priority is."

What ultimately is the chief end of life? To appropriate the Westminster Shorter Cathechism in its sex specific sense, what is the chief end of us men? To serve God. To fulfill our marriage contract, sworn before God. To love and enable our wives to become strong leaders in the army of God. To train our children to be stalwart faithful warriors under God's reign. To show others by word and deed the good things of God and attract them to follow our example of relational triumph.

If the scriptural imagery is true, if women express half the image of God, if they are, indeed, gifted by God, if they are, therefore, called by God to God's service, then we mutually complement each other. Together our one flesh becomes a breathing, ministering individual in God's sight. "For no one ever hates, or is indifferent to, one's own flesh," Paul wrote in Ephesians 5:29. For the married, self-nurture is spouse-nurture and, just as the single walk in the footprints of the models of Paul and of Mary and Martha, we married should reflect Peter and his wife, or Prisca and Aquila. Together we will all reflect in community the image of our great God.

A house divided against itself cannot stand, said our Savior (Mark 3:25). If Christ has saved us from the curse, why should we then divide ourselves and fall back under it?

Appendix
Suggestions For Group Study

The renowned first-century philospher, Philo, has some good advice on teaching. When Rebecca "let down the pitcher on to her arm" so that Abraham's servant could drink, Philo interprets the event allegorically:

By the "letting down" on to her arm we are shown how the teacher comes down to the learner and attentively studies him as one with whom he is intimately concerned. For teachers who when they set about giving their lessons keep in view their own great superiority and not the capacity of their pupils, are simpletons, who are not aware how vast is the difference between a lesson and a display. For the one who is giving a display uses to the full the rich yield of the mastery which he possesses, and without let or hindrance brings forward into the open the results of hours spent in labour by himself at home. Such are the works of artists and sculptors. In all this he is trying to gain the praise of the public. The one, on the other hand, who is setting out to teach, is like a good doctor, who with his eyes fixed not on the vastness of his science but on the strength of his patient, applies not all that he has ready for use from the resources of his knowledge—for this is endless—but what the sick person needs, seeking to avoid both defect and excess (*The Posterity and Exile of Cain* XLII [140-1]).

Similarly, these group and individual study questions have to be sifted through and chosen by the group coordinator or group members after attentive study of the specific individuals. What questions are most appropriate, important, and clear to you? Since accurate analysis is assisted by understanding our emotions, a possible introductory exercise might be to answer:

What do you think this book will prove?

What do you want it to prove or not prove?

What questions would you like answered?

All discussions could begin with a general introductory question:

What point was unclear?

Choose conclusions in the chapter with which you agree, disagree, or are unsure, explaining your reasons.

What would you need to research in order to confirm or disprove the point made?

What do you think has been proven to be true?

What ramifications can you draw, both theological and practical?

What action should you and will you take?

How do you feel?

The questions for each chapter are organized around three categories: discussion starters, research questions, and appropriation questions. The quotations in the discussion starters are thought-provoking, outrageous, controversial, insightful, or inspirational. Their goal is simply to cause animated response. The introductory quotation preceding every chapter or even contemporary movies (such as "Yentl") or events can also be used in groups as discussion starters. Since one of the goals is to encourage study of primary texts, I have also included research questions. Often these topics can be studied before the pertinent chapter is read. Sometimes the research topics can be completed together by the group. In any chapter an interesting research activity might include finding and studying a footnote of Scripture references. I have suggested only research options which necessitate this book, a Bible, and Bible concordances. The appropriation questions aim to help the readers apply the findings from each chapter. Many of them are truly open-ended questions to which several answers may be possible.

All in all, I hope the discussions become lively dialogues in which thought, research, and action come together with respect and mercy.

1
Introduction
Equal in Eden

Discussion Starters

1. It is happiness that I want for Germany. I would like to put men back onto the land and women back into the home. It is not necessary that life should be so complicated (Adolf Hitler).
2. For in human beings the mind occupies the rank of the man, and the sensations that of the woman (Philo, *On The Creation of the World* LIX).
3. Eve was "prompted by a mind devoid of steadfastness and firm foundation" to eat the fruit (Philo, *On the Creation* LV [156]).
4. The king asked, "How he could live amicably with his wife?" and he answered, "By recognizing that womankind are by nature headstrong and energetic in the pursuit of their own desires, and subject to sudden changes of opinion through fallacious reasoning, and their nature is essentially weak" (The Letter of Aristeas 250).
5. Why did God command the women first?—Because they are prompt in the fulfillment of the commandments. Another explanation is: So that they should introduce their children to the study of the Torah. Rabbi Tahlifa of Caesarea said that God said: "When I created the world, I only commanded Adam first, and then Eve, too, was commanded, with the result that she transgressed and upset the world; if I do not now call unto the women first, they will nullify the Torah"; for this reason does it say, THUS SHALT THOU SAY TO THE HOUSE OF JACOB (Middrash Rabbah XXVIII on Exod. 19:3).

Research Question

Read the book of Genesis.

Appropriation Questions

1. "Scriptures are authoritative and reliable." Discuss.
2. "There is a foolish and a wise way to wisdom." Discuss.
3. Since "helpmate" signifies "help meet," do you find any value in using the word "helpmate"?
4. Are "helpers" inferior or superior to those they help?
5. Discuss how God's image is and can be reflected in marriage and single relationships.

2
The Torn Curtain

Discussion Starters

1. Rabbi 'Azariah in the name of Rabbi Judah ben R. Simon expounded: A parable will illustrate. To what may [the Tabernacle (Exod. 35:22)] be compared? To a mortal king who had a daughter whom he loved exceedingly. So long as his daughter was small he used to speak with her. When she grew up and attained to puberty the king said: "It befits not my daughter's dignity that I should hold converse with her in public. Make a pavilion for her so that when I wish to speak with my daughter I shall do so inside the pavilion. (Midrash Rabbah on Num. XII.4).
2. "Jesus was a feminist."
3. Jerome's advice to Laeta for her daughter:
   a. Let them seek [Paula] upon the world's highway amid the crowds and the throng of their kinsfolk, and let them find her nowhere but in the shrine of the scriptures, questioning the prophets and the apostles on the meaning of that spiritual marriage to which she is vowed (*Letter* CVII. 7).
   b. Let [Paula's] treasures be not silks or gems but manuscripts of the holy scriptures; and in these let her think less of gilding, and Babylonian parchment,

and arabesque patterns, than of correctness and accurate punctuation (*Letter* CVII. 12).

4. In May 1954 the United States Supreme Court outlawed segregated public schools, reversing the doctrine of "separate–but–equal." "Separate educational facilities are inherently unequal," the court ruled, and created "a feeling of inferiority" in Black students "that may affect their hearts and minds in a way unlikely ever to be undone" (Brown v. Board of Education).

Research Questions

1. Read one gospel paying attention to Jesus' interaction with women.

2. Find and show a layout of the temple in Jerusalem.

Appropriation Questions

1. In what ways are the first century Jewish prohibitions for women similar or different from contemporary Protestant expectations of women?

2. How would you receive a female President or Pope?

3. With whom do you more identify, Mary or Martha? Why?

4. Jesus teaches: "cut away totally the thorny vines which were choking the ancient tree." Discuss.

5. Discuss the significance of God's sanctuary being God's people.

3
The Altered Prayer

Discussion Starters

1. May I indeed never devote study and pains to anything of which I am not afterwards to be a guardian. Study or practice is a mean, a half-way stage, not a perfect final achievement. It is seen in souls that are not perfect, but bent on reaching the summit. Watching or guarding is something complete, consisting in entrusting to memory those principles of holy things which were acquired by practice. To do this is to commit a fair deposit

of knowledge to a trustworthy guardian, to her who alone makes light of the nets of forgetfulness with all their cunning devices. "Guardian" is therefore the sound and appropriate name which he gives to the man who remembers what he had learnt. At an earlier stage, when he was in training, this man was a pupil with another to teach him, but when he became capable of watching and guarding, he obtained the power and position of a teacher, and appointed for the subordinate duties under the teacher his own brother, the word of utterance: for it is said "his brother shall minister" (Numb. viii.26). Accordingly the mind of the truly noble man will be guardian and steward of the teachings of virtue, while his brother, utterance, will minister to those who are seeking education, going over with them the doctrines and principles of wisdom (Philo, *The Worse Attacks the Better* XIX [64-6]).

2. Strange remote soul of a man that could pierce into the very heavens and discern God with such certainty and never see the proud and lonely creature at his side! To him she was only a woman. Since those days when I saw all her nature dimmed I have hated Saint Paul with all my heart and so must all true women hate him, I think, because of what he has done in the past to women like Carie, proud free-born women, yet damned by their very womanhood. I rejoice for her sake that his power is gone in these new days (Pearl S. Buck about Carie, her mother, and Andrew, her father, in *The Exile* [New York: Reynal & Hitchcock, 1936], pp. 358-9.)

3. You can turn out people in any shape you like, but it's easier to influence men than women. Kitchens and nurseries are a pretty solid background. Get men away from women and you can make them into machines. They won't think and they'll feel exactly the way you want. But you mustn't let them know it! (Dr. Goebbels, propagandist for Hitler's regime, cited by Rosita Forbes, *These Men I Knew*, [New York: E. P. Dutton, 1940], p. 59).

Research Questions

1. Read Galatians.

2. Read 1 and 2 Timothy. What can you learn about the people and their problems and assets? Do you know of a comparable situation?

Appropriation Questions

1. Silence is: "a state of calm, restraint at the proper time, respect, and affirmation of a speaker." How can you apply this principle to your own life?

2. If the Greek term *huios* signifies "son" or "descendant" and *anthropos* signifies "human" or "person," could Jesus be called the "Descendant of Humanity"?

3. Women's role as homemaker is not their first priority; rather, it is to learn the full knowledge of God's truth "in silence" as the men. Do you agree? Discuss the application.

4. What denotations and connotations do you have for orthodox and heterodox (or different) doctrine?

5. Do you ever exhibit a domination which destroys? How can you avoid it?

6. Discuss Jesus' saying, "A disciple is not above the teacher, but being instructed all will be as their teacher" (Luke 6:40) in light of the question, "Are women to be students who never graduate?"

7. What man in the Bible is like Eve in that he transgressed because of deception? Abimelech or Pharaoh (Gen. 20:12)?

8. Do you think sincere Christians should disagree on the interpretation of specific Bible passages? To what extent can people disagree with your own interpretation and you still appreciate them as family?

4
First Apostles, Second Prophets, Third Teachers

Discussion Starters

1. Vibia Perpetua was arrested in Carthage during the persecution by Septimus Severus in AD 202-03. She said:

While I was still with the police authorities my father out of love for me tried to dissuade me from my resolution. "Father," I said, "do you see here, for example, this vase, or pitcher, or whatever it is?" "I see it," he said. "Can it be named anything else than what it really is?" I asked, and he said, "No."

'So I also cannot be called anything else than what I am, a Christian" (*The Martyrdom of Perpetua* 3).

2. "Many women have received power through the grace of God and have performed many deeds of manly valour" (1 Clement to the Corinthians 55.3). Clement was the third or fourth bishop of Rome at the end of the first century.

3. Now, my most religious and industrious Ambrose and my most honest and manly Tatiana, from whom I vow womanish things, have vanished just as they did from Sarah (cf. Gen. 18:11) (Origen, *On Prayer* II.1).

4. "The Tyranny of the 'Ship' ": The day that *kephale* or "head" became Headship was a sad day indeed. From a simple metaphor or simile, Headship has become the antidote for all of society's ills. "Head" has merely one syllable. It certainly sounds to the point, crisp, firm. But "Headship" is so much better—*two* syllables. The "shh" sound is akin to the preacher's intonations, a bastion and a foundation and a hierarchy. "Headship" is a principle now, no longer an individual, a principle which ties together all of life—"Headship."

5. "A Gift of Sight: A Christmas Fable," a fictional story published by *Daughters of Sarah* 2 (November, 1976), 8-9.

It was the best Christmas gift that I have ever received and, perhaps, will ever receive. I suppose that I have journeyed through about the same number of bleak and empty Christmases as you have, dirty rain-spattered evenings when the shining strength of faith alone makes the heart glad. This one I sat alone as happens at times to us who have not taken or been taken in marriage. I had my memories as we all do. And these were sweet and bittersweet. You know how they are. It should have been a joyful Christmas for it was on a Monday night, and Sunday had given me candlelight and choirs, and their loveliness nearly drowned out the usual tired message about "Christmas/Easter Christians."

What marred it was Freddy hitting Artie on the nose. Of course, Artie probably jabbed Freddy first with his elbow which is his way. He has been a noted elbower since the second grade. Mary had been whining and Rhonda sick and Freddy and Sammy began to pester Chloe, who shoved Sammy, and while I was separating them, I suppose Artie did his famous elbow performance on Freddy, who I had in one hand beside me while with the other I was parting Sammy and Chloe, for Freddy squealed and squirmed out of my grasp and let Artie have it point-blank. Well, then there was a furor, and Ms. Matthews left her class and helped me calm it all down, taking Freddy in custody so I could conduct Artie to the kitchen and wash him off. When I came back Rhonda had thrown up and Chloe was crying and Sammy was gone. Freddy was giggling and holding his nose, and that imp Artie began to giggle, too. And it was only 10:30. I had 15 minutes more to atone, I guess, for my sins. The lesson had completely broken down. The spirit of the day was in shambles.

Ms. Punumba, the Superintendent, said not to be sad or upset about it, these things happened. But still I came home and cried a little. I suppose I want to be a success, so it is probable that my pride was hurt. Still, it had disgraced the sanctity and nobility of the day. The children were so small-minded, not merely childlike but childish-puerile in the worst sense, nasty little beasts, perverse as children sometimes are—seemingly more perverse on this day than on others.

So it was with discouragement that I faced what was to prove a further disappointment. Christmas day dragged on with its wearying drizzle, never raining hard, until the night came murking up all but the heavy, polluted smell that the city has on a close night.

I took myself to bed thanking God that this was not all I could expect from life. And so I went to sleep.

And what about the gift I mentioned? Christmas had come and gone—ragged and dulled and empty.

The gift came that night in a dream.

One moment I was in my bed and the next I was on a broad highway in a beautiful valley. The sun was in my eyes, bright all around. I was travelling and a beautiful strong woman was beside me, keeping pace.

I did not feel the need to speak and instead let the wonder of the place enchant me. We traveled on we two silent companions. And she with graceful step was in every way the definition of an Amazon. She was lithe, tall, with silver hair caught back for working or for war. She held a stave not for support and strode like a strong gazelle—a warrior queen. At last upon a gentle rise we stopped and saw across a placid sea an alabaster temple set with emerald, ruby, azure, and pearl. There were beautiful youths about the steps, an obvious guard, women and men together, themselves lithe limbed and mighty.

At last the Queen spoke. "Gaze long, Virginia. This is why you were summoned."

"Why?" I asked faltering.

"To gaze on them."

"They are beautiful."

"Not so. They are ugly, nasty, and brutish. It is the love of the God who bore them that is beautiful and has made them beautiful. Do you see that woman near the last pillar?"

"Yes, she is so lovely."

"Her name is Rhonda...."

I felt faint.

"...and Chloe and Samuel."

I turned to her in shock.

"Do you know me, Virginia?"

"No...I...."

"I am you in the sight of God."

I awoke and sat up in the close night. I was crying now—for joy. These children—myself—there was a meaning in our struggle. Beyond the veil of failing human sight a vision saw what we would be with the bright, clear sight of the Father of lights. Praise God.

Research Questions

1. Read 1 and 2 Corinthians and study the problems and assets of the Corinthians.

2. In Young's, New Strong's, or the Englishman's Concordance find all the Bible references to:

    a. "head" (*kephale* and its Hebrew counterparts) and see how *kephale* is used.

    b. "hands, place hands on" referring to "ordination."
What do you learn?

3. Study women or a couple not mentioned in chapter 4, such as Mary, Elizabeth, Sarah, or Rebekah. In what ways are they exemplary persons or leaders?

Appropriation Questions

1. Look at the lists of gifts in 1 Corinthians 12:8-10, 28-30, Romans 12:6-8, and Ephesians 4:11. What gift(s) might God have given you? What gift do you think another person in the group has?

2. Authority is legitimate power (to command, act, enforce obedience, or make final decisions) and definitive explanation or interpretation. To what extent do Christians, the Bible, and God have "authority"? What is an authoritative style and how does it differ from authority?

3. Do you think yesterday's overseer was the equivalent of today's "head pastor"?

4. Compare and contrast the ministering structure described in chapter 4 with your denominational structure.

5
The Full Vision

Discussion Starters

1. In the essay "Priestesses in the Church?" C. S. Lewis concludes: "Only one wearing the masculine uniform can (provisionally, and till the *Parousia*) represent the Lord to the church: for we are all, corporately and individually, feminine to Him."
   He says a priest is: "a double representative, who represents us to God and God to us." Women can speak "to God for us" but they cannot "speak to us for God," because "a good woman may be like God, but God is not like a good woman" (*God in the Dock: Essays on Theology and Ethics*, ed. Walter Hooper [Grand Rapids, Eerdmans, 1970], pp. 236-39.)

2. To us infants, who drink the milk of the Word of the heavens, Christ Himself is food. Hence seeking is called sucking; for to those babes that seek the Word, the Father's breasts of love supply milk (Clement of Alexandria, *The Instructor* 1.6).

3. "At the summit I saw an immense garden, in the center of which sat a tall, grey-haired man dressed like a shepherd, milking sheep" (Perpetua's vision in *The Martyrdom of Perpetua* 4).

4. All the beauty of the cavern, yes, of all [Curdie] knew of the whole creation, seemed gathered in one centre of harmony and loveliness in the person of the ancient

lady who stood before him in the very summer of beauty and strength" (George MacDonald, *The Princess and Curdie*, ch. 6 "The Emerald").

Research Questions

1. Read one book of the Bible such as Isaiah, Psalms, Revelation, or John. Tally the images of God which are clearly from females, males, either, or other. An image is something that represents something else. It includes metaphor, simile, personification, and, sometimes, synecdoche.

2. The reign of heaven is like leaven which a woman took and hid in flour until it was all leavened (Matt. 13:33). In light of Matthew 13, is the woman an image of God or of something else?

Appropriation Questions

1. What is the benefit and danger of employing images to describe God? To what extent do you use adjectives or acts in history or images to describe God? Do you have your own mental image of God?

2. If God employs feminine images for self-description:
   a. Should we be free to coin new feminine metaphors to describe God?
   b. Can God be called "She" as well as "He," heavenly "Parent" or "Mother" as well as "Father"?

3. Must God be masculine for you to be saved?

4. Do the feminine images in Chapter 5 show God's immanence or transcendance or both? How do they compare with masculine images for God?

5. What is your picture, if any, of femininity and masculinity?

Conclusion and Afterword

Discussion Starters

1. "The good news is supposed to be a proclamation of freedom for the captives. Some theologians have made it into a handbook for the guards. So the captives revolted and

rejected the bad news that was presented to them in place of the good news."

2. All happy homes run on mutual respect and mutual service.

3. "In Defense of The First Church of Tootsie," a fictional satire we published in *The Wittenburg Door* 72 (April-May, 1983), 26-27:

Our Church got started when several disgruntled pastors got together and shared their concern and their disappointment that splinter groups aren't going far enough. It's a fine move to split off from the ecclesiastical mainline to insure that women won't get into any of our pulpits, they argued, but present splinter church policies are mere shilly shallying. Why just insure women will be kept off all the ruling boards and out of the pulpit? Why not insure they will be definitely out of the Sunday School as well where they can't subvert all those tender little minds?

I don't remember who first recommended our new denomination, but the "Church of Tootsie" has been going along quite well now for several months.

A lot of liberals have been complaining because we don't allow women in our services, but as usual we're being flagrantly misrepresented. Women and Women's Concerns are fully represented in all our meetings. Just the way they did it in Shakespeare's time when women weren't allowed to act in the theatre, we men take turns portraying women with surprisingly effective results. What the liberals fail to understand is our consistency here.

Most people agree that Paul's explanation for women keeping silent in the church is that they can ask their husbands what happened when they get home. So, that's our basis for action. We let them stay home, and when their husbands return, they can ask what happened. Of course, none of them have asked yet, but they will, they will, especially when they get reconciled to our new obedience to a truly biblical stance. And you know, since they haven't been coming, it's amazing how much agreement we've had in church among all the boys. And this is just one of many fine reasons that commend our system.

After all, when women are present they invariably distract men to lustful thoughts. In addition, when references are made to God as a mother, mother hen, woman in labor, woman looking for a lost coin in the Bible, that's just figurative language. When Jesus and God are portrayed in the Scriptures as Males (Warrior, King, Father, Shepherd) that's literal. Besides, all the disciples were male. As for the other so-called biblical data, Phoebe could not be a minister because she was a woman. Junia couldn't be a woman because she was an apostle. The Elect Lady must be a Church because she couldn't be a lady. Stephana couldn't be a woman because people were subjected to her. Anna was a profitess (merchant?) and certainly not a prophet. Prisca of Priscilla and Aquila couldn't be a woman because she instructed Apollos. This last example calls for some careful exegesis. There are obviously two Priscillas here. The Prisca in the latter part of Acts 18 must be Aquila's brother who helped instruct Apollos. The second Priscilla mentioned in the former part of Acts 18 we are told is his wife, and her name is only listed first because the Gentiles (like author Luke) loved to mention people in reverse alphabetical order—as we see conclusively from this example here.

Really, women belong in the home and their sphere of influence should be curtailed to the family. Women are passive and emotional and think with the left side of the brain. A conclusive case for their unsuitability can be drawn from the example of women's suffrage. Ever since women have gotten the vote, they tend invariably to cast ballots cancelling out their husband's vote. We should take a sharp lesson from this!

In the light of these reasons, all the men present overwhelmingly agreed that the actions we took are totally logical. But for these brave steps we have been continually persecuted.

The conservatives have charged us with "dressing in drag." This is utterly false! What we *are* doing is maintaining our witness to the world. The unsaved wouldn't understand a Church moving on its principles and having only men attend, so we maintain our appearances as a witness to the community. I dress up as a female character I created every other Sunday. Assistant Pastor Johnny Adonis does his every second and fourth Sunday. Deacon Hank Narcissus and his guys handle the first and fourth, and Harry Jock dons his nylons every fifth Sunday and at all special services. Despite the attacks in the Church press, this *has not* damaged our ministry. The only part of our work that has had to be curtailed for the time being is our prison ministry. The inmates complained they "had enough of that in here without bringing it in from the outside."

But we're hoping that new laws will pass that we can take advantage of. After all, why should the legal aid types only help well-publicized weirdos when we obviously need help, too? With their clout, they'll make sure nobody keeps us out of prison!

Now I'd like to turn the tables on our critics. You so-called conservatives who feel it's not right women should preach or serve on the boards of elders and deacons are just a bunch of hypocrites. You allow them to run all the offices, all day-to-day Church business, fill up most of the constituency, sing in the service, and even discharge most of the teaching duties, even instructing all the future preachers of the Church! You might as well let 'em run the rest of the Church as well. For all our faults, we're at least consistent. We stand on our principle. If God had wanted women to be preachers and teachers and Pioneer Girls, He would have made them men!

Research Questions

Summarize all the principles for effective relationships in the afterword.

Appropriation Questions

1. What is your own history? How did you come to the place you are, as a woman or man in the church or society?

2. How can you avoid acrimonious debate and encourage respectful communication?

3. Can Christ be portrayed as black, oriental, Indian, female, white, or other?

4. In order "to share the same tasks" and "to do that as equals," go over actual and ideal division of household responsibilities.

5. "Built into our definition is limitation." How is such knowledge freeing and Christian?

6. The church can be a fragmenter for pastors and parishioners. Discuss how the church fragments and what can be done about it. How would you picture an ideal church where women and men and children all can minister together? What is the first step you can take to accomplish it?

7. How can you balance limiting an overextended schedule and responding to genuine needs?

8. "It's the little things that are killing us." What little things are killing you? How can you end that death?

9. Discuss the viability of employment "success" being evaluated by the quality of work accomplished rather than the hours of work completed. How can women and men be effective in their employment and in their homes?

10. What do you understand to be the "traditional" model

of parenting and homemaking? What do you think is essential for effective parents and teachers?

11. "Who one is rather than what one does defines identity." Do you agree? Compare to faith (e.g., James 2:17-26).

12. Are you willing to be oppressed because of association with and support of the oppressed?

13. "Where the text leads we have to follow." What does the Bible lead you to do?

Bibliography

Works Cited

Primary References

Alden, Raymond M., ed. *Readings in English Prose of the Nineteenth Century*. New York: Houghton Mifflin, 1917.

Bauer, Walter. *A Greek-English Lexicon of the New Testament and Other Early Christian Literature*. trans. W. F. Arndt and F. W. Gingrich. Chicago: University of Chicago, 1957.

Blass, F. and A. De Brunner. *A Greek Grammer of the New Testament and Other Early Christian Literature*. Oxford: Clarendon, 1907.

Boeckhius, Augustus, ed. *Corpus Inscriptionum Graecarum*. 4 vols. Berolini: Academica, 1828.

Brown, Francis, S. R. Driver and Charles A. Briggs. *A Hebrew and English Lexicon of the Old Testament*. trans. Edward Robinson. Oxford: Clarendon, 1907.

Butler, H. E., trans. *The Institutio Oratoria of Quintilian*. 4 vols. Loeb Classical Library. Cambridge: Harvard University, 1921.

Charles, R. H., ed. *The Apocrypha and Pseudepigrapha of the Old Testament in English*. 2 vols. Oxford: Clarendon, 1913.

Cohen, A., trans. *The Minor Tractates of the Talmud*. 2 vols. London: Soncino, 1965.

Colson, F. H. and J. W. Earp, trans. *Philo.* Loeb Classical Library. Cambridge: Harvard University, 1929, 1962.

Danby, Herbert, trans. *The Mishnah.* Oxford: Oxford University, 1933.

Dupont-Sommer, A. *The Essene Writings from Qumran,* trans. G. Vermes. 2d ed. Gloucester: Peter Smith, 1973.

Epstein, I., ed. *The Babylonian Talmud.* 35 vols. London: Soncino, 1948.

Feldman, Louis H. and H. St. J. Thackeray, trans. *Josephus.* Loeb Classical Library. 10 vols. Cambridge: Harvard University, 1926-7, 1934.

Freedman, H. and M. Simon, eds., trans. *Midrash Rabbah.* 5 vols. London: Soncino, 1939.

Hatch, Edwin and Henry A. Redpath. *A Concordance to the Septuagint.* 3 vols. Oxford: Clarendon, 1897.

Kilburn, K., trans. *Lucian.* 8 vols. Loeb Classical Library. Cambridge: Harvard University, 1959.

Lake, Kirsopp, trans. *The Apostolic Fathers.* 2 vols. Loeb Classical Library. Cambridge: Harvard University, 1912.

LeSaint, William P., trans. *Tertullian: Treatises on Marriage and Remarriage.* Ancient Christian Writers. Westminster: Newman, 1956.

Liddell, Henry George and Robert Scott. *A Greek-English Lexicon.* eds. Henry S. Jones and Roderick McKenzie. 9th ed. Oxford: Clarendon, 1968.

Milne, J. P., ed. *Patrologia Graeca.* 161 vols. Paris: 1857-66.

Moulton, James Hope and George Milligan. *The Vocabulary of the Greek Testament: Illustrated from the Papyri and other Non-Literary Sources.* Grand Rapids: Eerdmans, 1930.

Radice, Betty, trans. *Pliny: Letters & Panegyricus.* Loeb Classical Library. 2 vols. Cambridge: Harvard University, 1926-7, 1934.

Roberts, Alexander and James Donaldson, eds. *The Ante-Nicene Fathers.* 10 vols. Grand Rapids: Eerdmans, 1885 [1979].

Robertson, A.T. *A Grammar of the Greek New Testament in*

the Light of Historical Research. Nashville: Broadman, 1934.

Schaff, Philip, and Henry Wace, eds. *A Select Library of the Nicene and Post-Nicene Fathers of The Christian Church.* 14 vols. Grand Rapids: Eerdmans, 1979 [1892].

The Septuagint Version of the Old Testament and Apocrypha. London: Samuel Bagster, [n.d.].

Smith, Joseph P. *St. Irenaeus: Proof of the Apostolic Preaching.* Ancient Christian Writers. Westminster: Newman, 1952.

Thayer, Joseph Henry. *Thayer's Greek-English Lexicon of the New Testament.* 2d ed. Marshallton: National Foundation for Christian Education, 1889.

Secondary References

Aaseng, Rolf E. "Male and Female Created He Them." *Christianity Today,* Nov. 20, 1970, 5-6.

Banks, Robert J. *Paul's Idea of Community: The Early House Churches in Their Historical Setting.* Grand Rapids: Eerdmans, 1980.

Bloesch, Donald G. *Is the Bible Sexist? Beyond Feminism and Patriarchalism.* Westchester: Crossway, 1982.

Brooke, A. E. *A Critical and Exegetical Commentary on the Johannine Epistles.* The International Critical Commentary. Edinburgh: T. & T. Clark, 1912.

Cohen, A. *Everyman's Talmud.* New York: E. P. Dutton, 1949.

Drazin, Nathan. *History of Jewish Education from 515 B.C.E. to 220 C. E. (During the Periods of the Second Commonwealth and the Tannaim).* Baltimore: Johns Hopkins, 1940.

Ellis, E. Earle. "Paul and His Co-Workers." *New Testament Studies* 17 (July, 1971): 437-52.

Evans, Mary J. *Woman in the Bible: An Overview of all the Crucial Passages on Women's Roles.* Downers Grove: InterVarsity, 1983.

Foh, Susan. "What is the Woman's Desire?" *Westminster Theological Journal* 37 (Spring, 1975): 376-83.

Forbes, Rosita. *These Men I Knew.* New York: Dutton, 1940.

Freedman, R. David. "Woman, A Power Equal to Man: Translation of Woman as a 'Fit Helpmate' for Man is Questioned." *Biblical Archaeology Review* 9 (January/February, 1983): 56-8.

Gordon, A. J. "The Ministry of Women." *Missionary Review of the World,* 7 (December, 1894), 910-21. Reprinted in *Theology, News and Notes* (June, 1975): 5-8.

Gray, G. B. *A Critical and Exegetical Commentary on The Book of Isaiah.* 2 vols. The International Critical Commentary. Edinburgh: T. & T. Clark, 1912.

Groves, Richard. "Conservatives Dominate Southern Baptist Meeting." *The Christian Century,* July 18-25, 1984, 701-03.

Gundry, Patricia. *Woman Be Free! Free to be God's Woman.* Grand Rapids: Zondervan, 1977.

Hefele, Charles Joseph. *A History of the Councils of the Church, from the Original Documents.* trans., ed. Henry Nutcombe Oxenhan. 4 vols. Edinburgh: T. & T. Clark, 1876.

Howe, E. Margaret. *Women and Church Leadership.* Contemporary Evangelical Perspectives. Grand Rapids: Zondervan, 1982.

Hurley, James B. *Man and Woman in Biblical Perspective.* Contemporary Evangelical Perspectives. Grand Rapids: Zondervan, 1981.

Jeremias, Joachim. *Jerusalem in the Time of Jesus: An Investigation into Economic and Social Conditions During the New Testament Period.* trans. F. H. and C. H. Cave. 3d ed. Philadelphia: Fortress, 1969.

Kemelman, Harry. *Thursday the Rabbi Walked Out.* New York: Fawcett/Crest, 1978.

Kroeger, Catherine C. "Ancient Heresies and a Strange Greek Verb." *The Reformed Journal* 29 (March, 1979): 12-15.

Lacks, Roslyn. *Women and Judaism: Myth, History, and Struggle.* Garden City: Doubleday, 1979.

Leitch, Elisabeth Elliot. "Called to be Liberated Women." *The Christian Reader,* November/December, 1975, 42-51.

Leonard, Bill J. "Forgiving Eve." *The Christian Century,* Nov. 7, 1984, 1038-40.

Lewis, Clive Staples. *God in the Dock: Essays on Theology and Ethics,* ed. Walter Hooper. Grand Rapids: Eerdmans, 1970.

Lock, Walter. *A Critical and Exegetical Commentary on The Pastoral Epistles.* The International Critical Commentary. Edinburgh: T. & T. Clark, 1924.

McKenna, Mary Lawrence. *Women of the Church: Role and Renewal.* New York: P. J. Kenedy, 1967.

Madsen, Paul O., ed. *Leaven: An Interpretative Volume Originating in the American Baptist Convocation on The Mission of the Church.* Valley Forge: American Baptist Home Mission Societies, 1962.

Mattingly, Harold. *The Man in the Roman Street.* New York: W. W. Norton, 1966.

Meeks, Wayne A. "The Image of the Androgyne: Some Uses of a Symbol in Earliest Christianity." *History of Religions* 13 (February, 1974): 165-208.

Mollenkott, Virginia Ramey. *The Divine Feminine: The Biblical Imagery of God as Female.* New York: Crossroad, 1983.

—*Women, Men, and the Bible.* Nashville: Abingdon, 1977.

Moo, Douglas J. "1 Timothy 2:11-15: Meaning and Significance." *Trinity Journal* 1 (Spring, 1980): 62-83.

Morris, Joan. *The Lady Was a Bishop: The Hidden History of Women with Clerical Ordination and the Jurisdiction of Bishops.* New York: Macmillan, 1973.

Osman, Karen. "PMS Versus the Curse." *Daughters of Sarah* May/June, 1985, 16-17.

Patterson, Ronald P., ed. *The Book of Discipline of the United Methodist Church 1980.* Nashville: United Methodist Publishing, 1980.

Plaskow, Judith. *Sex, Sin, and Grace: Women's Experience and the Theologies of Reinhold Niebuhr and Paul*

Tillich. New York: University Press of America, 1980.

Safrai, S. and M. Stern, eds. *The Jewish People in the First Century: Historical Geography, Political History, Social, Cultural and Religious Life and Institutions.* Compendia Rerum Iudaicarum ad Novum Testamentum, Section 1. Philadelphia: Fortress, 1974.

Sanday, William and Arthur C. Headlam. *A Critical and Exegetical Commentary on The Epistle to the Romans.* The International Critical Commentary. 5th ed. Edinburgh: T. & T. Clark, 1902.

Scanzoni, Letha and Nancy Hardesty. *All We're Meant to Be: A Biblical Approach to Women's Liberation.* Waco: Word, 1974.

Scholer, David. "Women's Adornment: Some Historical and Hermeneutical Observations on the New Testament Passages." *Daughters of Sarah 6,* January/February, 1980, 3-6.

Shideler, Mary McDermott. *The Theology of Romantic Love: A Study in the Writings of Charles Williams.* Grand Rapids: Eerdmans, 1962.

Skinner, John. *A Critical and Exegetical Commentary on Genesis.* The International Critical Commentary. 2d ed. Edinburgh: T. & T. Clark, 1930.

Spencer, Aida Dina Besançon. "Eve at Ephesus: Should women be ordained as pastors according to The First Letter to Timothy?" *Journal of the Evangelical Theological Society* 17 (Fall, 1974): 215-22.

—*Paul's Literary Style: A Stylistic and Historical Comparison of II Corinthians 11:16-12:13, Romans 8:9-39, and Philippians 3:2-4:13.* An Evangelical Theological Society Monograph. Winona Lake: Eisenbrauns, 1984.

Spencer, William David and Aida Besançon Spencer. "In Defense of the First Church of Tootsie." *The Wittenburg Door* April/May, 1983, 26-7.

Stendahl, Krister. *The Bible and the Role of Women: A Case Study in Hermeneutics,* trans. Emilie T. Sander. Biblical Series, No. 15. Philadelphia: Fortress, 1966.

Swidler, Leonard. *Biblical Affirmations of Woman.* Philadelphia: Westminster, 1979.

—*Women in Judaism: The Status of Women in Formative Judaism.* Metuchen: Scarecrow, 1976.

Swidler, Leonard and Arlene Swidler. *Women Priests: A Catholic Commentary on the Vatican Declaration* New York: Paulist, 1977.

Tetlow, Elizabeth M. *Women and Ministry in the New Testament: Called to Serve.* New York: Paulist, 1980. Reprinted by Lanham: University Press of America, 1980.

Tucker, Ruth. *From Jerusalem to Irian Jaya: A Biographical History of Christian Missions.* Academie Books. Grand Rapids: Zondervan, 1983.

Additional Bibliography

Historical Studies, First-Century Background

Balsdon, J.V.D. *Roman Women: Their History and Habits.* New York: Barnes and Noble, 1962.

—*The Romans.* New York: Basic, 1965.

Brooten, Bernadette J. *Women Leaders in the Ancient Synagogue: Inscriptional Evidence and Background Issues.* Chico: Scholars, 1982.

Bruns, J. Edgar. *God as Woman, Woman as God.* New York: Paulist, 1973.

Cary, Max and T. J. Haarhoff. *Life and Thought in the Greek and Roman World.* London: Methuen, 1961.

Daube, David. *The Duty of Procreation.* Edinburgh: University, 1977.

Fowler, W. Warde. *Social Life At Rome in the Age of Cicero.* New York: Macmillan, 1924.

Goodwater, Leanna. *Women in Antiquity: An Annotated Bibliography.* Metuchen, N.J.: Scarecrow, 1975.

Lefkowitz, Mary F. and Maureen B. Fant. *Women's Life in Greece and Rome. A Source Book in Translation.* Baltimore: Johns Hopkins, 1982.

Macurdy, Grace H. *Hellenistic Queens: A Study of Woman-power in Macedonia, Seleucid Syria, and Ptolemaic Egypt.* The John Hopkins University Studies in

Archaeology, 14. Chicago: Argonaut, 1932.

Michel, O., ed., and others. *Studies on the Jewish Background of the New Testament.* Assen: Van Gorum, 1969.

Neusner, Jacob. *A History of the Mishnaic Law of Women.* Studies in Judaism in Late Antiquity, Vol. 33, Part 5. Leiden: E. J. Brill, 1980.

Pomeroy, Sarah B. *Goddesses, Whores, Wives, and Slaves: Women in Classical Antiquity.* New York: Schocken, 1975.

Schuerer, Emil. *The History of the Jewish People in the Age of Jesus Christ.(175 B.C.-A.D. 135).* eds. Geza Vermes, Fergus Millar, and Matthew Black. 2 vols. 2d ed. Edinburgh: T. & T. Clark, 1973-9.

Seibert, Ilse. *Woman in Ancient Near East.* trans. M. Herzfeld. London: George Prior, 1974.

Zinserling, Verena. *Women in Greece and Rome.* New York: Abner Schram, 1972.

Biblical/Theological Studies (Ministry and Marriage)

Baker, William P. *Women and the Liberator.* Old Tappan: Revell, 1972.

Bennett, Anne McCrew. "The God of Miriam, Deborah, and Huldah." *Right On 7,* September, 1975, 9.

Bilezikian, Gilbert G. *Beyond Sex Roles: A Guide for the Study of Female Roles in the Bible.* Grand Rapids: Baker, 1985. [Includes extensive bibliography compiled by Alan F. Johnson].

Boldrey, Richard and Joyce Boldrey. *Chauvinist or Feminist? Paul's View of Women.* Grand Rapids: Baker, 1976.

Brown, Antoinette. "Exegesis of 1 Corinthians XIV, 34, 35; and 1 Timothy II, 11, 12." *Oberlin Quarterly Review* 3 (July, 1849): 358-73.

Bushnell, Katharine C. *God's Word to Women: One Hundred Bible Studies on Woman's Place in the Divine Economy.* North Collins, N.Y.: Ray B. Munson, 1923.

Christian Reformed Church. *Agenda for Synod 1984.* Grand Rapids: Board of Publications, 1984.

Clark, Stephen B. *Man and Woman in Christ: An Exami-*

nation of the Roles of Men and Women in Light of Scripture and the Social Sciences. Ann Arbor: Servant, 1980.

Davis, John Jefferson. "Some Reflections on Galatians 3:28, Sexual Roles, and Biblical Hermeneutics." *Journal of the Evangelical Theological Society* 19 (Summer, 1976): 201-8.

Deen, Edith. *All of the Women of the Bible.* New York: Harper and Brothers, 1955.

Faxon, Alicia Craig. *Women and Jesus.* Philadelphia: United Church, 1973.

Fiorenza, Elisabeth Schuessler. *In Memory of Her: A Feminist Theological Reconstruction of Christian Origins.* New York: Crossroad, 1983.

Foh, Susan. *Women and the Word of God: A Response to Biblical Feminism.* Grand Rapids: Baker, 1981.

Ford, J. Massyngberde. "Biblical Material Relevant to the Ordination of Women." *Journal of Ecumenical Studies,* 10 (Fall, 1973): 669-99.

Gerstner, John and David Scholer. *Is Women's Ordination Unbiblical?* Hamilton, M.A.: Current Affairs Committee, Gordon-Conwell, 1980.

Giles, Kevin. *Women & Their Ministry: A Case for Equal Ministries in the Church Today.* Victoria, Australia: Dove Communications, 1977.

Graebner, Alan. *After Eve: The New Feminism.* Minneapolis: Augsburg, 1972.

Hoppin, Ruth. *Priscilla: Author of the Epistle to the Hebrews and Other Essays.* New York: Exposition, 1969.

Hosie, Lady. *Jesus and Woman: Being a Study of the Four Gospels with Special Reference to the Attitude of the Man, Jesus Christ Towards Women.* London: Hodder and Stoughton, 1946.

Hurley, James B. "Did Paul Require Veils or the Silence of Women? A Consideration of 1 Cor. 11:2-16 and 1 Cor. 14:33b-36." *Westminster Theological Journal* 35 (Winter, 1973): 190-220.

Jewett, Paul K. *Man as Male and Female.* Grand Rapids: Eerdmans, 1975.

Karssen, Gien. *Her Name Is Woman.* Colorado Springs: NavPress, 1975.

Knight, George W. III. *The New Testament Teaching on the Role Relationship of Men and Women.* Grand Rapids: Baker, 1977.

Kroeger, Catherine and Richard. "May Women Teach? Heresy in the Pastoral Epistles." *The Reformed Journal* 30 (October, 1980): 14-18.

Lockyer, Herbert. *All the Women of the Bible.* Grand Rapids: Zondervan, 1965.

Mason, Maggie. *Women Like Us: Learn More About Yourself Through Studies of Bible Women.* Waco: Word, 1978.

Mercadante, Linda. *From Hierarchy to Equality: A Comparison of Past and Present Interpretations of 1 Cor. 11:2-16 in Relation to the Changing Status of Women in Society.* Vancouver: G-M-H, 1978.

Mollenkott, Virginia Ramey. "Women and the Bible: A Challenge to Male Interpretation." *Sojourners,* February, 1976, 20-25.

Moo, Douglas J. "The Interpretation of 1 Timothy 2:11-15: A Rejoinder." *Trinity Journal* 2 (Fall, 1981): 198-222.

Nunnally-Cox, Janice. *Foremothers: Women of the Bible.* New York: Seabury, 1981.

Otwell, John H. *And Sarah Laughed: The Status of Women in the Old Testament.* Philadelphia: Westminster, 1977.

Payne, Philip B. "Libertarian Women in Ephesus: A Response to Douglas J. Moo's Article, '1 Timothy 2:11-15: Meaning and Significance,' " *Trinity Journal* 2 (Fall, 1981): 169-97.

Penn-Lewis, Jessie. *The Magna Charta of Women.* Minneapolis: Bethany, 1975.

Prohl, Russell C. *Woman in the Church: A Restudy of Woman's Place in Building The Kingdom.* Grand Rapids: Eerdmans, 1957.

Relk, Theodore. *The Creation of Women.* N.Y.: McGraw Hill, 1973.

Roberts, Mark D. "Woman Shall be Saved: A Closer Look at 1 Timothy 2:15." *Theological Students Fellowship Bulletin,* November/December, 1981.

Schneiders, S. M. "Women in the Fourth Gospel and the Role of Women in the Contemporary Church." *Biblical Theological Bulletin* 12 (1982): 35-45.

Scholer, David M. "Exegesis: 1 Timothy 2:8-15." *Daughters of Sarah,* May/June, 1975, 7-8.

— "Women in Ministry." *The Covenant Companion,* Dec. 1, 1983; Dec. 15, 1983; Jan. 1, 1984; Feb., 1984.

Siddons, Philip. *Speaking Out For Women: A Biblical View.* Valley Forge: Judson, 1980.

Sigountos, James G. and Myron Shank. "Public Roles for Women in the Pauline Church: A Reappraisal of the Evidence." *Journal of the Evangelical Theological Society* 26 (September, 1983): 283-95.

Spencer, Aida Besançon. "Equal in Eden." *Free Indeed 1,* October/November, 1978, 23-4.

— "Paul, Our Friend and Champion." *Daughters of Sarah* 2, May, 1976, 1-3.

Spencer, William David. "Equaling Eden," *Free Indeed,* October/November, 1978, 25-7.

Stagg, Evelyn and Frank Stagg. *Woman in the World of Jesus.* Philadelphia: Westminster, 1978.

Starr, Lee Anna. *The Bible Status of Woman.* New York: Fleming H. Revell, 1926.

Swidler, Leonard. "Jesus Was a Feminist." *South East Asia Journal of Theology* 13 (1, 1971): 102-10. Also in *Catholic World* 212 (January, 1971): 177-83.

Thrall, M.E. *The Ordination of Women to the Priesthood: A Study of the Biblical Evidence.* Studies in Ministry and Worship, 7. London: SCM, 1958.

Trible, Phyllis. *God and the Rhetoric of Sexuality.* Philadelphia: Fortress, 1978.

— *Texts of Terror: Literary-Feminist Readings of Biblical Narratives.* Overtures in Biblical Theology. Philadelphia: Fortress, 1984.

Wahlberg, Rachel Conrad. *Jesus According to a Woman.* New York: Paulist, 1975.

—*Jesus and the Freed Woman.* New York: Paulist, 1978.

Warkentin, Marjorie. *Ordination: A Biblical-Historical View.* Grand Rapids: Eerdmans, 1982.

Willard, Frances E. *Woman in the Pulpit.* Washington: Zenger, 1889 [1976].

Williams, Don. *The Apostle Paul and Women in the Church.* Glendale: Regal, 1977.

Witherington, Ben. *Women in the Ministry of Jesus: A Study of Jesus' Attitudes to Women and Their Roles as Reflected in His Earthly Life.* Society for New Testament Studies, Monograph 51. New York: Cambridge University, 1984.

Theological/Historical Studies

Bainton, Roland H. *Women in the Reformation.* 3 vols. Minneapolis: Augsburg, 1971, 1973, 1977.

Beaver, R. Pierce. *American Protestant Women in World Mission: A History of the First Feminist Movement in North America.* (alt. *All Loves Excelling*). Grand Rapids: Eerdmans, 1980.

Blake, Lillie Devereux. *Woman's Place Today: Four Lectures.* New York: John W. Lowell, 1883.

Bloesch, Donald G. *Battle for the Trinity: The Debate Over Inclusive God-Language.* Ann Arbor: Servant, 1985.

Borresen, Kari Elisabeth. *Subordination and Equivalence: The Nature and Role of Woman in Augustine and Thomas Aquinas.* trans. Charles H. Talbot. Washington: University Press of America, 1968 [1981].

Cade, Toni, ed. *The Black Woman: An Anthology.* New York: New American Library, 1974.

Christ, Carol P. and Judith Plaskow, eds. *Womanspirit Rising: A Feminist Reader in Religion.* New York: Harper & Row, 1979.

Clark, Elizabeth A. *Women in the Early Church.* Message of the Fathers of the Church. Wilmington: Michael Glazier, 1983.

Clark, Elizabeth and Herbert Richardson, eds. *Women and Religion: Readings in the Western Tradition from*

Aeschylus to Mary Daly. New York: Harper and Row, 1976.

Collins, Sheila. *A Different Heaven and Earth.* Valley Forge: Judson, 1974.

Daly, Mary. *Beyond God the Father: Toward a Philosophy of Women's Liberation.* Boston: Beacon, 1973.

—*The Church and the Second Sex.* New York: Harper and Row, 1968.

Dayton, Donald W. *Discovering an Evangelical Heritage.* New York: Harper and Row, 1976.

Deen, Edith. *Great Women of the Christian Faith.* New York: Harper and Brothers, 1959.

Demarest, Victoria Booth-Clibborn. *Sex and Spirit: God, Woman and Ministry.* St. Petersburg: Valkyrie, 1977.

Eller, Vernard. *The Language of Canaan and The Grammar of Feminism.* Grand Rapids: Eerdmans, 1982.

Gage, Matilda Joslyn. *Woman, Church and State: A Historical Account of the Status of Women Through the Christian Ages with Reminiscenses of the Matriarch.* American Women Series: Images and Realities. Chicago: C. H. Kerr, 1893.

Gurko, Miriam. *The Ladies of Seneca Falls: The Birth of the Women's Movement.* New York: Macmillan, 1974.

Hardesty, Nancy. *Great Women of Faith.* Grand Rapids: Baker, 1980.

—*Women Called to Witness: Evangelical Feminism in the 19th Century.* Nashville: Abingdon, 1984.

Harkness, Georgia. *Women in Church and Society, A Historical and Theological Inquiry.* Nashville: Abingdon, 1972.

Hull, Gloria T., Patricia Bell Scott, and Barbara Smith, eds. *All Women are White, All the Blacks are Men, But Some of Us Are Brave (Black Women's Study).* Old Westbury: Feminist, 1982.

Jewett, Paul K. *The Ordination of Women: New Testament Perspectives.* Grand Rapids: Eerdmans, 1980.

Lovejoy, Arthur O. *The Great Chain of Being: A Study of*

the History of an Idea. Cambridge: Harvard University, 1948.

Meeks, Cathy. *I Want Somebody to Know my Name.* Nashville: Thomas Nelson, 1978.

O'Faolain, Julia and Lauro Martines. *Not in God's Image: A History of Women in Europe from the Greeks to the Nineteenth Century.* New York: Harper and Row, 1973.

Palmer, Phoebe. *Promise of the Father; or, A Neglected Specialty of the Last Days.* Boston: Henry Degen, 1859.

Ruether, Rosemary Radford. *New Woman, New Earth: Sexist Ideologies and Human Liberation.* New York: Seabury, 1975.

—Ed. *Religion and Sexism: Images of Woman in the Jewish and Christian Traditions.* New York: Simon and Schuster, 1974.

—and Rosemary S. Keller, eds. *Women and Religion in America.* 2 vols. San Francisco: Harper and Row, 1981.

—and Eleanor McLaughlin, eds. *Women of Spirit: Female Leadership in the Jewish and Christian Traditions.* New York: Simon and Schuster, 1978.

Russell, Letty M. *The Future of Partnership.* Philadelphia: Westminster, 1979.

—*Growth in Partnership.* Philadelphia: Westminster, 1981.

—*Human Liberation in a Feminist Perspective—A Theology.* Philadelphia: Westminster, 1974.

—Ed. *The Liberating Word: A Guide to Nonsexist Interpretation of the Bible.* Philadelphia: Westminster, 1976.

Sawicki, Marianne. *Faith and Sexism: Guidelines for Religious Educators.* New York: Seabury, 1979.

Scanzoni, Letha. "The Great Chain of Being and the Chain of Command." *The Reformed Journal* 26 (October, 1976): 14-18.

Schneir, Miriam, ed. *Feminism: The Essential Historical Writings.* New York: Random, 1972.

Shaw, Anna Howard. *The Story of a Pioneer.* New York: Harper and Brothers, 1880 [1915].

Swartley, Willard M. *Slavery, Sabbath, War, and Women: Case Issues in Biblical Interpretation.* Scottdale: Herald, 1983.

Tavard, George H. *Woman in Christian Tradition.* Notre Dame: University, 1973.

Tolbert, Mary Ann, ed. *The Bible and Feminist Hermeneutics.* Semeia 28. Chico: Scholars, 1985.

Trout, Margaret. *The General Was a Lady: The Story of Evangeline Booth.* Nashville: A. J. Holeman, 1980.

Verdesi, Elizabeth Howell. *In But Still Out: Women in the Church.* Philadelphia: Westminster, 1976.

Williams, Selma R. *Divine Rebel. The Life of Anne Marbury Hutchinson.* New York: Holt, Rinehart & Winston, 1981.

Wilson-Kastner, Patricia and others. *A Lost Tradition: Women Writers of the Early Church.* Washington: University Press of America, 1981.

Studies on Shared Marriage

Boyce, David and Lori Boyce. "Mutuality: Marriage on the Growing Edge." *Daughters of Sarah 8,* November/December,1982, 9-11.

Demarest, Gary. *Christian Alternatives Within Marriage.* Waco: Word, 1977.

Gundry, Patricia. *Heirs Together: Mutual Submission in Marriage.* Grand Rapids: Zondervan, 1982.

Lindskoog, Kathryn. "The Lost Father." *Free Indeed 1,* October/November, 1978, 19.

McGinnis, Kathleen and James. *Parenting for Peace and Justice.* Maryknoll: Orbis, 1981.

Olthuis, James H. *I Pledge You My Troth: A Christian View of Marriage, Family and Friendship.* New York: Harper & Row, 1975.

Rallings, E.M. and David J. Pratto. *Two-Clergy Marriages: A Special Case of Dual Careers.* Lanham: University Press of America, 1984.

Rowatt, G. Wade and Mary Jo Rowatt. *The Two-Career Marriage.* Christian Care Books. Philadelphia: Westminster, 1980.

Scanzoni, John H. *Love and Negotiate: Creative Conflict in Marriage.* Waco: Word, 1979.

Scanzoni, Letha D. and John Scanzoni. *Men, Women and Change: A Sociology of Marriage and Family.* 2d ed. New York: McGraw Hill, 1976.

Spencer, Willam and Aida Besançon Spencer. "Equal Parenting: One Couple's Practical Aproach to Developing a New Paradigm." *ECW Update 7,* March-May, 1983, 1, 6-7.

Stapleton, Jean and Richard Bright. *Equal Marriage.* Nashville: Abingdon, 1976.

Tetlow, Elisabeth Meier and Louis Mulry Tetlow. *Partners in Service: Toward a Biblical Theology of Christian Marriage.* New York: University Press of America, 1983.

Yoder, Perry and Elizabeth. *New Men, New Roles: A Study Guide for Christian People in Social Change.* Newton, Kansas: Faith and Life, 1977.

General/Inspirational Studies

Booth, Catherine. *Female Ministry, or, Woman's Right to Preach the Gospel.* London: Morgan and Chase, 1859. New York: Salvation Army Supplies, [1975].

Callahan, Sidney Cornelia. *The Illusion of Eve: Modern Woman's Quest for Identity.* New York: Sheed and Ward, 1965.

Cardwell, Sue Webb. "Why Women Fail/Succeed in Ministry: Psychological Factors." *Pastoral Psychology* 30 (Summer, 1982): 153-62.

Carroll, Jackson W., Barbara Hargrove, Adair T. Lummis. *Women of the Cloth: A New Opportunity for the Churches.* New York: Harper and Row, 1981.

Cornwall Collective, The. *Your Daughters Shall Prophesy: Feminist Alternatives In Theological Education.* New York: Pilgrim, 1980.

Crotwell, Helen G. *Women and the Word: Sermons.* Philadelphia: Fortress, 1978.

DeVos, Karen Holder. *A Woman's Worth and Work: A Christian Perspective.* Grand Rapids: Baker, 1976.

Doely, Sarah Bentley, ed. *Women's Liberation and the*

Church: The New Demand for Freedom in the Life of the Christian Church. New York: Association, 1970.

Dumas, Francine. *Man and Woman: Similarity and Difference,* trans. Margaret House. Geneva: World Council of Churches, 1966.

Eldred, O. John. *Women Pastors: If God Calls, Why Not the Church?* Valley Forge: Judson, 1981.

Ermarth, Margaret Sittler. *Adam's Fractured Rib.* Philadelphia: Fortress, 1970.

Fischer, Clare Benedicks, Betsy Brenneman, and Anne McGraw Bennett, eds. *Women in a Strange Land: A Search For a New Image.* Philadelphia: Fortress, 1975.

Gibson, Elsie. *When the Minister is a Woman.* New York: Holt, Rinehart & Winston, 1970.

Guidelines for Nonsexist Use of Language. Urbana: National Council of Teachers of English, 1976.

Gundry, Patricia. *The Complete Woman.* Garden City: Doubleday, 1981.

— "A Theological Explanation As to Why Women Only Should Do Housework." *The Wittenburg Door* (1979), 6-7.

Hageman, Alice L., ed. *Sexist Religion & Woman in the Church: No More Silence!* New York: Association, 1974.

Hamilton, Michael P. and Nancy S. Montgomery, eds. *The Ordination of Women: Pro and Con.* New York: Morehouse-Barlow, 1975.

Haugerud, Joann. *The Word for Us: Gospels of John and Mark, Epistles to the Romans, and the Galatians.* Seattle: Coalition on Women and Religions, 1977.

Hestenes, Roberta and Lois Curley. *Women and the Ministries of Christ.* Pasadena: Fuller Theological Seminary, 1979.

Hewitt, Emily and Suzanne Hiatt. *Women Priests: Yes or No.* New York: Seabury, 1973.

An Inclusive Language Lectionary. Philadelphia: Westminster, 1983.

Lindskoog, Kathryn A. *Up From Eden: (An uncommonly candid look at the complex choices facing Christian* women today). Elgin: David C. Cook, 1976.

Malcolm, Kari Torjeson. *Women at the Crossroads: A Path Beyond Feminism and Traditionalism.* Downers Grove: InterVarsity, 1982.

Miller, Casey and Kate Swift. *The Handbook of Non-Sexist Writing for Writers, Editors, and Speakers.* New York: Harper and Row, 1980.

—*Words and Women.* New York: Doubleday, 1976.

Minard, Rosemary, ed. *Womenfolk and Fairy Tales.* New York: Houghton Mifflin, 1975.

Mollenkott, Virginia Ramey. *Speech, Silence, Action: The Cycle of Faith.* Nashville: Abingdon, 1980.

Neufer Emswiler, Sharon and Thomas Neufer Emswiler, eds. *Put on Your Party Clothes.* Normal: Wesley Foundation, 1977.

—*Women and Worship: A Guide to Nonsexist Hymns, Prayers, and Liturgies.* New York: Harper and Row, 1984.

Ohanneson, Joan. *Woman: Survivor in the Church.* Minneapolis: Winston, 1980.

O'Reilly, Veronica. "Changing Emphasis in Mission—New Ministries For Women." *International Review of Mission* 71 (July, 1982): 327-31.

Pape, Dorothy R. *In Search of God's Ideal Woman: A Personal Examinaton of the New Testament.* Downers Grove: InterVarsity, 1976.

Proctor, Priscilla and William Proctor. *Women In the Pulpit: Is God an Equal Opportunity Employer?* New York: Doubleday, 1976.

Royle, Marjorie H. "Women Pastors: What Happens After Placement?" *Review of Religious Research* 24 (December, 1982): 116-26.

Sayers, Dorothy L. *Are Women Human?* Grand Rapids: Eerdmans, 1971.

Schaef, Anne Wilson. *Women's Reality: An Emerging Female System in the White Male Society.* Minneapolis: Winston, 1981.

Schmidt, Elisabeth. *When God Calls a Woman: The Strug-*

gle of a Woman Pastor in France and Algeria, trans. Allen Hackett. New York: Pilgrim, 1981.

Sergio, Lisa. *Jesus and Woman: An Exciting Discovery of What He Offered Her.* McLean, VA: EPM, Hawthorn. 1975.

Shelly, Judith Allen. *Not Just a Job: Serving Christ in Your Work.* Downers Grove: InterVarsity, 1985.

Soelle, Dorothee. *Beyond Mere Obedience.* New York: Pilgrim, 1982.

Spencer, William David. "A Gift of Sight: A Christmas Fable." *Daughters of Sarah 2,* November, 1976, 8-9.

Stanton, Elizabeth Cady, ed. *The Woman's Bible.* 2 vols. New York: European, 1898.

Swidler, Arlene. *Woman in a Man's Church: From Role to Person.* New York: Paulist, 1972.

Troll, Lilian, ed. *Looking Ahead: A Woman's Guide to the Problems and Joys of Growing Older.* Englewood Cliffs: Prentice Hall, 1977.

Van Scoyoc, Nancy J. *Women, Change and the Church.* Nashville: Abingdon, 1980.

Van Vuuren, Nancy. *The Subversion of Women: As Practiced by Churches, Witch-Hunters and Other Sexists.* Philadelphia: Westminster, 1973.

Ward, Patricia A. and Martha G. Stout. *Christian Women at Work.* Grand Rapids: Zondervan, 1981.

Washbourn, Penelope. *Becoming Woman: The Quest for Wholeness in Female Experience.* New York: Harper and Row, 1972.

Watkins, Keith. *Faithful and Fair: Transcending Sexist Language in Worship.* Nashville: Abingdon, 1981.

Weidman, Judith L., ed. *Women Ministers: How Women are Redefining Traditional Roles.* New York: Harper and Row, 1981.

Williamson, Jane R., Diane Winston, and Wanda Wooton, eds. *Women's Action Almanac.* New York: Morrow, 1979.

Wold, Margaret. *The Shalom Woman.* Minneapolis: Ausburg, 1975.

Wyker, Mossie Allman. *Church Women in the Scheme of Things.* St. Louis: Bethany, 1953.

Bibliographies

Daughters of Sarah keeps updated a bibliography of books in print (2716 W. Cortland, Chicago, IL 60647).

Evangelical Women's Caucus has a bibliography, periodically updated, and a newsletter (P.O. Box 3192, San Francisco, CA 94119).

Kendall, Patricia A. *Women and the Priesthood: A Selected and Annotated Bibliography.* Philadelphia: Episcopal Diocese of Pennsylvania, 1976.

Richardson, Marilyn. *Black Women and Religion: A Bibliography.* Boston: G. K. Hall, 1980.

Syllabi/Bibliography Service, Women of Episcopal Divinity School and Women's Theological Coalition, Episcopal Divinity School, 99 Brattle St., Cambridge, MA 02138.

Women and Religion bibliography (Religion Indexes) indexed by author and subject.

Scripture Index

Subject Index

Adam, the, 21-23, 34, 41, 159.
  See also Eve
Akiba, Rabbi, 78
Analogy, 89-91, 94, 128, 134
Anna, 103-4, 120
Apostle, 72, 97, 100-2, 114
Augustine, 19
authentein. See Leadership
Authority, 96, 98-9, 109-10, 120,
  133, 135
Azariah, Eleazar ben, 69, 183
Bear, 127-8
Bema, 63
Beruria, 47, 55
Bible, interpretation, 7-8, 11-12,
  89, 141-2
Bishop, 73, 80, 94, 107-8, 116,
  156
Brooke, A. E., 110
Brothers, the, 119
Brown, Dee, 147
Brown, Francis, 25
Buck, Pearl, 165, 185
Caesar, 117
Chesterton, G. K., 138
Childbearing, 35, 92-4, 123
Chrysostom, 63, 101, 132
Church, house, 110, 112; mascu-
  line, 124; meetings, 151-2
Clement, of Alexandria, 80,
  110-11, 117, 151, 187, 191
Corinthians, 60, 104-5
Cornelius, 100
Coworker, 118-20, 128, 143
Curse, 14-15, 35, 39-42, 133-5.
  See also Fall
David, 70-1, 124, 126, 155
Deborah, 103, 120, 166
Dequincy, Thomas, 43
Didache, 80

Dorcas, 114, 166
Eagle, 125-7
Education, rabbinic, 57-61. *See*
  also Women
Elder, 98, 107-8, 116, 120
Elect, 111
Eliezer, Hyrcanus ben, 47, 50-3,
  55
Elliott, Elisabeth Leitch, 18-19
Ellis, E. Earle, 119
Endo, Shusaku, 147
Ephesus, heresy, 81-4
Essenes, 54
Euodia, and Syntyche, 73, 109,
  118-9, 120
Evangelical Theological Soci-
  ety, 139, 142-3, 151-2
Evangelical Women's Caucus,
  145, 151, 161
Evangelist, 98, 108-9, 114, 118
Evans, Mary J., 137
Eve, 15, 17, 21, 30-9, 52, 88-9,
  91-4, 100, 133-5, 182
Fall, 22, 29-39
Feasts, Jewish, 47-8, 66
Femininity 29, 127, 129, 130,
  135, 138, 156-7
Fence, 78
Foh, Susan T., 36
Freedman, R. David, 27
Friedan, Betty, 145
Gaius, 111
Gamaliel, Rabbi, 47, 77
Gift, 99, 187-90
God, 121, 124-6, 135, 142-3,
  175, 179; image of, 20-3;
  guardian, 126-7; mother, 123-
  4, 128-9; one, 21, 40, 65-7, 71,
  134, 177. *See also* Rule
Goebbels, 186

	DATE DUE		
11/13/96			
1/25/05			

261.8344SPE C.4

Spencer, Aida Besancon.
Beyond the curse.